Jo

Revolutionary Lives

Series Editors: Sarah Irving, University of Edinburgh;
Professor Paul Le Blanc, La Roche College, Pittsburgh

Revolutionary Lives is a series of short, critical biographies of radical figures from throughout history. The books are sympathetic but not sycophantic, and the intention is to present a balanced and, where necessary, critical evaluation of the individual's place in their political field, putting their actions and achievements in context and exploring issues raised by their lives, such as the use or rejection of violence, nationalism, or gender in political activism. While individuals are the subject of the books, their personal lives are dealt with lightly except insofar as they mesh with political concerns. The focus is on the contribution these revolutionaries made to history, an examination of how far they achieved their aims in improving the lives of the oppressed and exploited, and how they can continue to be an inspiration for many today.

Also available:

Salvador Allende:
Revolutionary Democrat
Victor Figueroa Clark

Hugo Chávez:
Socialist for the Twenty-first Century
Mike Gonzalez

W.E.B. Du Bois:
Revolutionary Across the Color Line
Bill V. Mullen

Frantz Fanon
Philosopher of the Barricades
Peter Hudis

Leila Khaled:
Icon of Palestinian Liberation
Sarah Irving

Jean Paul Marat:
Tribune of the French Revolution
Clifford D. Conner

Sylvia Pankhurst:
Suffragette, Socialist and Scourge of Empire
Katherine Connelly

Paul Robeson:
A Revolutionary Life
Gerald Horne

Percy Bysshe Shelley:
Poet and Revolutionary
Jacqueline Mulhallen

Toussaint Louverture:
A Black Jacobin in the Age of Revolutions
Charles Forsdick and
Christian Høgsbjerg

Ellen Wilkinson:
From Red Suffragist to Government Minister
Paula Bartley

Gerrard Winstanley:
The Digger's Life and Legacy
John Gurney

John Maclean

Hero of Red Clydeside

Henry Bell

PLUTO PRESS

First published 2018 by Pluto Press
345 Archway Road, London N6 5AA

www.plutobooks.com

British Library Cataloguing in Publication Data
A catalogue record for this book is available from the British Library

ISBN   978 0 7453 3839 2   Hardback
ISBN   978 0 7453 3838 5   Paperback
ISBN   978 1 7868 0354 2   PDF eBook
ISBN   978 1 7868 0356 6   Kindle eBook
ISBN   978 1 7868 0355 9   EPUB eBook

Typeset by Stanford DTP Services, Northampton, England

Simultaneously printed in the United Kingdom and United States of America

For Livi, my favourite socialist schoolteacher

Contents

Acknowledgements

I am extremely grateful to Katie Reid at Glasgow Women's Library, Barbara Neilson at the Mitchell Library, Carole McCallum at Glasgow Caledonian University Library, Thijs van Leeuwen at the International Institute of Social History, Fiona Hayes at the Glasgow Museums Resource Centre, Audrey Canning at the Willie Gallacher Memorial Library, and a great many people at the Scottish National Library, The National Archives, The National Records of Scotland, the Irish Military Archives, the Russian Embassy, Glasgow University Library, Stirling University Library, Strathclyde University Library, University of Warwick Archive, The People's Palace, The Marx Memorial Library, The Working Class Movement Library, and the Marxist Internet Archive, as well as for notes and support from Ewan Gibbs, Christopher Silver, Nick Bell, Fiona Brook, Robbie Guillory, Livi Crook, Jonathon Shafi, Tessa Cook, Kate Tough, Joey Simon, Dominic O'Hara, Harry Josephine Giles, Julia Taudevin, Rory Scothorne, Katy Hastie, Willy Maley, Sarah Irving, David Castle, Sara Shaarawi, Heather Mclean, Tom Coles, Jim Monaghan, John Foster, Alec Finlay, Dot Reid, John Couzin, Liz Lochhead, Hassan Abdulrazzak, Kevin Morgan, Scott Reeves, Donald Anderson, Gerry Cairns, Poppy Kohner, Fiona Jack, Rebecca Dewald, Svenja Meyerricks, Eddi Reader, Stephen Coyle, Josie Long, Christian Hogsbjerg, Kate Macleary, Sean Anderson, Craig Smillie, James Crisp, Mark Hesling, and John Maclean's grandchildren; Ellice Milton, Denis Maclean Wilson and Frances Maclean Wilson.

An excerpt from 'Freedom Come All Ye' by Hamish Henderson appears courtesy of the Henderson family, excerpts from 'Don't Sign Up for War' and 'Mrs Barbour's Army' by Alistair Hulett appear courtesy of the Alistair Hulett Memorial Trust, excerpts of poems by Sorley Maclean, Edwin Morgan and Hugh MacDiarmid appear courtesy of Carcanet Press.

List of Abbreviations

BSP – British Socialist Party

CLP – Communist Labour Party

Comintern – The Third Communist International, founded by Lenin in 1919

CP (BSTI) – Communist Party (British Section of the Third International)

CPGB – Communist Party of Great Britain

CWC – Clyde Workers' Committee

EIS – Educational Institute of Scotland

ILP – Independent Labour Party

IWW – Industrial Workers of the World

SDF – Social Democratic Federation

SLP – Socialist Labour Party

SNP – Scottish National Party

STUC – Scottish Trade Union Congress

SWRP – Scotish Workers' Republican Party

1

Out for Life and All That Life Can Give Us

John Maclean died on St Andrew's Day, 30 November 1923, at the age of just 44. Three days later, below the sandstone tenements of Eglington Toll on the Southside of Glasgow, more than 5,000 people gathered to begin the three-mile march to Eastwood Cemetery where he would be laid to rest. The Clyde Workers' Band marched in front, playing socialist anthems, and Handel's 'March of Saul'.[1] Some of the most famous socialists, communists, Labour MPs, suffragettes and trade unionists Scotland and the wider British Isles have ever produced greeted each other in the cold, and followed the silver band across South Glasgow. Glasgow's many unemployed men and women, as well as miners, teachers and shipyard workers held up banners and marched in silence.[2] Only the sound of their feet striking cobbles and tram tracks, and the strains of the band, rang out across the city.

As they passed through the streets of Govanhill, Pollokshields and Pollokshaws, black and red flags flapped from tenement windows and the pavements heaved with Glaswegians paying their respects. By the time the procession reached Maclean's home in Auldhouse Road, some estimates put the crowd at 20,000.[3] Along with the hearse and carriages, a horse-drawn cart carried a camera crew to capture the event. Soon the mass funeral march would be screened in cinemas across the west of Scotland, and shown on the anniversary of his death each year. To this day, the funeral of John Maclean, Britain's foremost Marxist revolutionary, remains the largest that Glasgow has ever seen. Tributes poured in from across the political spectrum. Obituaries were carried in Swedish, Russian and French, as well as British and Irish papers. Streets were named after him in Soviet cities, and Maclean was memorialised as an icon of Communism in the USSR right up until its collapse.[4] His coffin, draped in a red flag, was lowered into the ground as the huge crowd sang 'A Rebel Song' and 'The Internationale'.[5]

Despite the collective camaraderie of the marching men and women that day, divisions over Maclean's life were already long established. For the two years prior to his death, Maclean was disregarded by many as a political outsider; rejected by large parts of the Communist movement, estranged from his wife and family, and reported to be insane by both the secret police and those members of the left that rejected his increasingly Republican and Celtic Communist views. Over the coming century, Maclean would be alternately claimed and slandered by communists, liberals and nationalists – and charges of madness and foolish nationalism would come to stand alongside a mythology of John Maclean as a lost Scottish Lenin.

Without doubt, the punishment Maclean received in Scottish jails and his early death helped to enshrine him as a Marxist saint. He is remembered still as the revolutionary teacher whose vast classes, Labour College and speeches made sure that Marxist analysis took root in the slums of Glasgow and the coalfields of Fife and Lanarkshire – a man in many ways responsible for the self-conception of Glasgow, and by extension Scotland, as radical and 'red'. In the 18 years from Maclean joining the socialist movement to his release from jail at the end of the First World War, the Scottish Radical Left was transformed from the fringe eccentricity of a few hundred people, to a force that could muster 100,000 workers to cheer on the Russian, German and British Revolutions.

However, much of this internationalist outlook was overwritten in the century that followed. It was nation building, rather than Marxism, that emerged, perhaps, as the single most prominent cultural and political force in Scotland. Soon after his death, the poets of the Scottish Renaissance began to take up Maclean as a patron saint of their new Scotland. For left-nationalist intellectuals such as Sorley Maclean, Hugh MacDiarmid and Hamish Henderson, John Maclean became a key figure in the poetic re-imagining of the nation, even making it into the unofficial national anthem 'Freedom Come All Ye':

So come all ye at hame wi' Freedom,
Never heed whit the hoodies croak for doom.
In your hoose a' the bairns o' Adam
Can find breid, barley-bree and painted room.
When Maclean meets wi's freens in Springburn
A' the roses and geans will turn tae bloom,
And a black boy frae yont Nyanga
Dings the fell gallows o' the burghers doon.[6]

In a Scotland both synthetic and ancient, parochial and international, Maclean was the ideal cipher for that Caledonian Antisyzygy,
those duelling Scottish polarities: a Highlander and a Lowlander,
rural and urban, a Nationalist and an Internationalist, an atheist and
a Calvinist, a moderniser and a voice from history. What the poet
Edwin Muir once said of Burns can equally be applied to Maclean:
'to the respectable, a decent man; to the Rabelaisian, bawdy; to the
sentimentalist, sentimental; to the socialist, a revolutionary; to the
nationalist, a patriot; to the religious, pious; to the self-made man,
self-made'.[7]

A fitting national icon for a changing people, who in his lifetime
and after it, would be shaped by industrial revolutions, depressions,
world wars and the welfare state, the story of Maclean and his legacy
is a story of Scotland, its contradictory political identity, and its
tremendous wealth and poverty.

In the years immediately after the First World War, in penning
his 'Open Letter to Lenin' and demanding a distinctively Scottish
Communist Party, it was Maclean who helped open the rift between
Scottish and British nationalisms that continues to divide the
Scottish left, but it was also Maclean who formed the bridge between
socialism and nationalism that influences the institutions that govern
Scotland. Today, Maclean is celebrated by unionists and nationalists.
Both the Radical Independence Campaign and the Labour Party are
happy to march under his image. His stern-seeming face stares down
from banners just the same whether he is placed next to Robert the
Bruce, Keir Hardie, or Rosa Luxemburg. Maclean is a nationalist
to nationalists, a democrat to democrats, and a revolutionary to
revolutionaries.

His place at the epicentre of a decisive historical moment for the British Empire – in terms of the Great War and the Irish Struggle but also the very real potential of World Revolution – granted him a prime vantage point from which to witness the traumas and triumphs of twentieth-century politics. He may not have been the hero who delivered his people from capitalism or imperialism, but he was formed, destroyed and continues to be memorialised by those struggles.

Amongst the many competing views of Maclean, one uniting factor emerges: how exceptional the man was in his pursuit of his egalitarian values. He possessed a tenacity that distinguishes him from both comrades and enemies, as MacDiarmid acknowledged when he wrote: 'of all Maclean's foes not one was his peer.'[8] In the popular conception of the Maclean myth, he appears Christ-like in his endurance, single-mindedness and determination to liberate the oppressed masses. Anarchist organiser Guy Aldred, writing for Bakunin Press in Glasgow in 1925, claimed that:

> Scholars ... tell us that there were many Jesuses in the Jewish portion of the Roman Empire. Some time hence, we may suppose, other scholars will look back to our time, especially those who dwell in other lands, and learnedly dilate upon the fact that there were many John Macleans. Yet all Scotland, and all Labor, knows that there was and is only one — John Maclean, man and agitator, a martyr of the class struggle ... Apart from his class, he was nothing, because his class, its sorrows, its struggles, had become his life and being.[9]

Consumed by the struggle in his lifetime and afterwards, Maclean is a symbol of Scottish radicalism itself – an icon, divorced from his wit, his warmth and his human flaws. It is a curious irony that while his legacy has outlived the Communist Party of Great Britain, Maclean's dramatic fall-out with its founders has become a fundamental part of his myth. His life opens revolutionary possibilities and potential in legend, even as it gained and lost them in real life. He cut the fork in the road where the Scottish Labour movement, had it not fallen under the influences of Moscow and/or London, may – or may not

– have transcended those leaders and made revolutionary upheaval possible. At the same time, he forged the closest links between Scotland and the Kremlin, only to hamstring those relationships with his own equally energetic stubbornness.

At the time of his death, Maclean may have been a household name; the nation's most famous revolutionary, but he was isolated as a husband, father and politician. The socialist and suffragette Sylvia Pankhurst focused on Maclean's loneliness in her obituary for him:

> When we saw him a month ago he was holding great meetings and seemed stronger and more confident than ever. Yet he lived the bare lonely life of an ascetic. Parted from his wife and children he lived quite alone, doing his own cooking and housework ... declaring that 'pease brose' was one of his daily meals. His tone bespoke the cheerful frugality that was only too near to want.[10]

Yet the tragic solitude towards the end of his life belies the warmth and welcome that his home offered, and the love and hope included in all his letters to his wife and children – and indeed his final reconciliation with his family.

This biography seeks to view Maclean through all these prisms – as a nationalist and an internationalist, as a pacifist and a revolutionary, as a social democrat and a Bolshevik, as a father and a husband – and in those overlapping lights, shades and colours, to tell the story of a life devoted to revolution and popular struggle from Russia to Scotland, from Ireland to Egypt. It is not intended as an academic work, or a comprehensive history, but as a portrait of a great figure and the movement that surrounded him; subjective, but offering from its viewpoint a continuation of Maclean's lessons and legacy. His is a neglected but important chapter in Scotland's history, one which has more to say to us than William Wallace, Bonnie Prince Charlie, or many others in the pantheon of Scottish rebels. Maclean's life offers lasting lessons about how capitalist crises and war might be used to unite rather than to divide; how education can be a tool of liberation, not control; how Marxism may compete or combine with different nationalisms; and how physical and mental health, family life and comfort can be destroyed by oppression and resistance. Above all, it is a life lived for a cause, to the very edge of human limits. As Edwin Morgan writes in his poem 'On John Maclean':

> Failures may be interesting, but it is the firmness of what he
> wanted and did not want
> that raises eyebrows; when does the quixotic
> begin to gel, begin to impress, at what point
> of naked surprise?
> … Maclean was not naive, but
>   'We are out
> for life and all that life can give us'
> was what he said, that's what he said.[11]

Whatever the impressions made by Maclean's quixotic life, they have lasted a century, and continue to shape Scotland and the left. The steps of Maclean's funeral march through Glasgow's Southside are still retaken every November by a mix of pacifists, nationalists, republicans and communists, and hopefully this book – reflecting Maclean's life – has something in it of value for all those groups and others who wish to walk in his footsteps and imagine another world.

2

Dispeller of Ignorance

John Maclean's story begins in the 1850s with a different march, one more ordinary, yet more remarkable. Maclean's mother Anne MacPhee was born in 1846 in Corpach, a small Highland town at the foot of Ben Nevis, where Loch Linnhe meets Loch Eil. Her family were crofters and Gaelic speakers, and in the middle of the century, like many Highlanders, they were cleared from their land. The arrival of the Cheviot, a hardy breed of sheep that could survive the Scottish winter and generate more income for the lairds than tenant farmers could, combined with the abrogation of the clan system and the violent destruction of many villages by landowners had led to tens of thousands of Highlanders to flee. Anne's father, Donald MacPhee, went ahead of his family, leaving the Highlands to find work as a quarryman in the growing industrial heartland of Clydeside. Anne and her mother followed. They travelled from Corpach to Paisley with their belongings on their back. Driven from the lochs and mountains of the Gàidhealtachd,[1] they walked most of the hundred miles to start a new life amongst the industrial slums of Greater Glasgow. Anne MacPhee was not even ten years old. Both John Maclean's mother and his grandmother often told the story of their ordeal,[2] of the burnt crofts and police beatings meted out in the service of profit, and of the women who resisted.

When Maclean read *Capital* at the end of the century, less than fifty years after his mother's long walk to Scotland's Central Belt, Marx's lines about the clearances must have rung out:

> ... the 'clearing' made by the Duchess of Sutherland will suffice here. This person, well instructed in economy, resolved, on entering upon her government, to effect a radical cure, and to turn

the whole country, whose population had already been, by earlier processes of the like kind, reduced to 15,000, into a sheep-walk ... All their villages were destroyed and burnt, all their fields turned into pasturage. British soldiers enforced this eviction, and came to blows with the inhabitants. One old woman was burnt to death in the flames of the hut, which she refused to leave. Thus this fine lady appropriated 794,000 acres of land that had from time immemorial belonged to the clan.[3]

Maclean saw in this – the clear and contemporary relation of economic realities through stories that Scots knew first-hand – a way to explain class warfare to the masses. This would be his life's work, and the many new Glaswegians who arrived in Central Scotland fleeing violence, famine and aggressive landlordism in Ireland, the Scottish Highlands and Eastern Europe would be particularly receptive to it.

John's father, Daniel Maclean was also a victim of the clearances. Originally from the Isle of Mull, his family were cleared to Glasgow when he was a child. By the time he married Anne MacPhee in 1867, he was working as a potter, first in Bo'ness, and later at the Victoria Pottery in Pollokshaws. Like Paisley, where Anne had grown up, and Nitshill, where she married Daniel, Pollokshaws was a small industrial town on the outskirts of Glasgow, notable for a history of Chartism and militant miners and weavers.

Nan, John Maclean's daughter, gives the following account of Anne: 'a typical highland woman, stout and large-boned, with a rosy face and high cheekbones and twinkling blue eyes. She had more than her share of courage, determination, and independent honesty.'[4]

We know little else about her, other than that she worked variously as a weaver, a nurse and a newsagent. One photo of Anne survives, she is in Victorian dress – black cloth and white lace – and is broad-faced and stoic looking, with a strong family resemblance to her son. Maclean's friend Tom Anderson describes her: 'a woman with a great personality. As I see her now I see John – the same face, the same head, the same merry twinkle in the eye, the same quick impulse.'[5]

We know less still about John's father, Daniel – only that 'he had an active mind and was fond of discussion and argument'[6] and that he taught young men to read and write.[7] He, like Anne, was a Gaelic speaker. But though Maclean adopted the pseudonym Gael, there is no evidence that his parents taught him their language.[8]

Both Daniel and Anne belonged to the Original Secession Church in Pollokshaws. This church forbade music and religious decoration and the Sabbath was strictly observed. It has been suggested that, though Maclean rejected religion in his late teens, this puritanical strand to his upbringing never left him. He never drank or smoked. There is identifiable in the image of Maclean a Scottish and radical Protestant Marxism, and certainly his dedication to universal education and democracy stem from some of the more positive attributes of the Scots Calvinist John Knox.

Daniel and Anne Maclean had seven children and of the four that survived, John Maclean was the youngest boy, born at 59 King Street – now Shawbridge Road – in Pollokshaws on 24 August 1879. At the time, 59 King Street housed 24 people living in nine rooms, just a few hundred yards from Cogan Street, where Daniel worked in the Pottery.

When John was very young, his father began to suffer from silicosis, or as it was known at the time, 'potter's rot'. This occupational disease caused by the inhalation of dust leads to shortness of breath, coughing fits, fevers, and blueish skin, and can eventually cause lung cancer and organ failure. The illness meant that Daniel Maclean was unable to work his trade and so had to accept lower earnings as a labourer. His death in 1888, at the age of 43, would accelerate the family's slide into poverty.[9]

By 1891, Anne Maclean was a widow, and the head of a household at 84 King St, Pollokshaws, a three-room house in which she ran a newsagent. She lived with her four surviving children – Daniel, Margaret, John and Elizabeth – as well as her mother, Catherine MacPhee, and a boarder from Ireland. Besides Anne, only two members of the family were in work, Daniel as a teacher, and Margaret, aged 13, as a cotton factory worker. John and Elizabeth, the two youngest, were still at school.

Despite the tremendous hardship of bringing up the family as a single mother, Anne was committed to education and pushed her sons John and Daniel to stay in school beyond the normal leaving age. John Maclean worked as a message boy before and after school, during the summer holidays he printed calico at the Thornliebank Printworks, and at Christmas he worked as a postman. On Saturdays he was a golf caddie, and the Sabbath was, of course, kept holy.[10] By the time Maclean completed his education at Queen's Park School in South Glasgow, his brother Daniel, ten years his senior, had contracted tuberculosis. Daniel emigrated to South Africa in the hope that it would preserve his health. It did not. He died young, working all his short life as a teacher.

John Maclean, now a teenager, became the only surviving male member of his household.[11] But, despite the lack of money, in 1896 he became a pupil teaching assistant in Polmadie[12] before going on in 1898 to higher education at the Free Church Training College in the West End of Glasgow, where he was supervised by the great Scots educationalist Sir John Adams who – though they disagreed on social issues – John greatly admired.[13]

By the time Maclean began his journeys from his home in Pollokshaws to university in the West End, Glasgow was the fourth largest city in Europe and one of the world's great industrial centres. It had a vast modern transit system with more than a hundred train stations, and a subway system pre-dating those in Paris, Moscow and New York. Its unique position as a port city facing the new world, with just a short train and canal link to the ports of the East Coast and the old world, combined with large local coal fields, meant that Glasgow – and the whole Central Belt of Scotland – became industrialised and urbanised at a rate far outstripping the rest of Europe. This was met by a flow of cheap resources and labour from the Highlands, Ireland and the Colonies.

At the turn of the twentieth century, Glasgow had a population of more than 6,000 Muslims and 8,000 Jews, and languages such as Italian, Irish, Gaelic, Yiddish, Lithuanian, Chinese and Russian could be heard throughout the city. Within just a few generations, Glasgow had changed from a medium-sized town, rich from the proceeds of tobacco and slavery, to a major metropolis producing more than a quarter of the world's locomotives and nearly a fifth of all ships at sea. Glasgow was the Second City of the Empire, growing ever richer off industry and colonialism.[14]

Many in Glasgow amassed fabulous wealth. In consequence, others suffered terrible slum conditions, with tens of thousands of Glaswegians crammed into unsafe and unsanitary tenements rife with infectious disease.

In 1904, a paper presented at the University of Glasgow, entitled 'What The People Sleep Upon', showed that the untreated rags that made up the bedding of working-class Glaswegians harboured more bacteria than raw sewage.[15] By 1911, half of the Scottish population lived in one- or two-room flats. By contrast, the equivalent figure in England was just 7 per cent. Edwin Muir, coming to Glasgow from Orkney, described the city's industrialisation: 'it sets its mark on several generations of men, women and children by whose work it lived in shrunken bodies and trivial or embittered minds. In return for this it increased vastly the total wealth of the world.'[16]

Perhaps due to the sickness and slum conditions around him, and perhaps also due to his father and brother's lung conditions and his own sometimes poor respiratory health, Maclean maintained the belief throughout his life that air and exercise were crucial. As well as working holidays as a postman and a farm labourer, for two years from 1898 to 1900, Maclean walked every day from his home on the Southside of Glasgow to college in the West End, some six miles each way. On these walks through the slums and shipyards of central Glasgow, the young John Maclean would have seen up close the poverty and hardship of the inner city's working class.

In 1900, Maclean qualified as a teacher and took a job at Strathbungo School.[17] He continued to study for a master's degree, travelling to the university by train from the Southside. His friends included Tom Johnston, who would go on to found the socialist newspaper *Forward* and become Secretary of State for Scotland, and James Maxton, who would become leader of the Independent Labour Party.[18]

During these years of evening classes, Maclean stopped attending church, having become disillusioned with a church that courted the city's wealthy elite. He would later write that 'the only way to end all the trouble is by the establishment of Socialism (Christ having failed).'[19] By his twenty-first birthday, in August 1900, he was spending his Sundays at a local left-wing debating and discussion group called the Pollokshaws Progressive Union, and at this time he converted his mother to socialism.[20]

The Progressive Union was part of the late Victorian and Edwardian phenomenon that saw the middle and working classes questioning the social order and examining the contradictions of the wealth and the poverty around them – a contrast as stark in Glasgow as it was anywhere in the world. The objectives of the Progressive Union were published in *Pollokshaws News* as 'the social intercourse and mutual improvement – materially, mentally and morally – of the members; the discussion of philosophic, scientific and literary subjects, and all the problems of present day interest, especially those which concern the social and religious life of the people'.[21]

Anarchism, socialism, poetry and astronomy were all discussed at the Progressive Union and it served as a training ground for Maclean as an orator. In 1901 and 1902, he gave lectures on 'Poverty, Crime, and Drink', 'Plato and the Republic', and 'Shelley'. *Pollokshaws News* gave a flavour of the first lecture: 'the writer of the paper attributed poverty to the unequal economic conditions. Socialism would cure this. He argued that in a state where the government was a socialist one there could not be the same opportunities for drink, and the diminution of drunkenness would result in the diminution of crime.'[22]

Maclean's enthusiasm for education and political discussion was boundless, and he soon became secretary of the society. Two photographs of Maclean in his late teens and early twenties survive.[23] In one, he is pictured with two friends, Maclean standing in the middle. He has a hand on his friend's shoulder and a thoughtful expression on his face. He's handsome, with strong features and crew-cut dark hair. He seems more serious than his two friends, who are smiling and looking at the camera; Maclean is wearing a three-piece suit and looking off into the distance.

The other image is a class photo of Maclean at Strathbungo School. The children sit in rows, smart and clean. Most are infant girls wearing frilled collars and smocks. John is to the right, his hands behind his back, his hair longer, and parted at one side, wearing a soft jacket done up by one top button. He looks almost baby-faced, but the strong features and kindly, yet serious, expression are unmistakable.

His job at Strathbungo School, near Shawlands, did not last long however, and he was soon transferred for refusing to teach the Bible to his pupils. Anderson writes of Maclean's removal from this upper middle-class neighbourhood: 'There are no slaves in Shawlands, and so every respectable worm loathed the person of the class-conscious teacher.'[24]

Maclean's removal to a new school at Rutland Crescent in Cessnock and, shortly after, on to Kinning Park School would mark the beginning of a decade-long struggle with Govan School Board, as well as a life-long antipathy to religion.[25]

Maclean's focus, however, was not on respectable education. Among the members of the Progressive Union were many socialists and anarchists who would have lasting working and personal relationships with Maclean, including Will and Jim Craig who were members of the Marxist Social Democratic Federation.[26] But no one Maclean met in these years would have a more significant impact on him than the MacDougall family. John MacDougall was a former stonemason who devoted his time to study and to the Progressive Union. He alternated between his own armchair, and one in the Mitchell Library. His brother Daniel was a disabled cobbler and novelist with a deep interest in psychology and, later, in the pioneering work of Freud. They went on to introduce Maclean to their young nephew James MacDougall, who became Maclean's lifelong lieutenant and would stand by him through the many trials to come. Together, these three encouraged Maclean to read the English socialist and atheist Robert Blatchford, and the German philosopher Karl Marx.[27]

During these early years at the Progressive Union, John Maclean studied economics at Glasgow University, and devoted his free time to socialism. He came second in his class in Political Economics at Glasgow, and was by that time committed not just to socialism, but to Marxism. Maxton said that it was Maclean who introduced him to Marx in hurried lectures between work and university on the Cathcart Circle Line which orbits the Southside of Glasgow.

In a letter to the *Pollokshaws News* in September 1902, Maclean wrote:

To make wealth rapidly, capitalists have wrought men and women and children long hours at high speed and for wages that just keep them alive. Here the class struggle begins with the desire to steal the maximum from the workers. The workers feel the necessity for united effort, so that they may resist the attacks of the enemy, the capitalists. Trade Unions are formed and the strike is used to get as much of the wealth produced as possible. But wives and children starve and the unions must yield. Though united, the workers still fight an unequal battle ...

That the class struggle is bitter we need only reckon the annual death toll of the workers, the maimed, the poisoned, the physically wrecked by overwork, the mentally wrecked by worry, and those forced to suicide by desperation. It is a more bloody and more disastrous warfare than that to which the soldier is used. Living in slums, breathing poisonous and carbon-laden air, wearing shoddy clothes, eating adulterated and life-extinguishing food, the workers have greater cause for a forcible revolution than had the French capitalists in 1789.[28]

With this, Maclean began his life's work as a Marxist educator. His roles as an organiser, an agitator and a revolutionary would follow. For now, he was still young, living in two rooms on Burnhead Road in Pollokshaws. The household was now reduced to three: himself, his mother, and his 17-year-old sister, Lizzie who worked as a laundress. By this time, he had passed eight courses at Glasgow University in his spare time, and only the Latin exam stood between Maclean and a Master of Arts. He took it twice a year for some time and joked that he had taken out a season ticket, before finally graduating.[29] Although it might seem pompous to us now to see his name often signed 'John Maclean MA' on his writings and pamphlets, it is testament to the high regard in which Maclean held education. He told James MacDougall that it was the knowledge of the sacrifices made by his mother and his sisters to enable him to be educated that made him resolve to use his education in the service of the workers.[30]

In 1903, the 24-year-old Maclean filled out a psychological profile in Daniel MacDougall's 'Character Album'. His answers show us something of that earnest and passionate young man:

His favourite quality is: 'sincerity of purpose'

His idea of happiness is: 'long life with a woman I admire'

The calling that appealed to him the best is: 'dispeller of ignorance'

He could live anywhere: 'with true friends'

He would like to be living when: 'socialism is established'

His idea of unhappiness is: 'a life without friends'

His chief character inclination is: 'nobility of ideal'

His favourite painter is: 'Sam Bough'

His favourite authors are 'Marx, Blatchford, Shelley'

His favourite colours are: 'pink and white'

His favourite flower is: 'forget-me-not'

His favourite heroes in history are: 'John Ball, Socrates, and Jesus'

His favourite heroines in history are: 'Lady Macbeth, Rosalind, and Miranda'

The historical characters to whom he feels antipathy are: 'Queen Victoria and Edward the VII'

His greatest antipathy is to: 'selfish rivalry'

His temperament is: 'serious'

His favourite food and drink: 'porridge and water'

His motto is: 'to thine own self be true, And it must follow, as the night the day, thou canst not then be false to any man.'

His greatest fear is: 'poverty, false friendship, and being misunderstood.[31]

Of his fears, false friendship, and being misunderstood, would haunt Maclean's later life and legacy. Poverty, however, was something that he had long known, and he is remarkable among the revolutionaries of the early twentieth century in this. Lenin, Pankhurst, Luxemburg, Gramsci and Liebknecht were all born into relative wealth; they used their privilege for revolution. But Maclean knew grinding poverty and disease and it was only through education that he had a voice. He devoted his life to Marxism and education, friendship and understanding.

3

The Revolutionary Gospel

In the first years of the twentieth century, John Maclean joined the Social Democratic Federation, quickly becoming a regular contributor to its newspaper, *Justice*. The SDF, Britain's first Marxist party, was to become Maclean's political home for nearly twenty years.

In 1902 in the *Pollokshaws News* Maclean had declared his faith in a Labour Party that '[w]hen in parliament ... will find its true mission not to be the shortening of hours, increasing of wages, and bettering of conditions, but the overthrow of the capitalist class and the landlord class, so that land and capital be used to produce for consumption and not for profit'.[1]

But Maclean's idealistic view of parliamentary socialism quickly evolved into a faith in the education of the workers and autonomous working-class models such as the cooperative movement of shops and businesses. He believed that the working class must build its own institutions and liberate itself, while at the same time engaging in parliamentary democracy. Marxist education and propaganda, with an aim of achieving revolution by constitutional means, was the focus of the SDF, and by the summer of 1903 Maclean was conducting street corner meetings for the Social Democratic Federation.[2]

The SDF was founded in 1881 by Henry Hyndman, twelve years before Kier Hardie's less doctrinal Independent Labour Party. Hyndman was a Cambridge graduate and the son of a wealthy businessman. He worked professionally as a journalist and also played cricket for Sussex. His early writings were supportive of Empire and critical of Home Rule for Ireland. On his first attempt at running for Parliament – as an independent – Hyndman was denounced as a Tory by Gladstone.[3]

Despite all this, Hyndman found himself to be something of a radical and an outsider and, after encountering the work of Karl Marx and meeting Marx in person, he declared himself a socialist. Hyndman's book *England for All*, published in 1881, was the first publication to popularise the works of Marx in the English language. Although as a political text it was highly successful, it led to a personal break with Marx, who had not been credited in the book. For all these reasons and more, many socialists were suspicious of Hyndman. Many of the more utopian, anarchist and leftist members of his party – including Friedrich Engels, Eleanor Marx and William Morris – had left over the years, frustrated by Hyndman's traditionalism. Nevertheless, the SDF become the de facto Marxist party in Britain at the turn of the twentieth century, despite a further split in 1903 when James Connolly and others left to form the Socialist Labour Party, following the teaching of the American syndicalist Daniel De Leon.

After the split with the SLP, Maclean became a member of this smaller SDF. The 23-year-old schoolteacher spent his weekends and holidays touring industrial Scotland and building up branches of the party. Whilst other socialist organisations such as the Labour Party, the Socialist Labour Party and the Independent Labour Party had a greater reach, more members and paid organisers, it was the SDF's strictly Marxist position which particularly appealed to Maclean. During this time, Maclean formed the Glasgow Press Committee which began a campaign of letter, leaflet and manifesto writing. He helped to organise demonstrations by the unemployed, took summer speaking tours, and founded new branches of the SDF in Pollokshaws and Greenock, even organising the Pollokshaws branch into a band of cycling propagandists who would tour the Southside neighbourhoods of Kinning Park, Polmadie and Thornliebank.[4]

In 1904, on a summer tour, Maclean met Agnes Wood in Hawick. Agnes was the niece of a Christian socialist widower who was hosting John. John and Agnes struck up a friendship which progressed to courtship when Agnes moved to Glasgow in 1906 to train as a nurse. Like John, Agnes had grown up in a religious family and become a committed socialist. She is described as having 'a strong personality and a lovable nature',[5] and her grandchildren remember her as endlessly kind and caring, warm, quiet and calm.[6] A photo from the time shows a pretty woman in a high-collared nurse's uniform; she wears her short, wavy hair up, and has large dark eyes and a smiling face.

Both aged 29, John and Agnes were engaged on Christmas Day 1908. Agnes was employed as a nurse and John was working full-time as a teacher, now at Kinning Park School. Harry Ross, one of Maclean's colleagues at the school, described him:

> John was one of the most popular members of staff. There were half-a-dozen of us who did not go home for dinner and John was one of our most enthusiastic whist and nap players. Latterly we dropped cards for chess ... After 1908 I did not see him so often unless on Christmas day which he usually spent at the football match followed by the pantomime with myself and some of my bosom friends.[7]

In these early years of Maclean's career, he was a respected teacher, known affectionately by his pupils as 'Daddy Maclean'[8] and involved in campaigns against homework and corporal punishment.[9] He was a keen football supporter, attending league games of Queens Park and

Figure 1   John Maclean, possibly at Lorne Street School (Glasgow Museums archive)

Third Lanark,[10] and at the same time carrying on his other life as a dedicated Marxist in the evenings and weekends. Sylvia Pankhurst describes Maclean:

> Thick-set, and swarthy as a Neapolitan, he recalled to me irresistibly the thought of a great brown bear. His small eyes dark, and twinkling, his mouth, as he talked, his entire set of white teeth, like a dog, at times playfully opening his mouth in a game, at others drawing his lips back with a snarl. Both expressions were common to him. A kindly fellow, gentle and probably incapable of belligerent action ....[11]

Another description appeared in the SDF newspaper, *Justice*, in 1907:

> John Maclean, than whom no better man has been produced by the SDF ... It is quite safe to say that Maclean has addressed meetings in different parts of the country at a rate of one per day since the beginning of May. He has sometimes held as many as five meetings in one day! ... Nor is he less active in the winter. As in addition to addressing indoor meetings he usually conducts as many as four economics classes – all of them meeting once a week.[12]

Despite all this activity, socialism was not a significant force in Scotland and, at the time, Maclean was an anomaly working as a Marxist in a public profession. In 1905, SDF membership in Scotland was estimated at 200, and the spring conference of 1906 was judged by John's friend McNabb to be 'easily the best that the Scottish district council ever held because twenty delegates were in attendance'[13] Marxism, socialism and trade unionism were not mainstream pursuits in Edwardian Scotland, with trade union membership remaining below 150,000, or around 3 per cent of the population, until at least 1910.[14]

During this time, Scotland also saw the distribution of a great deal of anti-socialist propaganda and the formation of organisations such as the Tariff Reform League, the Anti-Socialist Union, and the Middle Class Defence League. The *Scotsman* published articles throughout these years declaring that 'the aim and goal of socialism is a return to the conditions of life and work in the African "savage states"',[15] and warned its readers against the 'dangerous and untrustworthy hands of the Social Democratic Federation'.[16]

Behind this anti-socialist pressure were high-ranking military figures, aristocrats and conservative politicians who sought to counter the work of the Independent Labour Party (ILP) and the SDF.[17] In 1906, the Conservative and Unionist Party distributed a pamphlet entitled 'Socialism or Freedom':

> The strident voice of the medical quack proclaims that the unholy potions or pills that he vends will cure every ill – from spotted fever to house-maid's knee. Similarly the Socialist Quack tells that Socialism is a universal panacea for our social ills; that it will banish hunger and thirst, poverty and want, and make everybody happy and healthy, well-fed and well-dressed, that at the same time it will reduce our necessary work to a minimum, leaving us perhaps 22 hours out of the 24 to eat and sleep and attend music-halls and football matches and generally enjoy ourselves. It is an alluring picture for the 'average sensual man' but it is all a sheer delusion.[18]

While socialism and Marxism had a very small foothold in Scottish life – there were fewer than 15,000 members of the ILP in the whole of Britain and Ireland[19] – the threat of a working-class break with the Liberal Party and the success of democratic socialism on the Continent had begun to spread fear amongst the establishment.

The Independent Labour Party, however, only gained its first two seats in Scotland in 1906. With the exception of the cooperative movement, there was little organised working-class activity at the time. But Maclean viewed the cooperative not just as a collective system for lowering prices, but as a vanguard working-class initiative to secure the means of distribution, if not production:

> In my eyes, just as trade unionism is playing its part, so also must co-operation in the great human impulse towards that time when, the world-wide Co-operative Commonwealth having been established, man for the first time shall rise dictator over the forces and resources of nature, and ensured through life of the material,

mental and moral requisites of a grand and noble existence, shall also for the first time cease from robbery and cease from conflict.[20]

In the General Election of 1906, Maclean got his first taste of electioneering. Tom Kennedy contested Aberdeen North for the SDF and John Maclean dedicated himself to the campaign. Kennedy came second with 25 per cent of the vote. James MacDougall remembered this period later in life, writing:

> The fixed pole around which all Maclean's aspirations and plans for the advancement of socialism in Scotland revolved was the street corner meeting. He was like a charged body at this time, a young, vigorous man, who had undergone an almost religious conversion to a noble doctrine, and the whole remainder of his life was the incessant pouring out of this charged energy in a sustained series of street corner meetings.
>
> He spoke in every quarter of Glasgow, in every industrial town in Scotland, from Hawick in the South to Aberdeen in the North – aye and further than Aberdeen, for he addressed the fisherman in the Summer Herring season in Lerwick.[21]

During this time Maclean started his economics classes, another defining feature of his career. His classes in Advanced Economics were held at the SDF branch office off Glasgow's Great Western Road. In addition, Maclean taught classes in Economics and Industrial History in Greenock. Pankhurst wrote of the classes, 'I have heard him in his hoarse voice, with delighted smiles, expounding to his class on Marxian economics the parable of the three coats, as though the very hearing of it were the universal cure all, the wine of life … he caused young men and women to read and think for themselves.'[22] The suffragette and political prisoner Helen Crawfurd described the students that Maclean's classes produced:

> Three types were turned out by these classes. There was the type who learned a few clever phrases and got a smattering of economics … There was another, who equipped himself in these classes with one objective – to get a good position in the official trade union,

political or co-operative movement. Many of these men who later became the bitter enemies of the workers ... Finally there was the minority who got a rooting and grounding in Marxist economics and industrial history. Among these were Arthur McManus, Tom Bell, William Gallacher.[23]

In Maclean's classes from this time onward he laid a groundwork for the leadership of Red Clydeside and much of Scottish socialism and communism. Few notes from his lectures survive, though from what does it seems the classes focused on an explanation of the labour theory of value, on the inevitability of unemployment under capitalism,[24] and of the function of gold and currency, combined with examples from industrial history and contemporary life.[25] This was, as Royden Harrison said, 'Marxism as a nineteenth century critique' rather than 'a twentieth century ideology'.[26]

A third aspect of Maclean's lifelong propaganda campaign had its beginnings in 1907, when he published his first pamphlet, 'The Greenock Jungle'. As much a piece of investigative journalism as a political treatise, 'The Greenock Jungle' was a practical intervention in the living conditions of the Clydeside working class, and an exposition of the illegal trade in diseased meat which was poisoning the people of Glasgow and Greenock.[27] Maclean wrote 'So long as profit can be made out of the sale of diseased carcases, just so long shall these be sold ... If the people of Greenock are wise, they will bestir themselves and never rest till the beef and other food-stuffs are sold for the benefit of the consumers and not for the enrichment of a few privileged merchants'.[28]

The pamphlet sold well and resulted in an inquiry and, eventually, in the appointment of a meat-inspector for the Greenock slaughter-house. This practical concession was a victory, but the real interest for Maclean lay in presenting the everyday experience of the people as an expression of class war. Maclean had used an immediate local issue to try to illustrate to the public that, under the current system, their lives were worth less than the profits of capitalists.

The next year, Maclean was introduced to what would become two driving forces in his political life: Irish politics, and the industrial strike. He had met the Irish trade unionist James Larkin in late 1906 and the following summer, at the culmination of three months of the Belfast Dock strike, Larkin invited Maclean to speak to the workers there.

The unrest in Belfast that summer was one of Irish trade unionism's first great battles, with Larkin having unionised more than 4,000 dockers and carters across the sectarian divide. After their demand for union recognition was refused, the dockers and carters went on strike, and were joined over the summer by shipyard workers, sailors, firemen, boilermakers, transport workers, and women from the city's largest tobacco factory, Gallaher's. The strike saw unprecedented solidarity between the city's Protestant and Catholic communities and in July more than 100,000 workers marched down the Shankhill Road accompanied by Loyalist *and* Nationalist flute bands.[29]

Though the usual violence of Ulster Protestant celebrations on 12 July had not been seen, fighting in the streets soon broke out when blackleg labourers were brought in to replace the striking workers. The Royal Irish Constabulary was deployed to break up pickets and to escort the blackleg carters across Belfast. On 19 July, Constable William Barrett refused his orders to escort workers breaking the strike and he was suspended. In response, more than 800 police officers, two-thirds of the total number in Belfast, mutinied. The forces of capital and labour were in direct and open conflict when, on 1 August 1907, John Maclean arrived in Belfast. He wrote in *Justice*:

> To read capitalist newspapers, one would imagine that these excitable Irishmen were the most turbulent rowdies within our isles; but the Socialist speaker gets the impression that they are the most mannerly and best-tempered section of the British workers … The men were justly entitled to strike because of the miserably low wages paid and the general treatment meted out to them by their slave-drivers; the men were justly entitled to upset carts and scatter the goods when the employers introduced blacklegs to beat their attempts at paralysing trade. If soldiers were needed in Belfast, then their services should have been given gratis to the workers who were being starved into surrender or incited on to revolt by the employment of blacklegs and constables.[30]

Maclean had never before seen a mass strike and was clearly intoxicated by it. In the same article, he stated that 'The workers have gone mad on Trade Unionism, and are rushing up to all the prominent men in the strike, wanting to join a Union – any Union. They are flocking into the Co-operative Society. They are rolling up in tens of thousands to the Custom House Steps on the Sundays to listen to the revolutionary gospel of Socialism.'[31]

However, with martial law enforced in Belfast, warships in Belfast Lough and the trade unions crippled by strike payments, the end of the dispute was near. In August, newspaper propaganda increased in the city, with suggestions that the strike was acting as a front for Irish Nationalism and, when British soldiers killed two Catholic workers on the Falls Road in mid-August, the fragile solidarity across the religious divide was broken.[32] The strike ended in defeat, with no concessions won. But, for both James Larkin and John Maclean, it was a taste of the potential power of organised labour.

In 1907, Maclean made another acquaintance who would define his political life. That autumn, Russian exile and socialist organiser Peter Petroff arrived in Glasgow. A slight man with a full moustache, Petroff had been active in the Russian Revolution of 1905 leading a liberated battalion of soldiers to the city of Voronezh during that year's mass unrest. During the uprising, he had been injured, captured and exiled to Siberia. Subsequently, he escaped and made his way to London, where he made contact with Russian socialist émigrés, eventually being sent to meet a ship of Russian sailors at Barrow. He hoped to convert the sailors to the Menshevik cause, Petroff's faction of the Russian Social Democratic Labour Party. When the ship later docked at Clydebank, Petroff quickly made contact with the Social Democratic Federation, which sent Petroff to John Maclean in Pollokshaws. There he stayed in Anne Maclean's flat, even sharing a bed with John.[33] Maclean and Petroff became firm comrades and, via Petroff's Russian and wider European connections, Maclean experienced his first real connection with international socialism. From Petroff, he was able to hear the ideas of figures such as Lenin, Luxemburg, Plekhanov and Trotsky.[34]

Unemployment was a growing problem in Scotland in these years and, despite more than 200,000 Scots emigrating between 1901 and

1910, many thousands of workers struggled to find work as the effects of the cotton industry's collapse and a contraction of ship building on the Clyde continued to be felt.[35] With no relief available from central government, thousands in Glasgow faced either starvation or the poor house. In 1907, Maclean led a march of the unemployed into the Glasgow Stock Exchange on Buchanan Street, both to instil fear in the capitalists within, but also to show the unemployed men the vast wealth that was not being deployed to help them. A disturbance and clashes with the police followed and Maclean saw the theatre and panic that direct action could create.[36]

In 1908, Peter Petroff visited again, and he and Maclean addressed Glasgow's workers on May Day. The demonstration had grown dramatically in size and, a year later, an emboldened Maclean was demanding that May Day be held in Glasgow on the first day of May, rather than on the nearest weekend – a battle still being fought by anarchists in the twenty-first century on Glasgow Green. He wrote in *Pollokshaws Review*:

> In 1889 the International socialist congress determined to call upon workers to Strike work on the first day of May ... We in Scotland have, so far, selected the first Sunday in May. This year the fine weather enabled over 40,000 to muster on Glasgow Green. Such a huge turnout indicates the growth of militant Socialism in and around Glasgow. Ere long we expect the workers to follow their continental comrades and celebrate the 1st of May as the workers' self-elected holiday.[37]

In these formative years of his political career, Maclean's position was social democratic, and his engagement with parliamentary politics was in the hope that socialism could be established through representative democracy. But in his experiences of industrial strikes and direct action, he was moving towards a tendency more radical than that of Hyndman and the SDF leadership. Maclean had begun to reject their idea that industrial and civil unrest would not have a key role to play in the establishment of a Marxist society. Another incident from Maclean's campaign for the unemployed in 1908, recorded in the diary of the Earl of Crawford, illustrates this militancy:

8 SEPTEMBER 1908 The Duchess of Connaught and Princess Patricia came to tea ... distressed at the hostile reception afforded to Prince Arthur when he visited Glasgow two or three days ago. The local socialists seized the opportunity of inflaming the unemployed workmen – a solid mass of these wretched men stood outside the Town Hall and were well drilled into hooting the Prince on each occasion of his appearance ... I doubt whether a Royal Prince has been thus persistently attacked for a hundred years.[38]

A socialist was arrested following the booing of the prince, charged with inciting the crowd 'to blind the police with cayenne pepper and to use deadly force',[39] and further clashes with police took place at Glasgow Cathedral.[40] The following Saturday, Maclean and others organised a march of unemployed workers to Glasgow's West End. The papers reported that 'Inflammatory speeches were made, and the police were ordered to disperse the mob.' The police then repeatedly charged the large crowd, but were unable to control it. Eventually 3,000 unemployed men and women banded together and began to race to the West End with its 'better-class residential quarters' around the Lord Provost's house in Park Circus:

> When the crowd passing along Woodlands Road reached within a quarter mile of the Lord Provost's residence the clatter of mounted police at the gallop was heard, and the next moment the mob was scattered in all directions ...
>
> A few arrests were made, and as the police used their batons with freedom many cut heads were treated; but in the main those injured preferred to suffer in silence lest request for medical treatment might lead to their detention.[41]

With a repeat demonstration expected the next night, 'large bodies of police were held in reserve, many being mounted and on foot secreted in the City Chambers ... The King's 'Own Scottish Borderers in Maryhill Barracks were also available for extraordinary duty if called upon.'[42] It is clear that by 1908 Maclean and the socialist movement in Scotland felt emboldened to move further than they had previously in order to achieve their goals, and here we also see Maclean combining his socialism with republican and militant actions for the first time. In these incidents, there is an intensity not often attributed to Clydeside or Maclean prior to the Great Unrest of the next decade. But by 1908, the tactics he was willing to adopt were already prefiguring the radical street politics that would dominate the coming decades.

4

The Rapids of Revolution

In early 1909, Maclean's lieutenant James MacDougall was fired from his job at the Clydesdale Bank because of his political activities: MacDougall and Maclean had been protesting against a slum landlord who happened to be a significant client of the bank. A campaign by Maclean and his Federation branch to have MacDougall reinstated was unsuccessful.[1] The Pollokshaws SDF had, however succeeded in getting two of their candidates elected to the Eastwood School Board – a small democratic victory that the party intended to use to full effect.[2] Maclean spent the first half of the year teaching at Kinning Park, lecturing on economics in Greenock and in Glasgow's West End, and conducting occasional speaking tours of factories and coal fields. His recent engagement to Agnes Wood was a happy backdrop to everyday life.

In August, Maclean forwent some of his speaking tour and took a holiday with his comrade James McNabb. The two men joined a Mediterranean cruise aboard the Ttramp steamer *Ravensheugh*, and Maclean's letters home to his fiancée provide an insight into his more playful side. This from 6 August:

> All the fortnight we have dozed and read lazily novels. In fact it has been the laziest holiday I have ever spent … We intend to break the bank at Monte Carlo. You will marry a millionaire yet my dear. If my purse were in proportion to my love for you I certainly would. However if the millions don't come we shall try, won't we dearest, to make love cover all the defects otherwise. How I have been longing for you all the voyage and how I begin to weary till Xmas when we shall be locked away in one another's arms for the

rest of our dual existence. My word how happy we shall be, we two, with an Italian sky of joy unalloyed over our heads.[3]

A further letter adds that they were knocked back from the casino in Monte Carlo for not possessing passports. It also describes 'sunbathing ... perfectly nude in the scorching sun. I wish you were here to enjoy the mosquito bites.'[4] Later during the trip Maclean visits North Africa:

All the French towns in Africa are walled in for the purpose, I suppose, of protecting the French should the natives ever dream of revolting ... I have become a Mohammedan as I took off my shoes at the porch of the Mosque and entered to worship Allah. Allah be praised!!! Arab women have to cover their faces with a white cloth, leaving only one opening for one eye, and frequently they fix that optic on us. Yesterday we had a typical French breakfast, which took us two hours to round off ... I could suffer five years of this and more if the weather were good and we were taken from new scenes to new scenes ... If we get off early and have no storms or fog we should reach Granton on Tuesday forenoon. Oh! That will be joyful, joyful, joyful, as I shall have a chance of seeing my own darling girl again. How I have been longing to smack your lips and give you a bear's hug.[5]

Returning to Glasgow, Maclean spent the autumn holding his usual economics classes.[6] In October 1909, he led a deputation of a hundred people to the Spanish Consulate in Glasgow to protest against the execution of Francisco Ferrer Guàrdia. Guàrdia was a Spanish anarchist and school teacher, who founded the Modern School to spread left-wing anti-authoritarian ideas among children.[7] Ferrer Guàrdia's last words as he faced the firing squad had been: 'Aim well, my friends, you are not responsible. I am innocent; long live The Modern School.'[8] The persecution and state murder of this radical educator must have struck a chord with Maclean.

He himself was already making a name as a seditious teacher. The Education Act of 1908 allowed local residents to petition Education Boards for adult education classes, and young SDF members in

Glasgow's Southside successfully applied to Eastwood School Board
– which now included two SDF members – for John Maclean to be
made a Tutor of Marxist Doctrine at the Sir John Maxwell School.[9]
Maclean was the only person in the country to be receiving a public
salary for teaching Marxism. *Forward* reported on the class:

> ... even more will be gained in one session at this class than in
> a lifetime at Ruskin College ... one of the ablest expounders of
> the *mysteries* of Marx in Scotland. His course includes not only
> the elucidation of basic principles, but also a criticism of the
> various schools and theories of economics and a skeleton course
> of industrial history from primitive society up to the present day.[10]

All the while, Maclean was preparing for his wedding. On 30
December 1909, John and Agnes were married at 50 Nicholson Street
in the Gorbals, with Rose Wood and James McNabb as witnesses.
Maclean wrote to Agnes before the wedding: 'Less than three days
now and you are mine. I wish these days were passed and we were
joined to part no more.'[11]

It seems clear from their letters that Agnes and John were deeply
in love. But the marriage would be a troubled one, and the conflict
between their love for each other and John's commitment to the
cause would in the end bring suffering. However, in the years before
the war, their life together was a happy one.

John and Agnes Maclean were married at the end of 1909, appro-
priately enough, on the eve of the Great Unrest. They took a house
together at 159 Albert Road in Govanhill, Glasgow, just a few streets
from where John's team, Third Lanark, played. In those peaceful
days, he would even occasionally miss a socialist committee meeting
to watch a game.[12] Agnes worked as a nurse, John as a teacher, and
they had three rooms to themselves. In their limited free time, they
would go on walks and cycle rides together.[13] The couple bought
new furniture for each room of the house, and made their first home
together.[14] Nan Milton writes that her mother was a 'very shy and
retiring person' and that she made up her mind early on that she
could best serve the cause of socialism by providing a steady and
comfortable home-life for her husband.[15]

Though they did not often campaign together, the early years of Agnes and John's marriage saw a sudden increase in trade union militancy across the country. The Great Unrest of 1910–14 saw the militancy of the working class shake the British Establishment to its core. The economic revival that had followed the long depression of 1873–96 had slowed to a stop and the new reality for British employers in an increasingly global market left them eager to cut wages and re-organise production. These threats to workers' livelihoods were met with unprecedented militancy from both the rank-and-file membership of many unions, and a strong response from the government, who during these years stationed warships on the Mersey and used soldiers against striking railwaymen.[16] In a speech to the Renfrewshire Cooperative Conference in November 1911, John Maclean would say of the period:

Truly, the development in every branch of industrial, commercial, political, social, and intellectual activity is so apparently quick that even the dullest must admit that the old order of society is passing away, to give place to one that with our aid will eradicate for ever the inequalities, the injustices, and the oppression that characterises the present. We have but to think of the increasing thousands of inventions and discoveries that facilitate production; of the swift spread of the most perfect modes of transit and communication; of the amazing expansion of capitalism through the export of capital from developed to underdeveloped countries; of the unprecedented grabbing of occupied lands for the extension of trade and of empires; of the sudden arrival of mammoth trusts controlling colossal masses of capital and slaves; of the tremendous uprise of the masses in the co-operative, the trade union, and the socialist movements, to find a growing expression in productive and distributive activity, economic revolt, and political agitation; of the modern political upheavals, starting six years ago in Russia, and passing in rapid succession through Turkey, Persia, Portugal, and Mexico, to find a momentary culmination in China, in what may ripen into the most magnificent and dramatic transformation ever witnessed by man—I say, we have but to think of all this to catch but the faintest outline of a world change that is so truly indicative of the triumph of knowledge and its application over the chaos of the past, and of the ultimate ascendancy of the organised masses over the forces and resources of the world.[17]

As he rode the Glasgow Underground, or watched the giant cranes along the Clyde, John Maclean was able to witness technology and progress unimaginable even to his father. For Maclean, the incredible march of capitalist progress only led to the glorious society that he believed must follow.

However, the red future that beckoned to him was even then not being realised by the established socialist parties. In 1910, after the January General Election saw a weak and largely moderate Labour grouping in the House of Commons, Maclean wrote that: 'The Labour Party is a miserable caricature of Marxism ... the reactionary Liberal element in the Labour party has carried the day and swept it into Liberalism of a dangerous kind.'[18] A disappointing result in a second General Election later that year – in which the Labour Party again secured just 6 per cent of the vote – confirmed Maclean's distaste for the moderates. But still Scotland was behind the rest of the country, with the Labour share of the vote in Scotland falling from 5.1 to 3.6 per cent in the second of 1910's two elections.

On May 6 that year, Edward VII died. The *San Francisco Call* reported that 'the King's friends are convinced that worry over the political situation aggravated, if it did not cause the fatal Illness.'[19]

Maclean gave a lecture shortly after Edward's death, pointing out that through the king's treaties with France and Russia he had determined to limit Germany's ability to undercut Britain in foreign markets. And he went on to explain how the king had hoped to prevent German imperial advances in Africa, and so had set the stage for an imperialist war in Europe. Maclean suggested that the title popular in the press, 'Edward the Peacemaker', should be replaced with 'Edward the Warmaker'. Maclean's mother was convinced that her son would be arrested for treason.[20]

A week after the king's death, the Great Unrest, which had begun in the North of England, reached the West of Scotland, with the Neilston Strike breaking out on 12 May 1910. Neilston is a small town in East Renfrewshire and, from its opening in 1792 to its closure in 1992, the town's most prominent feature was the Crofthead Thread Mill, with more than a thousand workers. By 1910, the mill was one of the great employers of the area. The women working there were largely daughters from coalmining families from Nitshill. A couple of these young women in the cop-winding department had demanded higher wages and were refused. In response, the workforce had walked out. The workers were young, inexperienced and not unionised, but the local people knew that a strike needed organisation, and Maclean was summoned to Neilston.[21] As James D. Young notes, 'Maclean was often a prominent figure in the midst of the struggles of working women',[22] be it in factories, housing, education, or destitution.

MacDougall recalled that 'Maclean came and infused his own vigour and courage into these girls. He instructed them how they must act in order to win, not only this immediate wage demand, but to be able in the future to protect themselves against the tyranny of the foremen or any unjust demand that might be made upon them. They must get into a Trade Union.'[23]

Maclean brought in Mary Macarthur, the famous Scottish suffragist. The dispute seems to have come to a head with something akin to a carnival, when the workers marched from Neilston to Pollokshields where the mill's manager lived. They made rough music, banging pots and pans, and carried effigies of the management to burn. The 'respectable inhabitants were thoroughly disturbed' and a meeting was held next to the manager's house and higher wages granted.[24]

The Neilston Strike marked the start of a series of strikes that swept across Scotland as female and semi-skilled workers found their wages cut while all around them the fabulous profits of the bosses rose. The incredible surplus of wealth for the middle and upper classes of this time can still be seen across Glasgow in its countless now-derelict department stores, cinemas and public spaces. Mrs Cranston's famous tearooms, designed by Charles Rennie Mackintosh, dotted the city, serving wealthy young men their tea, and at the same time providing poorly paid work for young women. An article in *Forward* written in 1911 was entitled 'How Mrs Cranston Treats her Workers' with the subtitle, 'the limits of tearoom generosity'.[25]

At the same time, in the City's West End, the most startling demonstration of wealth and leisure in early twentieth-century Glasgow was being constructed: the Scottish Exhibition of National History, Art and Industry. Palaces and pavilions were built in Kelvingrove Park, along with exhibitions of painting, photography and Scottish history. An aerial railway was constructed reaching from Gilmorehill across the River Kelvin to Park Circus. Most astonishing of all, three villages were built – the West African, Arctic and Highland villages – where natives from Equatorial Africa, Lapland and the Scottish Highlands would live for the summer. Maggie Craig notes that 'the Laplanders, complete with reindeer, had been persuaded to spend several months there for "as much milk as they could drink."'[26] How the Africans were paid in this human zoo is not related.

Further west, in Clydebank, the Singer Factory, one of the largest industrial plants in the world, with its own six-platform train station, was producing 13,000 sewing machines a week and paying its workers a pittance. At Singer, on 20 March 1911, twelve female cabinet polishers struck work over their increased workload and decreased wages. Within two days, 11,000 workers at the factory had joined the action.[27]

Though the workers were not unionised, there existed a strong but small network of labour activists within the factory. Many, like Tom Bell, were members of the Industrial Workers of Great Britain, the local branch of the IWW. Others were members of the Socialist Labour Party – the syndicalist grouping inspired by De Leon which had split from the SDF years earlier.[28]

Maclean was not directly involved in the organisation of the strike, but he played a significant role as a propagandist supporting it, and as a reporter documenting it. He wrote for *Justice* on 1 April 1911 that:

> The whole circumstances are uniquely appropriate for the immediate application of industrial organisation of the up-to-date type. A monopoly centred in one workshop; minute division of labour; unskilled labour; absence of trade unions; a growing group of enthusiastic, hard-working industrial unionists; a sudden and spontaneous strike of unprecedented dimensions ...
>
> The result will largely depend on the course and the conduct of the strike. The strikers have no means behind them, except what may be yet collected from a sympathetic public. If the ranks

are held in hand unbroken, if discipline is maintained in a loyal manner ... then nothing will stand in the way of an immediate organisation embracing the workers in every part of the factory.

It is my earnest desire that all this should happen.[29]

The strike lasted three weeks and saw huge demonstrations in support. But it was eventually broken by a ballot that assured work to those who voted to end the strike. Maclean declared that this was nothing more than 'a veiled threat'.[30] Four hundred of the workers who opposed ending the strike were fired, including all the organisers and every member of the Industrial Workers of Great Britain. Though the action ended in defeat, it had two major effects: it gave a large body of workers the experience of organising a mass strike on the Clyde, and also, due to the reprisals, the experienced trade-unionists and strike organisers, including Tom Bell and Arthur MacManus, now found work in other factories across Clydeside. Maclean believed that the strike had been broken wholly by a lack of solidarity, and was clear then that the power of strikes could only be advanced in tandem with increased class consciousness: 'We must blame the lack of the feeling of, and confidence in, class solidarity ... Essentially, we must get the masses to test their confidence in one another by giving them ample opportunity of voting "class" at every election.'[31]

Soon after the Singer strike, Maclean was able to explore these ideas further when he travelled to the Rhondda Valley, spending a week with the striking Welsh miners. Impressed by their militancy and disappointed by the lack of solidarity from miners in Scotland, Maclean saw here a sharpened example of the political value of the strike. Maclean was not a natural supporter of syndicalism. He believed that the State had to play a role which went beyond nationalisation, to the socialisation of industry under worker control, but within a greater planned economy. However, like the anarchists and syndicalists, Maclean believed that greater demands could be made through the strike, to highlight the internal contradictions of capitalism – and to awaken the workers to the truth that their interests were in direct opposition to those of their bosses. This was in contrast to the SDF's position that only the ballot box could bring about socialism. Maclean wrote in 1913:

It is now our duty to try and direct the aroused workers not only to strike for an unstable temporary advance but to concentrate at the same time on a legally fixed, definite minimum below which no adult's wage must fall … rising with every increase in prices and increased productivity. That the state would not grant this is a foregone conclusion … But that is all the more reason why we should fight. If we get the masses behind us, every capitalist resistance will bring us nearer the revolution.[32]

This argument, that the strike should be used for political ends, to make a transitional demand – that is to say, one which cannot be granted within capitalism – shows that as the outbreak of war approached Maclean was already quickly moving toward a more radical position.

Figure 2   John, Agnes and Jean Maclean, 1911 (Ellice Milton)

He was, however, still at odds with those anarcho-syndicalists who built up revolutionary unions and rejected the state.

In the summer of 1911, John and Agnes Maclean had their first child, a daughter, Jean. She was born at the family home in the early hours of 24 May, and John was present at the birth. When she was a few months old, the family sat for a portrait. Maclean in a black three-piece suit, with the chain of a pocket watch visible, stands relaxed, hand in his pocket, next to Agnes who holds baby Jean. Jean is in a white frock, and Agnes wears a decorative high-necked dress and jewellery. Her family remember her always wearing an amethyst pendant. The young family look happy, even proud. It is a dramatic irony that Jean and Agnes would be cut out of this image countless times as it became the classic image of John for pamphlets, posters and even Soviet stamps in the decades that followed.

That summer John began a regular column for *Justice* entitled 'Scottish Notes', which he signed as 'Gael': a pseudonym marking his first explicit connection with a Celtic otherness in a public and British context. Its regular updates included strike reports, and attacks on the local council, employers and the Church. A typical entry from the end of December reads:

… the Dundee battle burst forth with meteoric suddenness. Dockers and carters made a combined and almost unanimous effort to raise wages. At once orders were sent to Aberdeen, Edinburgh, and Glasgow, to fetch along blacklegs, whose arrival naturally meant sport. At once the working class rose in revolt, and in a determined way handled the traitors and the police sent out to protect them in the interests of the employers. Terrified lest the workers should gain the upper hand, the Lord Provost, to be in the fashion, I suppose, sent to Edinburgh for the Black Watch, 300 of whom received hissing hospitality from the starved wage-slaves of Bonnie Dundee.

So far as my limited knowledge goes, this is the first occasion within a lifetime, if not longer, on which the soldiers have been called out in Scotland ready to shoot down their fellow-members of the wage-slave class. The Lord Provost must feel proud after his feat of daring.[33]

The excitement that Maclean felt is tangible. The wave of industrial disputes engulfing factories, mines, railways and docks during the Great Unrest is evoked in his famous speech to the Cooperative Society in 1911: 'The times we live in are so stirring and full of change that it is not impossible to believe we are in the rapids of revolution.'[34]

Maclean believed that even if a revolutionary moment did not arrive, the experience was still a workshop for revolution. In every strike, every street corner meeting, every Marxist class, the workers' understanding of their own oppression could be raised. Maclean's idea of a 'fighting theory' was that lessons learnt about the nature of capitalism and the ruling class during these conflicts must inevitably propel the movement forward. He ceaselessly toured the industrial and mining towns of the Central Belt and Fife, at a time when the liberalism of the miners receded and more radical figures, such as Bob Smillie, emerged as leaders. In 1912, Maclean addressed 2,000 workers in Falkirk, and helped to organise committees demanding rent caps. The following year he addressed a packed Glasgow Pavilion Theatre, keeping to his regular theme of moving politics beyond the leadership of the moderate socialists in the House of Commons: 'Karl Marx is dead. He died in 1883. Since then he has been killed many times, most recently by Ramsay Macdonald ... I want you to go home and read the works of Karl Marx ... what we want in this country today is an educated working class. The millennium, if it is to come, must come from an educated working class.'[35]

That year the Macleans had a second daughter. Named after John's mother, Annie, or Nan as she would be known, was born just before midnight on 24 April in the flat on Albert Road. Nan would go on to be her father's chief biographer and to carry on his political legacy, rising to prominence in Trotskyist, socialist and Scottish nationalist circles. At the time of her birth, her father was busy with a strike at Weir's Works in Cathcart as well as a dispute at the Coalburn cooperative. But soon after, the young family took a rare holiday, with John, Agnes and their two young daughters heading to Tarbet on Loch Fyne. The holiday was cut short when a strike broke out at a linen factory in Fife, and John was sent for to organise the workers.

However, the energy of the previous years' unrest was dissipating. The rapids of revolution had passed. But, as Maclean had insisted, the experiences of strikes, negotiations and demonstrations were valuable ones, and left those movements acting for the rights of working people far stronger by 1914 than they had been just four years earlier. Despite the many defeats which the workers had endured in those years, the Great Unrest provided a training ground for the industrial, social and political unrest which the coming war would bring.

In the same months, as that war loomed, John and Agnes bought a house at 42 Auldhouse Road for £130.[36] It was a new-build terrace backing onto the Newlands Tram Depot. Agnes and John furnished the three-bedroom house, and began covering the walls of the cellar with the gold foil from chocolate boxes and cigarette packets to create a glittering den for Jean and Nan.[37]

Maclean remained an active member of the Social Democratic Federation or, as it became, the British Socialist Party. Still under the same leadership, and deploying policy and tactics as before, with Hyndman remaining in control, the BSP was a new, larger, Marxist grouping. Although he remained within the party, Maclean began more often to express his opposition to the leadership, particularly with regard to Hyndman's support for the build-up of armaments. Hyndman had written an article in the *Morning Post* suggesting that an extra £100 million be spent on the British Navy. A memorandum from Maclean's branch of the party appeared in the *Pollokshaws Review*: 'this branch recognises the international solidarity of the working class and therefore depreciates Comrade Hyndman's agitation for a Big Navy as tending rather to break down than to build up the essential unity of the workers of the world.'[38]

This division between Left Internationalism – as embodied by Maclean – and Leftist Jingoism – as embodied by Hyndman – would be echoed in socialist parties across the continent as war approached. The Second International – which had as its aim the unity of the global working class, and was endorsed by socialist parties across Europe and the world – had avowed at its congress in 1907 and again in 1912 that it was the duty of all socialists to disrupt their countries' steps towards war. The 1912 manifesto stated that the great powers must face strikes and even revolutions if they continued to increase their armaments and position themselves for an imperialist war. It was the duty of socialists to 'exert every effort in order to prevent the outbreak of war by the means they consider most effective, which naturally vary according to the sharpening of the class struggle and the sharpening of the general political situation'.[39]

However, at the same time that Hyndman was encouraging the build-up of the British Navy, in Germany the dominant Social Democratic Party broke with the Second International and granted war credits to the Kaiser. In August 1914, their theorist Karl Kautsky despaired, as their chairman Hugo Haase announced 'We will not desert our fatherland in its hour of need.' The Second International had collapsed and socialist parties had given in to jingoism and set the stage for mass slaughter. Catherine Merridale relates that Lenin was said to have remarked on hearing of the betrayal in Germany: 'From this day I am no longer a social democrat, I am a communist.'[40] A similar shift took place for many socialists in the face of the Second International's failure. As Nan Milton writes: 'it revealed ultimately a strong, resolute, revolutionary movement ... a tiny movement which swelled in the struggle against the war and became symbolized to future generations by Lenin and Trotsky in Russia, Liebknecht and Luxemburg in Germany ... and Connolly and Maclean in Britain.'[41]

Small wonder, perhaps, that this resistance and revolt would take place in Glasgow and Dublin, Turin and Hamburg, away from the centres of nationalism and monoculture, in the industrial cities at the countries' fringes. Whilst the largely Protestant and Lowland craft trade unionism of Glasgow was a major factor in unrest during these years, Red Clydeside was also fuelled by Highland and Irish identities – fractures in British identity, as symbolised by the two Gaels: Connolly and Maclean.

5

Internationalists First, Last, and All the Time

On 4 August 1914, the United Kingdom declared war on Germany. Cheering crowds gathered in front of Buckingham Palace to celebrate. The Second International's commitment to end the conflict by a general strike had collapsed before the war had begun, and socialists on Clydeside braced themselves against a wave of patriotic enthusiasm for the war. In Glasgow, the Independent Labour Party called a halt to its weekly meetings at the Glasgow Metropole.[1] As Ripley and McHugh note, decades of agitation by socialists and trade unionists had barely left an impression on the staunch liberalism of most of Scotland's working class.[2] The gulf between the liberal and patriotic Glasgow of 1914 and the hotbed of radicalism and unrest that the city would soon become was vast.

The declaration of war was received enthusiastically by many on Clydeside; 20,000 Glaswegians joined the army in August alone.[3] Trams bedecked in union flags bore slogans such as 'Men of Glasgow, to arms'. The public were told that the war was necessary in order to ensure Belgium's right to nationhood, and that it would last only a few months.

But from the very start, there were those who declared their resistance to the conflict. On 9 August 1914, a peace rally was held on Glasgow Green. Called the day prior by the ILP, the BSP and the Peace Society, it saw 5,000 people gather to protest against the declaration of war and the anticipated profiteering. *Forward* reported that the crowd contained doctors, dock labourers, and every brand of rebel from mild peace advocates to 'the wildest of revolutionaries'. The reporter also noted that the meeting was boycotted by the capitalist press.[4] This boycott was likely an effect of the Defence of the Realm Act which came into force on 8 August. The Act, as well as banning the flying of kites and the feeding of bread to ducks, gave the government wide-ranging powers of social control and censorship, proclaiming: 'No person shall by word of mouth or in writing spread reports likely to cause disaffection or alarm among any of His Majesty's forces or among the civilian population.'[5] This new law was to have a defining impact on Maclean's life.

After the first flurry of protest against the war, the British Socialist Party found itself split. A group of young members supported Maclean's anti-war position and stood against militarism, but the old guard stayed loyal to Hyndman and argued in favour of British involvement in the war. That September, the Executive Committee of the British Socialist Party even encouraged branch members to take part in recruiting for the army[6] – this policy was quickly dropped.

Even amongst the caustic nationalism of 1914, John Maclean continued to campaign fiercely against the war. Willie Gallacher writes in his memoir that from this time onward Maclean declared 'war against the war makers'.[7] He held street-corner meetings across the city agitating against the conflict and explaining in Marxist terms who would profit from war and who would pay for it. He sent MacDougall to organise at the gates of the shipyards and factories, in particular the key munitions producer Weir's of Cathcart. The legendary ability of MacDougall and Maclean to keep a street meeting orderly, honed by years of confrontation and disruption by conservatives, drunks and hecklers, came to the fore in these early months of the war when jingoism was rife, and uniformed men often sought to break up anti-war meetings.

The divide between the BSP Executive, and Maclean and his Glasgow comrades deepened. The Executive issued a manifesto proclaiming that 'the party naturally desires to see the prosecution of the war to a speedy and successful issue.'[8] And the party's paper *Justice* contained articles encouraging members to hate the Prussian Army and state. Maclean responded:

> Our first business is to hate the British capitalist system that, with 'business as usual,' means the continued robbery of the workers.

After that I, for one, will transfer the larger portion of my hate to Russian soil against the devilish autocracy that prevents the peaceful development of the workers' organisations by organised murder ...

It is our business as Socialists to develop a 'class patriotism,' refusing to murder one another for a sordid world capitalism. The absurdity of the present situation is surely apparent when we see British Socialists going out to murder German Socialists with the object of crushing Kaiserism and Prussian militarism. The only real enemy to Kaiserism and Prussian militarism ... was and is German Social-Democracy. Let the propertied class go out, old and young alike, and defend their blessed property. When they have been disposed of, we of the working class will have something to defend, and we shall do it.[9]

Maclean is unapologetic in his view of the working class as international, and his presentation of the propertied class as the enemy. This was to be the last thing that Maclean wrote for the BSP paper *Justice*. He and his comrades switched their allegiance to *Forward*, before launching their own paper, *Vanguard*, in 1915. Published in Glasgow by the local BSP, it sold some 3,000 copies per issue. Maclean remained a member of the party, but his disagreement with Hyndman over the war now cast him and his comrades in the Glasgow branch adrift from the BSP in London.

The year 1914 continued with much of Glasgow embracing the war. Eight thousand Belgian refugees arrived in the city, and workers poured in from Ireland and the Highlands. Production increased on the Clyde, with ships and munitions orders soaring and Glasgow's already dominant shipyards increasing in capacity by a third during the war. Thousands joined the army, with Glasgow raising three battalions in 1914, the first mainly from the city's tram workers, the second from the Boy's Brigade, and the third largely made up of students and white-collar workers. Most believed that the war would be over soon, unable to imagine the deadlock of the trenches that was to come. Willie Gallacher wrote, remembering that time, 'What terrible attraction a war can have! The wild excitement, the illusion of wonderful adventure and the actual break in the deadly monotony of working-class life!'[10] The terrible attraction of the armed forces to the alienated and the dispossessed has long been a feature of the West of Scotland. Then as now, enlisting was a result of patriotism, peer-pressure, lack of opportunity, and overcrowding and unemployment at home. For others, joining the army was a result of more direct threats: in 1914, the Earl of Wemyss offered continuing half-pay to all the men working on his estate who joined up, and threatened that able-bodied men who did not enlist would be sacked.[11]

Against this backdrop, the Glasgow Branch of the British Socialist Party decided in late 1914 to call a weekly meeting to oppose the war. Every Sunday night, Maclean and others addressed crowds on Bath Street in the centre of Glasgow. The first meeting attracted enough socialists and pacifists to block the street, and attendance grew week after week, as rumours of the slaughter in France arrived back in Glasgow with the first casualties. Collections were held to fund the anti-war activity and regularly £20 or £30 in small change was raised from the crowd.[12] MacDougall recalled:

Men who had never before in their lives taken any interest in Socialism … flocked to Bath Street to hear what Maclean had to say, for by this time his name was a household word in the city … At the foot of the street stood the tramway office, brilliantly lit, plastered with poster appeals to men to join the army. Up the street, standing on a table, in the midst of a dense crowd of the proletariat, stood John Maclean exhorting men in explicit terms under no circumstances to join the army! The war, he told them, was not an accident. It was the continuation of the peace competition for trade and markets already carried on between the powers before hostilities broke out …

The men they were asked to shoot were their brothers, with the same difficulty on Saturdays to find rent for their miserable dwellings, who had to suffer the same insults and impertinence from their gaffers and foremen … What did it matter if they looked a little different? And spoke a different language? …

He told them that the main thing for them to know was that their real enemy was the employers, and that as long as turning lathes, ploughs, looms, ships – all the tools of wealth production –

were possessed by a small class of privileged people, then so long they would be slaves. To get free from this slavery was their real concern ... The victory of Socialism must be world-wide.[13]

Maclean, MacDougall, Willie Gallacher and the ILP member and suffragette Helen Crawfurd addressed the huge crowds week after week. Everyone knew that the speakers were risking their liberty, if not their lives, with their seditious speeches. These Bath Street meetings could be considered the birthplace of Red Clydeside and, along with Maclean's economics lessons, they provided the fuel that would power the socialist and pacifist resistance to the First World War in Glasgow.

That same year, James Ramsay MacDonald, the leader of the Labour Party, resigned in protest against the £100,000,000 of War Credits that his party had voted through. Ramsay MacDonald had urged that his party take a pacifist position and asked his MPs to abstain on the vote to finance the war. The Labour MP John Hodge replied that he would not abstain, as 'surely the Labour Party must be either for its country, or against it', and the vast majority of Labour MPs voted in favour of financing the war.[14] Ramsay MacDonald was replaced by Arthur Henderson who as leader marshalled the TUC into a commitment that there would be no strike activity for the duration of the war. He became the first Labour cabinet member, joining Asquith's coalition government.[15]

Socialists on Clydeside were horrified by the betrayal. Alistair Hulett's song 'Don't Sign Up for War' tells the story:

See yon Arthur Henderson, heid bummer o the workin men
When war broke oot he pressed his suit and he ran tae catch the
    train
He signed a deal in London, nae mair strikes until the fightin's
    done
In Glesga toon the word went roon, 'Tak tent o John Maclean!'
He said 'A bayonet, that's a weapon with a workin man at either
    end
Betray your country, serve your class
Don't sign up for war my friend, don't sign up for war'[16]

As the war stretched on, prices that had in many cases remained stable since the 1890s began to rise sharply. Between 1914 and 1918, the cost of living would double.[17] This hardship was felt particularly sharply in Glasgow where the massive influx of labour for the Clyde's shipyards and factories was putting pressure on housing and rapidly driving up rents. With their representatives in Parliament now in support of the war, and their representatives in the trade union movement denying their right to strike, workers looked elsewhere for support, and so the socialist street corner meetings took on a new significance.

In 1914, engineers across Glasgow requested a pay increase of 2 pence per hour to meet this rising cost of living. The dispute escalated and when their trade union, the Amalgamated Society of Engineers, refused to back members, an unofficial Labour Withholding Committee was formed.[18]

A wildcat strike followed, and Gallacher relates that 'John Maclean, through his Marxist classes, was supplying a continuous stream of material for the agitation ... he demonstrated in the clearest manner that the war was a war for trade.'[19] The strike lasted for three weeks, with workers out on strike across eight factories. In the United States, the socialist magazine the *New York Call* reported '14,000 out in Clyde strike, Berlin hears.'[20] But without the support of the unions, and with no strike pay available, the defeated workers were soon forced back to work. This first strike of the war proved that – despite the condemnation of the government and the capitalist press, despite the constant patriotic propaganda, and without the support of the unions – some of Glasgow's workers were nevertheless willing to take action against their employers.[21]

In the first few months of the war, the German Army had advanced on Paris and was within sight of the Eiffel Tower. Over the autumn it had been pushed back nearly a hundred miles, but by the end of the year the new landscape of industrialised war had emerged, with the trenches of the Western Front stretching from the Swiss border to the North Sea.[22] Rosa Luxemburg articulated in Germany what was felt by increasing numbers in Glasgow: 'the cannon fodder that was loaded upon the trains in August and September is rotting on the battlefields of Belgium and the Vosges, while profits are springing like weeds, from the fields of the dead. Business is flourishing upon the ruins.'[23]

On 3 January 1915, a meeting of the Glasgow BSP passed a resolution which summarised John Maclean's view on the war: 'That this meeting of Glasgow members of the BSP recognising that this war has been brought about by the intrigues of the capitalist and landlord interest of all the countries involved; and that the workers of the world will obtain no advantages out of the war, determines to do all it can to peacefully stop the war at the earliest moment.'[24]

At the same time, the production of pamphlets criticising the war and its profiteers increased, and a further confrontation between Maclean and Hyndman, the pro-war leader of his party, emerged. Hyndman accused the authors of an Independent Labour Party anti-war pamphlet of being traitors, funded by the German Government.[25] Maclean responded forcefully, never one to praise the ILP, but always keen to support fellow socialists whatever their allegiances:

> It is just a stretch or two beyond the limit for our 'cultured' comrade [Hyndman] … to suggest with the subtlety of the serpent that MacDonald, Hardie & Company have stooped to the basest treachery any socialist could be guilty of – acting as paid agents in the interests of German Imperialistic Capitalism.
>
> I have never admired MacDonald's or Hardie's tactics, nor do I suppose I ever shall admire their outlook or method; I look forward yet 'with pleasure' to criticising both but I would rather cut out my tongue than suggest the utterly base thought, attributed to Hyndman, at such a juncture as this, when British Capitalism is ready to use *Vorwärts* and Karl Liebknecht against German Capitalism, and Hyndman's suggestions against British Socialism.[26]

He wrote a further letter three weeks later clarifying that his criticism of Hyndman should not be mistaken as support for the position of the ILP and adding that he and James MacDougall were the only figures in Glasgow advertising openly anti-war meetings.[27]

Whilst socialists themselves sabotaged left-wing opposition to the war, the British Government was mobilising the courts against the nascent resistance. On 2 July 1915, Parliament passed the Munitions of War Act, which was intended to ensure the steady production of armaments under the close supervision of the government. It quickly became clear to the workers of Glasgow and elsewhere that the Act would do this by strengthening their employers' power and dramatically curtailing hard-won workers' rights.

The new Act made it a penal offence to leave your job without permission, and ensured that workers would be punished if they refused a new job offered by their employer, regardless of pay. It also became an offence to refuse overtime, again regardless of pay. At the same time, the Act provided for the dilution of labour, with unskilled workers being introduced into the factories in order to increase production. Up and down the Clyde, tens of thousands of factory-workers and ship-builders who made their way from their overcrowded tenements to their often dangerous workplaces now lost those few rights they had to refuse work or change employer. The provisions of the Act were enforced by new Munitions Tribunals, special courts that oversaw the enforcement of the Act – against which there was no appeal.[28] This new legislation greatly increased the power of employers and became known in Glasgow as the Industrial Slavery Act.[29]

Between 70 and 80 cases a day were heard by Munitions Tribunals in Glasgow,[30] and in October 1915 three shipwrights from the Fairfield Yard in Govan were imprisoned under the Act for non-payment of fines issued after they took strike action in solidarity with a colleague who had been dismissed.[31] It was clear that, before conscription had even been introduced, forced labour was being supported by the government at home.

The Labour Withholding Committee, still active after the engineers' strike, issued an ultimatum to the government. It declared that if the Govan shipwrights were not released within three days, there would be strikes across the Clyde. Three days later, the workers were released. Their fines had been paid anonymously, though many suspected that it was trade union officials who had covered the fines, desperate to avert strikes that would be beyond their control. With the small victory of the shipwrights' release secured, the socialists and shop stewards of Glasgow formed the Clyde Workers' Committee (CWC), to defend workers against the Munitions Act.[32]

The Clyde Workers' Committee drew together trade unionists from across Glasgow's industries and included members of the Socialist Labour Party, the Independent Labour Party, and the British Socialist Party. It was a group that comprised at different times 200–300 representatives,[33] elected by tens of thousands of workers across 29 Clydeside factories and shipyards. Prominent figures included Willie Gallacher, Tom Bell, David Kirkwood, James Maxton, Arthur MacManus, Harry McShane and John Maclean. The committee began to agitate for higher wages in early 1915 and later produced a weekly paper, the *Worker*.[34]

Maclean was the only member of the CWC who was neither a trade unionist nor an industrial worker. Teachers were not part of the trade union movement in Scotland at the time, though Maclean was a member of professional bodies including the Educational Institute of Scotland, and the Scottish Socialist Teachers Society[35] – which had organised the first ever Scottish teachers strike in and around Barrhead and Neilston in 1913.[36] In early 1915, Maclean was again engaged in a dispute with his employer, Govan School Board. His head teacher, Mr Fulton, had taken to having a female teacher in his office all day, with other staff having to do her work. When the issue was raised, Fulton insulted the staff. In response, Maclean drafted a letter, signed by 26 members of staff at the school, demanding an apology.[37] In the months that followed, Maclean is mentioned more often in the Govan School Board minutes than almost any other subject. After several investigations and interviews, and a board split between its one socialist member – Harry Hopkins – and the many conservative and religious members,[38] John Maclean was transferred from Kinning Park School to Lorne Street School in the nearby area of Plantation, though he continued to try to represent the unhappy staff at Kinning Park. In 1915 Maclean also publicly criticised the curriculum, in which children were taught 'thou shalt not kill' but also celebrated British military victories, and in which they heard 'thou shalt not steal', before learning about British rule in India and Canada. Maclean suggested that primary education was being used not to create critical minds, but to 'mask the reality of things'.[39]

At the same time as Maclean battled the School Board, and the Clyde Workers' Committee campaigned in the factories, Mary

Barbour was organising the women of Govan. Barbour had been an active member of the Co-operative in Kinning Park, and became involved in the Govan Women's Housing Committee, emerging as a leader. As thousands of workers poured into Glasgow, rents continued to increase throughout 1915, unaffordable in particular for the wives and families of servicemen who, unlike munitions workers, were seeing no increase in pay. The Scottish TUC announced at the time that since the outbreak of war wages had decreased in real terms by 19 per cent.[40] When appeals to Barnes and Henderson, the Labour members of the coalition government, fell on deaf ears, Mary Barbour – supported by others such as Helen Crawfurd, Agnes Dollan, John Wheatley and the ILP – planned direct action. In May 1915, a rent strike was called in Govan and organised women, known as 'Mrs Barbour's Army', made 'rough music' with pots, pans and trumpets, and drove back any factors or bailiffs who tried to carry out evictions. Maclean and MacDougall toured the shipyard gates, galvanising the workers' support for the women's crusade.[41]

By the middle of June, the landlords of Govan were defeated and rents were lowered to their previous level.[42] News of the victory in Govan soon spread, and the struggle became city-wide, with Mary Barbour addressing crowds in every corner of Glasgow, and windows in every neighbourhood bearing signs that read 'We are not paying increased rent.' Bailiffs and sheriff's officers were hounded in the street and pelted with flour.[43] Rent couldn't be collected, and evictions were impossible.[44] Children carried placards proclaiming 'my father is fighting in France, we are fighting the huns at home.'[45] Jessie Barbour, one of the strikers, recalled the experience: 'It was great fun! … They werenae just labourers' wives that were on strike against the factors. No matter who you were, what you were or what you did. That was it. You were on strike against the factors. In fact, you were on strike against the whole blooming thing.'[46]

The strike had spread beyond those households affected to become a greater cause. As the tensions mounted on Clydeside, the government began for the first time to focus on Maclean. His Marxist Economics class now had more than 400 students enrolled, and the weekly meetings on Bath Street had continued to swell, as had his street and factory-gate meetings throughout the city.[47] All this had attracted the attention of irate patriots and of the secret police. A letter in the *Herald* on 15 October read:

> At 9.30 last night at the foot of Kilbowie Road, I heard a man preaching treason. He was telling a crowd of working men that the war was not being fought in the defence of Belgium, but in the interests of greedy capitalists … Why is he allowed to go on in this way? What is the D.O.R.A for? Are there no men in Clydebank to stop him without waiting for the law to act?[48]

Days later, Maclean was summoned to court under the Defence of the Realm Act for making statements likely to prejudice recruiting. John Wheatley wrote in *Forward*: 'John's ability and fearlessness have singled him out as one of the great rebel leaders of our time, and consequently one of the first subjects of persecution. Our rulers fear Maclean more than they do the whole Labour Party.'[49] A Free Speech demonstration was held by Maclean and the local branch of the BSP at Shawlands Cross with over 2,000 people in attendance – perhaps the largest demonstration ever seen in that neighbourhood.[50]

Maclean pleaded not guilty on 27 October and a trial was held on 10 November, with the viewing gallery swamped with socialists, trade unionists and members of the Free Speech Committee, which Maclean had formed in response to his charges.[51]

The court heard from various police spies, who could remember only snatches of Maclean's speeches at Bath Street and outside Langside Hall at Shawlands Cross. The prosecution claimed that at Langside Hall Maclean had said that soldiers were murderers. When the presiding Sheriff asked the officers why they did not stop the treasonous speech as it happened, they replied that 'our interference would have started a riot.'[52]

Maclean took to the stand and responded: 'I certainly did not say that the soldiers were murderers. The soldiers belonging to the working class are those who will not get any benefit from this war. I say here and now that the soldiers themselves are not murderers, but those who sent them and are sending them to war are murderers.'[53]

Another officer claimed that Maclean had said 'God damn the army' at a meeting of more than 300 people in Bath Street. Again

John clarified: 'I said "I have been enlisted in the Socialist Army for fifteen years, the only army worth fighting for. God damn all other armies." Take out of that what meaning you like.'[54]

He added, 'I have friends, and dear friends, in the British Army. But I am opposed to the present military system.'[55]

Maclean was found guilty and sentenced to a fine of £5 or five days' imprisonment. Someone in the gallery shouted 'Three cheers for Maclean, three cheers for the revolution', and Maclean's comrades in the gallery cheered in response before singing 'The Red Flag'.[56] Petroff remarked that this song had never been heard before in front of a judge, but would soon become customary in Glasgow courts.[57] Maclean then returned to the Southside where he was summoned in front of the Govan School Board and dismissed from his job – there too crowds booed the decision and sang 'The Red Flag' and 'The Internationale'. Both Maclean and the school board insisted that his dismissal was as a result of the dispute over his former headteacher, Mr Fulton's, treatment of the staff in Kinning Park,[58] though it seems unlikely that his conviction did not play its part. Either way the decision of the Govan School Board was reported in the international socialist press. *Nashe Slovo*, Trotsky's newspaper in Paris, reported that 'When it became known that Maclean's sacking was upheld, the people's anger reached new limits. In all districts there were protest meetings at which harsh resolutions were adopted.'[59] The Govan School Board and the Free Speech Committee received hundreds of messages supporting Maclean. Manny Shinwell, the Clydeside trade unionist who would go on to serve as a minister in Clement Atlee's government, wrote on behalf of the Seafarers Union, stating that more than a thousand of their members lived in the Plantation area of Glasgow where Maclean taught and demanded his reinstatement. The Clyde Workers' Committee asked members to withdraw their children from the school,[60] and the workers at the Weir's Factory in Cathcart passed the following resolution:

> that we immediately get in touch with all conveners ... with a view of levying 1d, 2d or such sum as would be sufficient to employ our victimised fellow-worker, John Maclean, as an independent organiser, at a salary equivalent to what he was in receipt of from

the Govan School Board. Furthermore that we henceforth labour unceasingly until Comrade Maclean is reinstated in his former position.[61]

The authorities no doubt felt that the threat of jail and poverty would be enough to restrain Maclean, and he faced criticism at the time from the likes of Sylvia Pankhurst who was disappointed by the plaintive, liberal nature of his defence, relying as it did on the idea of free speech.[62] But despite these pressures, Maclean remained committed to the cause and still found time to publish a short but excitable report on the Internationalist conference that had just taken place in Zimmerwald:

> The conference was attended by seven delegates from the anti-war section of the German Democratic Party, two from the French trade unions (the French Socialist Party being hopeless), three from the Italian Socialist Party, and others representing Bulgaria and the other Balkan States, Norway, Switzerland, and Russia. 'Socialist patriots' were excluded.
>
> Both sections of the Russian social democrats at the conference are internationalists and are fighting the Russian government with all their might. The 'majority' [Bolshevik] section declares that the defeat of the Tsar's army would be the lesser evil for the Russian and European democracy. They urge civil war for the establishment of a democratic republic in Russia, and international action to stop the war and defeat the bourgeoisie ... We learn that a gigantic political strike has already been declared in Petrograd ...
>
> We assure our comrades that we in Glasgow are international-ists first, last, and all the time.[63]

Maclean increasingly located his movement in an international context, observing that the struggles on the Clyde were mirrored in Germany and Russia. The likes of Lenin and Zinoviev – the Bolshevik delegates – were rebuilding the International and Maclean saw himself as a part of it. The divide within his party in London and the collapse of the Second International drove him to look more keenly for allies abroad, and his connections with comrades in Russia, Ireland, and America became increasingly central to his politics.

Whilst Lenin and his comrades were meeting in Zimmerwald, up to 40,000 households across Glasgow were participating in the rent strike following the initial victory in Govan.[64] Unable to enforce the increased rent themselves, landlords had resorted to the courts and begun to sue individual households for rent arrears. The Small Debt Courts could then have the rents deducted directly from the wages of striking households. Tribunal Courts were forcing men to work while Small Debt Courts handed their wages directly to the landlords. On 18 November, 18 men were due in court for non-payment, and Mrs Barbour's Army planned a grand show of force.[65]

As day broke, many of the shipyards and engineering works came out on strike. Workers marched from Cathcart, Parkhead and Dalmuir towards the Sheriff Court, whilst Mrs Barbour marched with thousands of women, carrying candles to see through the November fog, and led by a band with whistles, drums and improvised instruments. On their way from Govan, they stopped at Lorne Street School in Plantation and carried Maclean out of his classroom and through the streets – Maclean was there working his last day under notice of dismissal.[66] The great crowds passed a column of soldiers on their way to Central Station and the Western Front – some from both sides cheered, and others shouted at the soldiers to join the strike.[67] By mid-morning, the huge crowds of striking women and workers had met, and the centre of the city was filled with protestors. The great neo-classical Sheriff Court on Wilson Street was besieged. Willie Gallacher recalls the scene:

All the streets were packed. Traffic was completely stopped. Right in front of the court Maclean was on a platform addressing the crowd as far as his voice could reach. In other streets near the court others of us were at it. Our platforms were unique. Long poster-boards had been picked up from the front of newspaper shops. These were placed on the shoulders of half a dozen husky, well-matched workers and the speaker was lifted on to them. It was a great experience, speaking from a yielding platform and keeping a measure of balance while flaying the factors and the war-makers.

Roar after roar of rage went up as incidents were related showing the robbery of mothers and wives whose sons and husbands were at the front. Roar followed roar as we pictured what would happen if we allowed the attack on our wages.[68]

At one point, police rushed the crowd and attempted to seize the poster-boards.[69] A 'sharp struggle' ensued.[70] Contingents from other factories sent messages to the Sheriff saying that if the men up in court were fined they would strike too. The huge crowd threatened at any moment to overwhelm the guards of the court. Maclean was sent in with a message for the city officials to pass on to Prime Minister Asquith: 'That this meeting of Clyde munition workers requests the Government to definitely state, not later than Saturday first, that it forbids any increase of rent during the period of war; and that; this failing, a general strike will be declared on Monday, 22 November.'[71]

The Sheriff was left with no option. It was clear that it would be impossible to keep order in Glasgow if the case against the strikers went ahead, and that even throwing it out would not be enough to placate the crowds. According to Gallacher, the Sheriff then telephoned Westminster and spoke with Lloyd George, the Minister for Munitions, informing him that the workers had left their factories and had the court and municipal buildings surrounded. Lloyd George replied: 'stop the case, a rent restriction act will be introduced immediately.'[72] Ripley and McHugh dispute this account, finding no record of the conversation, though they concede that the immediate implementation of the Rent Restriction Act was undoubtedly due to the strike.[73]

The victory was celebrated in the streets. The workers of Glasgow – along with fellow rent-strikers in Dundee, Aberdeen and Leith – had secured a rent freeze not just for themselves but for the whole of Scotland, England, Wales and Ireland. The workers had forced the hand of the government, and celebrations continued into the night.[74]

Tragically, almost no record of Mary Barbour's speeches or writings has been preserved, despite her key role in one of the defining moments of Scottish working-class history, her long political career, and her achievements as one of the first women elected as a Glasgow councillor. She went on to be one of the city's first female Baillies and the city's first female magistrate, and in 1925 she opened the first family planning clinic in Glasgow.[75]

Maclean wrote about the strike that Mary Barbour led in *Vanguard*:

The strike having taken place, the workers were bent on letting the Government know that out they would come again unless it restored rents to their pre-war level. It now transpires that a Rent Bill will be passed ... to reduce the rents to the level prevailing immediately prior to the outbreak of the Great Slaughter Competition.

It should be noted that the rent strike on the Clyde is the first step towards the Political Strike, so frequently resorted to on the Continent in times past. We rest assured that our comrades in the various works will incessantly urge this aspect on their shop-mates, and so prepare the ground for the next great counter-move of our class in the raging class warfare – raging more than even during the Great Unrest period three or four years ago.

Bear in mind that, although the Government has yielded to enormous pressure, it must do something to balance the victory. Remember how Lloyd George came out with the Munitions Act as a reply to the victory of the striking Clyde engineers ...

A victory at football, draughts, or chess, is the result of many moves and counter-moves ... So in the game of life. It advances from move to move, ever on grander and grander scale. Let us be up and doing all the time never giving the enemy time to settle down to a peaceful enjoyment of victorious plunder. Prepare, then, for the enemy's counter-stroke to our victory on the rent question![76]

On 19 November, Maclean went to Duke Street Prison to serve his five-day sentence. He refused to pay the fine, not acknowledging his guilt. On the day of his release, 40 miners arrived at Glasgow Central Station from Lanarkshire, dressed in their pit clothes and with their lamps burning. They had struck work for the day in protest at the imprisonment of their comrade John Maclean, whom they had come to welcome home from the jail. Once Maclean was safely home, the miners held a mass meeting with the workers at the gates of Fairfield Shipyard, passing resolutions in defiance of the Munitions Act and in support of John Maclean.[77] James Connolly wrote in his paper *Workers' Republic* that 'the fight against Maclean is a conspiracy against the working class',[78] and the foremost American socialist paper *Appeal to Reason* celebrated Maclean to its half a million readers.[79]

The war dragged on through a second winter, with the terror of poison gas in the trenches and Zeppelin raids in London now making a deep impression on the public. Maclean was uncowed by his time in jail, and on 12 December he was again arrested – along with Gallacher, MacManus, Dollan, Crawfurd and others – for obstructing North Hanover Street and North Frederick Street in central Glasgow with a horse and lorry, and delivering speeches, to a large crowd. They were fined 20 shillings each.[80] Maclean spent the end of 1915 holding street meetings such as these; lecturing on economics; and warning the public of the coming threat of conscription: 'Quick and firm action is needed if slavery is going to be abolished and conscription defeated. We must now fight boldly for the common ownership of all industries in Britain.'[81] Maclean studied Luxemburg's book *The Mass Strike*, and hoped that such a political strike as had defeated the landlords could now be used to defeat the government on conscription.[82]

6

The War Within a War

Glasgow's reputation as a centre of political unrest grew. London socialist paper the *Daily Herald* reported: 'Glasgow in these days is wonderful. It is a place of many meetings; a place rumbling with revolt ... I seemed to see a meeting at every street corner, and late in the evening the theatres poured forth huge masses of people who had been, not at entertainments, but at serious deliberations ... a mad whirl of meetings, strikes, and little revolutions.'[1]

In Autumn of 1915 two more of London's socialists came to Glasgow; Peter and Irma Petroff moved to the city in order to take on Maclean's teaching and propaganda commitments, should he be re-arrested.[2] Petroff came to stay in Maclean's home and found it to be the 'centre of the movement and headquarters of a manifold activity.'[3] The further association between Maclean and Petroff – both unpopular among the pro-war elements of the BSP – created suspicion among their party and the authorities.

Willie Gallacher aired his concerns about Petroff in his memoirs. He criticises his politics, claiming that the Russian was forever whispering conspiracies in Maclean's ear, and describing Petroff as having 'a sharp, dark face with black restless eyes, hooked nose'[4] – the anti-Semitic implications are clear. Petroff left his own account of Gallacher in his unpublished autobiography, in which he describes him as a 'muddle-head ... wobbling between anarchism and SLP dogmatism.'[5]

In December 1915 an anonymous letter attacking Petroff appeared in *Justice*, almost certainly written by Hyndman: 'Many of us have known of Peter Petroff for some years, though we have known little about him save that he has usually acted as a disintegrating nuisance...

He has now been for some weeks on the Clyde. What he is doing there, and what may be his object is best known to himself.'[6]

A day before this letter appeared, Petroff had been arrested. Maclean wrote to *Justice*, defending his friend and comrade:

[Peter Petroff] was invited to Glasgow by the Glasgow District Council of the B.S.P. to address a meeting in the Panopticon. He spoke on the Russian Revolution [of 1905] to an audience of over a thousand. After arrangements for this meeting were made, I was summoned under the Defence of the Realm Act. Expecting six months, I wished to see that my 'withdrawal' would involve no hitch in the conduct of our Economic Class, the issue of the 'Vanguard,' and the other activities that are helping to make the Clyde Valley the danger spot to capitalism. I therefore suggested to the G.D.C. that Petroff be kept in Glasgow as our second organiser. This was agreed to, and here he remains, with his wife, as a B.S.P. organiser.

The authorities thought a collapse would come with my dismissal. We gained as a consequence, and we are making straight for a Labour College …

I had arranged to go to Bowhill and speak against conscription, but by mistake the Anderston B.S.P. Branch ticketed MacDougall and myself for the same night. MacDougall had to go to Lesmahagow. My choice fell on the Anderston meeting to prime the comrades up for Lloyd George …

I consequently asked Petroff to go to Fife. I am responsible, and I shoulder the blame absolutely.[7]

After Peter's arrest he was tried and held for a week at Duke Street prison. His wife Irma kept a constant vigil, afraid he would be secretly deported to Russia[8] and soon she too was called to court. The Sheriff found that she had been living falsely as the wife of Peter Petroff and was in fact a German, and so an enemy alien. When asked by the Sheriff why she had not married Petroff, if they were indeed partners, Irma replied that she considered marriage degrading to women. Unsympathetic to this answer, the court sentenced her to 10 days in prison.[9]

Ripley and McHugh note that this period of time he spent with the Petroffs distinctly sharpened Maclean's critique of the BSP and of militarism, and helped to forge a view of his own place within an international socialist movement, with Peter Petroff bringing him news of his fellow-travellers Lenin, Trotsky, Adler and Luxemburg. It reinforced in his mind the impossibility of remaining loyal to Hyndman's clique whilst supporting the Zimmerwald conference.[10]

At the same time the conflict between Clyde workers and the Government was mounting, as Prime Minister Asquith intended to introduce a Conscription Bill. The bill would force men into the army with a view to counteracting the heavy losses being suffered on the Western Front. Maclean warned that the government 'had better not enlist us, for we will prove more dangerous with arms than without them.'[11]

At the same time the government instituted a policy of dilution of labour, bringing women and unskilled workers into the factories in order to free up more men for service and increase productivity, whilst lowering costs and reducing the power of the skilled workers. Maclean and the Clyde Workers' Committee didn't oppose dilution of labour per se. They were happy to embrace it if they were given more control over the running of the factories, seeing automation of their industries and the introduction of unskilled labour as inevitable. However, they wanted assurances that wages and bargaining power would not be weakened. Maclean also saw in the twin threats of conscription and dilution an opportunity to radicalise previously liberal members of the working class.

Whilst there were many in the trade union and socialist movements who opposed allowing women into the workforce, Maclean and his comrades on the other hand viewed the dilution of labour not in terms of conflict between the sexes but rather as a threat to gains won by the workers, and the future power of organised labour.[12] Maclean throughout his life viewed any sectional struggle by one group of workers with disdain, and instead thought tactically that the rights of skilled workers must be defended so they could better improve the conditions of unskilled workers.

MacDougall wrote for *Vanguard*:

As women enter out into production in huger and huger numbers, as they take their place alongside the men, their importance to society will come to be fully realised, not merely as producers of wealth, but as producers of men. Women themselves will become more conscious of the decisive part that they play in human development, and will no longer be content to sit at the feet of the male sex, or should we say, remain under the heel? They will arise in their power and demand their rightful position as equal friends and comrades of men. There will be no question of treating women as inferiors by refusing them the vote or in any other way. For women with practice will acquire just as great an influence over society in the future as she has today in the home. That influence will, I am convinced, be used for the humanising of this mankind which is today wallowing in filth and beastliness.[13]

In November of 1915 a meeting against conscription planned for Glasgow City Halls was banned by the Lord Provost. Petroff recalled having tea with Maclean and Pankhurst at 42 Auldhouse Road, and described George Lansbury running in to say the meeting had been prohibited and predicting violence if the event weren't cancelled. Maclean replied: 'Sit down and have tea, no police will prevent us from having the meeting.'[14] Maclean was right, and many thousands met in the snow outside the City Halls that night, where Lansbury and others stopped Sylvia Pankhurst and John Maclean breaking down the doors of the hall. Instead, the two spoke to full houses at the Pavilion, the Metropole and the Panopticon.[15] Maclean wrote in *Vanguard*:

we warn then that conscription means the bringing of all young men under the control of the military authorities ... and thus the old as well as the young will be bound hand and foot to Mr. William Weir and his capitalist friends. Military conscription implies industrial conscription ...

To the old, as to the young, we appeal for stern opposition to conscription.[16]

A correspondent from the *Daily Herald,* who had travelled with
Lansbury and Pankhurst to Glasgow reported on the mood in the city:

> Glasgow is a tonic, a holiday, and a pick-me-up all in one. Is
> there any other place where the movement can run six or seven
> successful large meetings within the space of a few hours? ... I
> am quite convinced that no other people in the world could sell
> literature with the apparent ease that the Glasgow women can ...
>
> It was not generally known that George Lansbury or Sylvia
> Pankhurst were going to be in Glasgow on Sunday, and consider-
> ing that the Lord Provost had banned the meeting arranged for
> Monday evening, it was assumed that they would not be there at
> all; yet we whirled into the crowded Metropole, where the Editor,
> amidst thunderous applause, denounced the theory of single
> men first; we dashed to Govan; back again to the Pavilion just in
> time to see the meeting pour out of the hall; and then on to the
> Panopticon ...
>
> Personally, I think the Govan meeting the most wonderful.
> There on the platform were three men who had been in gaol for
> defying the Munitions Act; men who declined to have their fines
> paid for them, and men who could ill afford to idle away their time
> within prison walls. The people of Govan were met to honour these
> men and their wives, and one felt that it was a historic occasion.
> It was not as though the men were well-known leaders of any
> movement in the neighbourhood—they were just ordinary men.
> But they were men ... There was a good proportion of women at
> this Glasgow meeting—the very women who might rightly regard
> themselves as the founders of the Rent Bill.[17]

In response to this growing unrest on Clydeside, David Lloyd George,
then Minister for Munitions, famed for his charm and rhetorical
skill, was sent to Glasgow in December 1915. The government hoped
Lloyd George could smooth the way for the unpopular government
policies of conscription and the dilution of labour.[18] He was due to
address a meeting at St Andrew's Hall – now the Mitchell Library –
on 25 December.

Christmas Day was hardly celebrated in Scotland at this time and John Maclean's daughter Nan recalls Irma Petroff's shock at the lack of festivities. Irma had gone out and found a tree, and, to the delight of the two Maclean daughters, she decorated it in the front room of their Pollokshaws house.[19] Having a German houseguest may have been difficult in the winter of 1915, but Peter Petroff remembers the great applause his wife received on being introduced to a meeting in Govan as an 'opponent of the war, and oppositional member of the Social Democratic Party of Germany.'[20]

Maclean, the Petroffs, and their comrades were out throughout December holding meetings and campaigning against conscription.[21] And on Thursday 22 Lloyd George – described in *Forward* as 'the best paid munitions worker in the country'[22] – had arrived in Glasgow. He first visited Beardmore's Forge at Parkhead where Clyde Workers' Committee member Davie Kirkwood introduced him to his colleagues, saying: 'he has come specially to speak to you, and no doubt you will give him a patient hearing. I can assure you that every word he says will be carefully weighed. We regard him with suspicion because every Act with which his name is associated has a taint of slavery to it.'[23] Kirkwood went on to say that the workers would embrace dilution if they were put in full control of the means of production, but otherwise would fight it tooth and nail.[24]

Lloyd George would face worse that afternoon when the workers of the Weir's factory in Cathcart refused to give him an audience at all, carrying on with their work instead.[25] Maclean and others spent the evening arguing about Arthur MacManus's suggestion to carry out a violent attack on Lloyd George.[26] Maclean opposed such a move, believing that it was unjustified, would bring harsh reprisals, and turn the public against the cause. From this time at least Petroff viewed MacManus with suspicion as a potential agent provocateur.[27]

When Christmas Day arrived, the members of the Clyde Workers' Committee made their way to the hall at Charing Cross where they found the 4,500 seat theatre packed with both workers and policemen. A Union Jack covered the speakers' table, women in uniform lined the front row, and a patriotic choir sang for the crowd. Some workers responded by singing the Red Flag until Arthur Henderson MP stood up to introduce Lloyd George.[28] The appearance of Henderson was the cue for disorder, and the crowd refused to let him speak; after a few minutes, Henderson gestured to Lloyd George for him to try instead. The crowd continued to roar as Lloyd George took to the stage.

The official report authorised by the censor suggested that it had been a small minority who had caused a disturbance. Other accounts state that the vast majority of the audience had been involved. Either way, the disruption had been sufficient to render the meeting a humiliation for Lloyd George.

Johnny Muir of the Clyde Workers' Committee was the next to take the stand. Willie Gallacher's memoirs here state that an instantaneous silence fell as Muir lectured the hall.[29] The account in *Forward*, however, concludes that as 'it was impossible to hear either Mr Muir or the Minister, the Chairman closed the proceedings and the meeting broke up in disorder.'[30] Lloyd George's attempt to pacify the Clyde and to persuade its workers of the need for dilution of labour had been a failure.

The extent of Lloyd George's humiliation at the Christmas Day meeting can be surmised from his response. Following *Forward*'s uncensored report of the meeting, he had their offices raided, their printing press confiscated, and the newspaper suppressed, even ordering police to ensure that the publication be removed from the shelves of every newsagent in Scotland. Some newsagents were even required to hand over lists of subscribers to the police.[31] This reaction by Lloyd George was viewed at the time as an escalation, and questions were asked in Parliament about the rights of the press.[32]

The atmosphere on the Clyde remained hostile both to conscription and to the dilution of labour, and packed out meetings continued to be held in halls, theatres and at factory gates.[33] Gallacher writes:

During all this period the general campaign against the war was proceeding more actively than ever. McLean was everywhere. His indoor meetings were packed out, with crowds outside clamouring for admission; until he was forced to run two meetings a night. He was the centre of the anti-war movement; and all the other movements, whatever their tendencies, supported the general line he was taking. He demanded an immediate armistice, with no annexations and no indemnities; along with this went his drive for the revolutionary overthrow of the capitalist class.[34]

Maclean's fame as a speaker and organiser was growing; his economics classes now had nearly 500 students, and more people still attended his Bath Street meetings each Sunday.[35] However, the government was also making its preparations for what it saw as an impending conflict in Glasgow, and over the course of January 1916 sufficient munitions were stockpiled in order to ensure that the country would be able to withstand a six week strike.[36] On 8 January, Maclean's newspaper *Vanguard* was also banned and the January issue confiscated.[37] The Clyde Workers' Committee responded at once with a new socialist publication, the *Worker*.

In late January, Petroff was re-arrested and confined to Edinburgh Castle.[38] The Home Office dismissed the many messages it received from trade unions demanding Petroff's release as being 'all traceable to Maclean.'[39] Meanwhile, the Defence of the Realm Act was extended to criminalise any actions which 'might impede or restrict the production, repair or transport of raw materials, or any other work necessary for the prosecution of the war.' After a lengthy correspondence between the Scotland Office, the Glasgow Police and the Scottish Military Command,[40] John Maclean was detained under this new law. He was arrested after his Sunday meeting at Bath Street, held overnight at Glasgow Central Police Station, and transported the next day to Edinburgh Castle.[41] In the castle he communicated with his fellow inmate Petroff, via books and messages passed between them by socialist soldiers.[42] John wrote to Agnes from his cell: 'I can be tried by the High Court of Judiciary, or by Court Martial. Naturally I will select the High Court ... I have been well treated so far, no need to feel anxious ... I trust you got Jimmie to arrange for Saturday's conference – a report, the paper, and purvey.'[43]

While in jail Maclean missed an event which he had been greatly looking forward to: the conference marking the foundation of the Scottish Labour College.[44] It had long been his belief that the workers needed their own form of education if they were to take control of industry. His proposal was for a Labour college which was to receive a donation of a penny a week from the wages of the workers of all of Scotland's factories, mines and shipyards, with the sum raised enabling workers at each plant, mine, or trade union to send students to the college. There they would receive three months of intensive education in Marxism, Mathematics and Public Speaking. Maclean wrote part of an article which was completed and then read by MacDougall at the event: 'The Universities and other institutions for higher education have for their object the training of men and women to run capitalist society in the interests of the wealthy. We think the time has come for an independent College, financed and controlled by the working class, in which workers might be trained for the battle against the masters.'[45]

Students would be selected by a ballot of the workers, and return to their places of work after training to hold classes themselves, thereby spreading their knowledge among their colleagues. Maclean saw the Labour College as an engine room for dissent. He had no interest in being the figurehead of a revolution and believed that his responsibility was to spread ideas and prepare the working class for its inheritance.

With Maclean in jail and much of the socialist press of the Clyde suppressed, the Government continued their offensive. They arrested Gallacher, Bell, and Muir for an article published in the *Worker* entitled 'Should the Workers Arm?'[46] The article concluded that the workers should not, arguing that 'if the internal clash of armed forces can be avoided in this country it should be avoided.'[47] But whether the title alone had been considered inflammatory, or whether the authorities simply had not read the piece, is unclear. Regardless, five of the key figures in the Clyde unrest were now jailed in Edinburgh, and word was spread that the socialists were traitors paid with German gold. It was even suggested that they had received a letter from the Kaiser thanking them for their cooperation.[48] The accusation was so prevalent that, before his arrest, Maclean would open his case of leaflets after giving a speech and call out 'German gold, who wants German gold.'[49]

Maclean was released on a bail of £100 and returned to his activities in Glasgow. His trial for breach of the Defence of the Realm Act was fixed for 11 April, and Maclean spent the intervening months ensuring that his Economics classes, anti-war meetings and, most importantly, the Scottish Labour College, would be able to carry on without him.[50]

A strike broke out at Beardmore's in Parkhead when shop stewards from the Clyde Workers' Committee were refused contact with new workers brought in under the dilution of labour. Over the following days, three more munitions plants struck in sympathy. The government feared that the Workers' Committee was gaining further influence on the Clyde and so increased its repression. A government paper argued that convicting Maclean alone would only create a martyr, and that the 'whole gang' had to be removed.[51] On 24 March ten shop stewards from Cathcart and Parkhead were arrested and deported to Edinburgh. In Edinburgh they were forbidden from taking part in political activity and ordered to report to a police station three times a day.[52]

A demonstration was called on Glasgow Green in defence of the deported trade unionists, and the crowd of 10,000 was addressed by Helen Crawfurd, Pat Dollan, James Maxton and James MacDougall. The speakers urged a strike. However, this in turn brought another blow from the authorities: on the 31 March Maxton and MacDougall were arrested and held at Duke Street Prison.[53] A few days later Jack Smith – another trade unionist at the Weir's munitions factory – was arrested for sedition. The fear of jail was now extremely real among the socialists and anarchists of Glasgow. While the BSP had undertaken to provide for Maclean's family in his absence, many of the other arrestees had left their families destitute, and a call for funds to support them was published in the newly re-instated *Forward*.[54]

Fear and confusion spread among the workers and the mass strikes with which Maclean believed arrests should be met did not emerge. Lloyd George had appointed William Weir, the owner of the Weir's factory in Cathcart, to the unpaid position of Director of Scottish Munitions in 1915 and, in that role, he had instigated the new hardness with which the state was meeting the 'war within a war' on the Clyde.[55] With the movement's leadership dispersed, anti-war activity decreased among the main body of the public and workers in Glasgow.

As the movements for peace and socialism lost momentum, Jingoism and anti-German sentiment increased, reaching new heights when, just over a week before Maclean's trial, Edinburgh was struck by Scotland's first air-raid. Thirteen people were killed and twenty-four were injured in the Zeppelin raid.[56] The atmosphere was tense in Edinburgh ahead of the High Court trial of John Maclean.

7

Convict 2652

On the morning of 11 April 1916, a crowd of supporters travelled with John Maclean on the train from Glasgow to Edinburgh. As well as his wife Agnes and sister Lizzie, the carriage was packed with engineers and miners who had taken the day off work.[1] Over the sound of the train, the workers played the fiddle and sang the Red Flag with a new poignancy to the line 'come dungeons dark or gallows grim'.[2]

The courtroom was full when Maclean arrived and many hundreds had already been turned away.[3] But whereas the court in Glasgow had been packed with Maclean's supporters at his previous trial, the courtroom here was already filled with the denizens of bourgeois and conservative Edinburgh – only a few of Maclean's comrades were able to gain entry – and the jury Maclean faced was made up entirely of property-owning men, including a 'jeweller', a 'farmer', a 'stock-broker' and a 'traveller'.[4] The six counts of the indictment against Maclean were read to the court. All related to statements he had made that January when there had been what was referred to by the prosecution as 'a somewhat anxious situation on the Clyde'.[5]

No civilians testified against Maclean and instead evidence was given against Maclean by 18 policemen, who each repeated and corroborated the charges. It was alleged that John Maclean had said that:

1. Conscription was unnecessary, as the government had plenty of soldiers and munitions; that after the war, conscription would be used to secure cheap labour; that should the government enforce the Military Service Act and the Munitions Act, the workers should 'down tools'; that if the British soldiers laid down their arms, the Germans would do the same, as all were tired of the war.
2. The workers should strike in order to attend a meeting.

3. The workers should 'down tools' and resist conscription.

4. If conscription became law, the workers would become conscripts to industrial labour – the real aim of the government.

5. The workers should strike and those who had guns should use them.

6. The workers should sell or pawn their alarm clocks, sleep in in the mornings and not go to work.[6]

Helen Crawfurd, Manny Shinwell and James Maxton among others spoke in Maclean's defence. Witnesses from Weir's Factory confirmed that they had been at the meetings described by the police, but that they had never heard anything about guns.[7] Helen Crawfurd in particular took the opportunity to criticise Maclean for not attacking the government enough and instead focussing his ire on the Clyde Workers' Committee which he saw as too moderate and too anxious not to come out strongly against the war. But she denied that he had encouraged armed rebellion.[8]

Maclean had pleaded not guilty, and on the second day of the trial he gave his own testimony to the court. He described his activities as a socialist and as an educator, stating that he was 36 years old, a school-teacher by profession, and a member of the British Socialist Party, concerned with securing better housing for the working class. He then explained that lately his time was devoted to the most important thing in the world: the establishment of a Scottish Labour College. He confirmed, though, that he was strongly opposed to military conscription and that he had taken part in an active struggle against it as he believed the current war to be a war of capitalist aggression.

In his defence, he went on to deny saying that if Scottish soldiers were to lay down their arms, German soldiers would do the same, suggesting that this was a utopian view. He added, though, that it had happened at Flanders on Christmas Day.[9]

Maclean did accept that he had frequently used the phrase: 'slaughter and be slaughtered' and declared that this phrase was a truism. He raised a laugh from the gallery when he also admitted to having used the phrase 'bloody English capitalists' but adding that he had only used it because it was 'a classic phrase'. He also confirmed that he had told the workers to pawn or sell their alarm clocks, because they were German made and as patriots it was their duty not to use them, and, if that meant that they would sleep in and miss work, then so be it.[10] This was followed by a denial that he had ever urged workers to use their guns, due to the fact that he had never met a worker who had a gun.

Under cross-examination, Maclean confirmed that he had been a socialist for 17 years and that he held an economics class in Glasgow attended by nearly 500 students.[11] When asked if it was his objective to encourage strikes with a view to forcing the government to end conscription, he answered that his objective was only to explain the dangers of conscription. On being asked, however, whether he was in favour of strikes at the current juncture, he answered that he had never considered the matter. It has been remarked that this seems a surprisingly poor defence from Maclean.

When the prosecution asked whether at the meeting in question he had referred to the prime minister as 'Assassin Asquith', Maclean replied that he was unable to remember, as he had used the phrase so many times.[12] The Lord Justice General ended by asking 'You are very much opposed to Mr Lloyd George and the government?' To which Maclean replied, 'I am, when their actions seem to me to be against the interests of the people. I quite admit that I would say at any moment that Lloyd George is a liar (laughter). I have said he was a liar often (renewed laughter).'[13]

Maclean told the court that he would not ask for leniency, as the police who had testified against him 'have their knees on the chest and their hands on the throat of the working class and I do not ask them for mercy. I am not here to ask for mercy, I am here to fight.'[14]

The judge reminded the jury that if they were to find Maclean innocent, they would be suggesting that the police officers had concocted the six statements which Maclean had denied uttering. The jury retired at 3.15 to deliberate for 65 minutes and returned to deliver guilty verdicts on the first four indictments, not proven on the fifth, and not guilty on the sixth.

Lord Strathclyde passed the sentence:

John Maclean, after a patient and prolonged consideration of your case, you have been found guilty, not for the first time, of contravening the regulations for the defence of the realm. On the former occasion a very light sentence, I observe, was passed on you with the intention no doubt of being a warning and to act as a deterrent. It seems to have failed. To a man so intelligent and highly educated as you appear to be it would be idle for me to dwell upon the gravity of your offence which a jury of your country-men have found you guilty of today. It is thoroughly well known to you, as it is no doubt to the whole of the community. The sentence of the court is that you be sent to penal servitude for a period of three years.[15]

Maclean waved his hat to his friends in the gallery on hearing the sentence, later saying 'The greatest "crime" I have committed in the eyes of the British Government and the Scottish capitalist class has been the teaching of Marxian economics to Scottish workers.'[16]

Those workers who had made it into the court cheered and sang, and a great crowd outside applauded Maclean as he was placed in a police van and driven to Calton Jail. The *Daily Record* reported that, after the verdict was read, a disturbance had broken out in the gallery, the Red Flag had been sung, and four men had been arrested.[17] The *Fife Free Press* summed up the response of most newspapers to the sentence, concluding that 'three years penal servitude serves the traitor well.'[18] However, Maclean's sentence was considered harsh by many Liberal and left-wing figures and newspapers, with the *Labour Leader* describing the sentence as an example of Britain 'being Prussianised'.[19] Letters and articles in the *Courier* and *Aberdeen Press and Journal* referred to the sentence as 'savage'[20] and 'severe' and remarked that three years' hard labour for such a crime was unprecedented.[21] The *Scotsman*'s editorial, however, remarked that 'the penalty does not unduly mark the heinousness of the offence' for such a 'parasite'.[22]

Fears over how Maclean would be treated intensified a fortnight later after the Easter Rising took place in Dublin. Several hundred men and women led an armed rebellion against British rule and intense street fighting took place. Thousands were arrested and interred. The ringleaders – including Edinburgh-born James Connolly – were executed, and the seeds were sown for the Irish Republic.

Though a supporter of home rule for Ireland as well as for Scotland, and a firm friend of the Irish trade unionist James Larkin, Maclean had up until this point written and said little about the prospect of an uprising in Dublin. But in 1916, Maclean's actions on the Clyde and Connolly's martyrdom on the Liffey would unite these two figures in the popular consciousness and, over the coming years, Maclean would often look to the Irish Struggle as an inspiration. Perhaps the first connection between the two was made by Trotsky in *Nashe Slovo* in May 1916 where he stated in a report on the Easter Rising: 'Scottish soldiers broke down the barricades in Dublin. But in Scotland itself the miners unite around the Red Banner raised by Maclean and his friends. Those very workers, who at the moment the Hendersons are trying to chain to the bloody chariot of imperialism, will revenge themselves against the hangman Lloyd George.'[23]

Many have sought to connect Connolly and Maclean as firm friends and comrades and part of a nascent Leninism. However, there is no evidence that they ever met or even corresponded. Although Connolly was briefly a member of the Social Democratic Federation before he left to form the Socialist Labour Party, it seems their membership did not overlap. James D. Young notes that Maclean was not converted to the cause of Irish independence until 1919, and it was not until 1922 that Maclean suggested a link between the unrest on Clydeside and the martyrdom of 'Jim' Connolly.[24] In his April 1916 High Court appearance, the record in Nan Milton's papers states that Maclean said armed struggle might be good enough for Dublin, but that it was of no use at that time in Glasgow. As the case was not reported in the Law Records and there are no other notes on the proceedings, this is difficult to verify.[25] However, as this assertion was described as having been made a fortnight before the Easter Rising, it is hard to see to what Maclean was referring and it is entirely possible that it is a deliberate invention to suggest that Maclean had had prior knowledge of the rebellion, much in the same way that Tom Bell falsified accounts of Connolly in Glasgow in 1915 to show that he and other communists had supported him.[26] In fact, it was not until early May that year that comment was passed on the Easter Rising in Scottish socialist circles, and then it was Tom Johnstone lamenting what he portrayed as the 'futile' death of their comrades.[27]

Either way, by the time James Connolly was executed in Dublin Castle in May 1916, Maclean, now Convict 2652, was in a cell in Calton Jail – just a few hundred yards from where Connolly was born. Maclean was soon joined by Gallacher, Bell, Muir, Maxton and MacDougall, who were all found guilty in the days following Maclean's conviction – although none defended themselves with the vigour of Maclean.

Of his own trial, Gallacher said, 'If Maclean held high the banner of revolutionary struggle, we dragged it, or allowed it to be dragged, in the mire.'[28] None of the other Red Clydesiders put up a revolutionary defence, and all received more lenient sentences. Maxton and MacDougall even asked the court to take into account the 'regret they now felt for their quite inexcusable action'.[29] They were, however, still afforded no special privileges as political prisoners.

The food provided was porridge and buttermilk for breakfast, soup for lunch, and porridge again for dinner.[30] Prisoners were kept 'silent and separate' with just half an hour's exercise in the courtyard each day.[31] Nevertheless, Maxton and his fellow prisoners managed to persuade the warders at Calton Jail to form a branch of the Police and Prison Warders Trade Union, and even talked a few of them into joining the ILP.[32] David Kirkwood recalled that the warders also allowed the deported shop stewards from Parkhead and Cathcart to come by Calton Prison to see the prisoners.[33] Maclean appeared to keep his spirits high and concluded his first letter to Agnes from Calton Jail: 'Now I must close with love to you all again, and bright hope as well.'[34]

The unrest on the Clyde continued to receive global attention and, in late May, Georgy Chicherin wrote a five-part series on the socialist agitation in Scotland for *Nashe Slovo*, with a portrait of John Maclean appearing on the front page of the 28 May issue. Chicherin, who was to become the Commissar for Foreign Affairs under both Lenin and Stalin, wrote:

The quick succession of repressions in Glasgow, the closure of newspapers, the arrests, the interning of Comrade Petroff and his wife, the recent trial of Comrade Maclean, which was unheard of in its severity and resulted in him being sentenced to three years' penal servitude, the administrative deportations, a number of court proceedings completed or pending – all of these blows are aiming for the very core of the revolutionary class movement in England [*sic*], for the splendidly and expansively developing Scottish labour movement ...

An exceptionally important role, as yet unparalleled on the Continent in this area, is played in the recent Scottish movement by the network of educational establishments created over many years of efforts by a large number of dedicated activists who had devoted themselves to this cause, of whom the most exceptionally talented, knowledgeable, energetic, enthusiastic and revolutionary minded man is Comrade Maclean, Comrade Petroff's constant ally.[35]

Meanwhile, the leaders of the Scottish movement were suffering the torment of jail and isolation. Both Muir and MacDougall suffered nervous breakdowns, and Maxton was, by the time of his release, an extremely ill man. Gallacher described Calton Jail: 'It was by far the worst prison in Scotland; cold, silent and repellent. Its discipline was extremely harsh and the diet atrocious.'[36]

After a month of solitary confinement at Calton Jail, Maclean was moved to Peterhead Prison on the Buchan coast, north of Aberdeen. Here he was to endure the hard labour to which he had been sentenced. Whilst the conditions of imprisonment were perhaps slightly improved, the daily work outside brought its own dangers and the authorities had packed more than 400 convicts into a jail built for no more than 208. Maclean was kept in a cell 4 ft wide, 8 ft long and 7 ft high and spent his days working in a quarry.[37] He complained of regular strip searches and cruel treatment by the guards,[38] adding that he was kept 'clean and sanitary' by having his underwear washed once a fortnight.[39]

From the summer onwards, there was pressure for Maclean's release. In August, Philip Snowden, the Labour MP for Blackburn, asked the Scottish Secretary if he would consider the remission of the three-year penal servitude sentence for Maclean in the light of the more lenient sentences being handed out to socialists and pacifists in England, and the unreliable character of the evidence given by

Figure 3   John Maclean in Peterhead Prison, 1916
(National Records of Scotland, HH16/132/1)

the police. The Secretary for Scotland replied, 'No, sir, I cannot undertake to give any promise of remission on either of the grounds stated, and I must enter a protest against the suggestion implied in the concluding portion of the question.'[40]

Maclean continued to work outside and those who cared about him, particularly Agnes, worried a great deal about his health. Like his father and his brother, he had always suffered with respiratory complaints. A petition for Maclean's release was prepared, but the case was not strong. One option was to appeal against the evidence given. But, as the evidence was entirely provided by police officers, it was unlikely to be thrown out. The second option was to appeal for leniency and to show contrition but, as Maclean had made plain, he was not willing to sacrifice his principles and ask for mercy.[41] Agnes visited John in July to ask what action should be taken and he made it clear that he did not want to beg for his freedom; he had squared his action with his conscience.[42]

The meeting left Agnes concerned about her husband. She described his situation to Albert Inkpen, the secretary of the British Socialist Party:

… he is a *convict* and is having no privileges whatever. I saw him for twenty minutes … with two warders present. We did not even get shaking hands – we were separated by bars. The regulations are that he gets no visit till a year of his time is up. He will be due one letter in November. He gets reading no newspapers and has to work out of doors all day. They get a summary of the war news read out daily.[43]

An appeal was sent to socialists around the world. They were told 'Comrades, stir yourselves, an injury to one is the concern of all … Get your ambassadors to approach the British Government on your behalf. Remember however, John Maclean does not ask for mercy, but merely demands justice.'[44]

Agnes wrote to John in November 1916:

It must be dreadful for you, the awful monotony for so long, the dreary winter days we now have … When I saw you in July I never thought for one minute you would still be in jail [in November]. Don't get downhearted. Your cause is more alive today than it ever was, and although there is nothing but silence for you meantime, your day is coming. It would take pages to tell you of all the people who are always asking after you and thinking of you. Our fund for maintenance is being closed already. There is enough to keep us although you are away the whole time, and enough to keep you for some time until you are in good condition to take up your life work again.

A John Maclean Sale of Work was held in the central halls which realised £180. This Sale originated at the women's guild, so don't say it has been no use! … they could have got double if the hall had been larger. Crowds of people could not get near the stalls at all …

... the class is going well. They enrolled upwards of 300 and attendance is excellent.[45]

Maclean was allowed to reply a few days later and his letter is characteristically breezy:

On no account worry about me. I am keeping the promise I gave you on 12 April. I have no reason to feel depressed even if kept here three years ... More than 2 months ago I heard rumours that a good fight was being made for me. Supposing I knew there wouldn't be a Soc. in Scotland when I came out I would not let that worry me, but resolve to come out and begin the good work again. Believe no one that would hint or suggest that I can be depressed. Glad to know you are secure. Thank The Guild for me ... As my throat was a bit worse I go inside for good to patch shirts etc. It's much better ... During the heat I ate little or no porridge and lost weight but now I'm heavier than ever. I sleep well at night and have a good nap every day after dinner. I have never been ill yet, not even indigestion. I can eat more than ever, the air's so bracing ... The winter is passing quicker than the summer as we eat less and sleep more! ... I read steadily a book a week, and having no distractions enjoy the books more than I did all my reading for years. Tell Jean she has to be able to read stories to me when I come home and Nan must be able to tell me all about giants and faeries and everything. I'll give them lots of fun and swings in Rouken Glen. They must get a penny from me every Sunday and I'll speak to good old S. Claus to see if he'll carry something nice for them at Xmas ... the bye-word here is 'Cheer Up'! Apply it![46]

The jollity of the letter seems unmistakably an act of will by Maclean, keen not to add his own misery to that of his family. We do not know to what extent he is telling the truth about his conditions, but we do know from the prison doctor's reports that his claim to be in good health and gaining weight were not true. Nevertheless, the relief that his young family was being provided for while he was in prison must have been significant. It was certainly not the case, as he jokes in his letter, that there might not have been a socialist left in Scotland. But, with many of the leaders imprisoned, and with the threat of heavy fines and sentences clearly established, industrial unrest in Glasgow was greatly reduced.

Despite the de-escalation of tensions on Clydeside, Maclean's presence in the international socialist consciousness continued to grow throughout his imprisonment. Lenin, at the time in exile in Switzerland, mentions Maclean at least eight times in his essays of this period, stating that 'the Scottish school teacher and socialist, MacLean, who was sentenced to hard labour by the bourgeois government of England for his revolutionary fight against the war, and hundreds of British socialists who are in jail for the same offence. They, and they alone, are internationalists in deeds.'[47] And 'MacLean and Liebknecht—those are the names of socialists who are putting the idea of a revolutionary struggle against imperialism into practice.'[48]

By 1917, Lenin was explicitly linking the struggle in Russia with the actions of the jailed Maclean:

But the socialists who 'fight for peace'—not in words, not to deceive themselves or the workers—started their fight long ago, without waiting for any international conferences. They started their fight by renouncing national unity, precisely in the way it was done by MacLean in Britain, Karl Liebknecht in Germany and the Bolsheviks in Russia.[49]

Though from today's perspective, a century of Soviet Russia and Communism in Asia has resulted in the idea of Marxist revolution seeming foreign to the United Kingdom, from the time Marx and Engels began writing – with their focus on London and Manchester – it was imagined that the industrialised West would be the place where Communism would begin. Even in early 1917, Lenin and his comrades thought Marxist revolution to be more likely either in Britain or in Germany than in Russia, and to the Bolsheviks it appeared that Maclean had the potential to be a revolutionary leader.

Maclean of course received little communication from the outside world during his imprisonment, with the exception of a letter allowed to him as a special privilege with news that Nan, his daughter, had caught scarlet fever but was improving.[50] Soon after that letter was sent, Agnes and their other daughter Jean also fell victim, and Nan was sent to live with John's sister Lizzie while they recovered.[51]

In early March 1917, Agnes received a letter saying that John's health had deteriorated and that he had been transferred to Perth Prison, and the prison hospital there. He had now been in jail for a year, and had received no visitors for ten months. But in his letter to Agnes in May, he continued to insist that his health was fine:

> I have nothing to add to what I said to you re my health on your last visit. I am the same as then and will be the same till I am free. Draw no conclusions from hair or tongue … I am glad to hear that you yourself are feeling stronger and I trust you will continue improving until my release when we could do no better than spend a good holiday at Perth and Peterhead – outside His Majesty's Hotel however! Remember me to all relatives, friends and comrades.
>
> Your *living* husband, Johnnie[52]

This adamant declaration of good health was characteristic. The popular view concerning Maclean at this time is that he was in fact suffering a great deal both physically and mentally. It was undoubtedly the case that Maclean suffered throughout his life from respiratory illnesses, and the cold, damp and unsanitary conditions of Peterhead Prison exacerbated his condition.

What is far more contentious, however, is the state of Maclean's mental health. Many have asserted that Maclean had a breakdown in Peterhead Prison, though there is little evidence. The view that he suffered from paranoid delusions arises in part from Maclean's claim after his release that prison guards had been poisoning his food, and also, more substantially, from suggestions spread by members of the intelligence agencies, and former comrades in the Communist and Labour Parties in the years leading up to and after his death, that John Maclean lost his mind in prison.

The separate question of whether Maclean had been poisoned while in prison is also contentious. After his release, Maclean stated repeatedly in public that he believed he had been drugged whilst in prison. He believed this largely because he felt sure that his prison

diet was making him ill. His suggestion that his food was being deliberately contaminated in order to reduce his political efficacy could
certainly be construed as paranoia, but it is nevertheless hard to
dismiss his allegation out of hand as being wholly irrational. Maclean
was in prison for political reasons and he did become ill in prison.
To link his persecution and his illness, in the context of a British
government that certainly did kill its political enemies in jail, was
not illogical. It may be fair to say that Maclean over-valued the idea
that his food was being adulterated, but not that it was a delusion. In
fact, the Secretary for Scotland noted at the time that 'Such delusions
are held by many of the inmates who write to this office.'[53]

However, the prison doctor in Peterhead felt that the prisoner's
assertion that he was dangerous to the British State, and that its
agents were trying to poison him, was clearly madness. The view that
Maclean's fear of poison was a sign of insanity persisted after Maclean
was transferred to Perth Prison Hospital, where official papers reveal
that the authorities were anxious to 'avoid giving anyone the chance
of using the mental breakdown of Maclean and MacDougall as a
basis for attacks on the government or prison system'.[54] MacDougall's
breakdown is clearer, he suffered terribly in jail and, after a second
stretch in prison, was unable to return to political campaigning. Contemporary letters and his own account of his life refer to a nervous
breakdown at this time. None of this is true for Maclean, whose
mental health is not discussed by him or his comrades.

Dr James Devon, the Prison Commissioner of Health for Scotland
and Dr Hugh Ferguson Watson, the medical superintendent of the
Criminal Lunatic Department at Perth Prison, both made notes on
Maclean's case. Dr Devon commented that, whilst Maclean 'reasons
quite clearly ... it is evident that he has not got rid of his suspicions
and of his insane delusions of persecution.'[55] And Dr Watson found
that Maclean would not take medicines prescribed for his chronic
catarrh, though this changed after the doctors put him on a special
diet and his health recovered.[56]

The extent to which Maclean was suffering with mental illness
remains unknowable. It was inarguable that he saw himself as being
persecuted as a threat to the government, and it is possible that
the diet in Peterhead had been making him ill; certainly life there

had aggravated underlying respiratory problems. Connecting these separate matters does not seem to lie outside the realms of sane reasoning, but the same time the nervous strain on him seems to have been immense.

However, Maclean's apparent 'persecution-mania' as described by the prison doctors was confined to concerns about the prison food and, when Dr Gilbert Garrey, the medical officer at Peterhead Prison, was asked to certify Maclean as insane, he refused.[57] It seems that, despite what they perceived as a mental health crisis, not one of the three doctors who saw Maclean was prepared to certify him as insane. Maclean himself wrote on a later release that

> ... the prison people did their utmost to accomplish the usual. The doctors this time made the most thorough test of my mind and character to find out such weaknesses as they might play upon in future to corrupt me into the betrayal of my class. It was beautifully done, but I can assure comrades that I beat the doctors at their game. I let them know that I was obsessed about nothing, not even life itself, and that they could burn all they thought they knew about me and have in tabulated and indexed form, as it would be of no use to them in my future fight against capitalism.[58]

The only evidence we have, other than that of the prison doctors, are John Maclean's letters and articles, which in tone and rationality are unchanged after this episode. The debate over Maclean's sanity is unlikely to ever be settled – fuelled as it was by enemies later in life – but the suffering he endured in prison and the powerful impact it had upon him are clear. What is clearer still is that prison in no way broke Maclean's determination to destroy capitalism.

8

We are Going to Live to See the Day

In January 1917, MacDougall, Maxton, Muir and Gallacher were released and returned to the Clyde. All but Gallacher were in poor health. Nevertheless they immediately joined in the struggle for the release of John Maclean. In late February, they addressed a packed meeting at St Mungo's Hall in Govan. Willie Gallacher writes that

> ... when I and subsequent speakers declared for all our forces being brought into the fight to release John Maclean, the roof was nearly lifted off the building ...
>
> Soon the Government had to take note of the fact that the 'unrest' on the Clyde was assuming serious proportions once again, and the centre of the trouble was the continued imprisonment of John Maclean.[1]

Less than a fortnight later, the Russian Revolution began. The February Revolution installed a provisional bourgeois democracy and heralded a new liberal Russia. Almost no one imagined that another Revolution might take place later that same year. Huge meetings in support of the new regime were held around Scotland. Russian sailors docked on the Clyde came ashore and celebrated the fall of the Tsar in the International Hall in the Gorbals.[2] Rebels and revolutionaries everywhere were bolstered by the news from Russia, and the *Call* remarked that, were Maclean to have been in a Russian jail, he would be at home with his wife and children by now.[3]

'Free Maclean' and 'Free Russia' were the two main socialist campaigns of early 1917, and support continued to be strong among the trade unions, left-wing parties and Clyde workers' organisations. Agnes received letters from friends of her husband who had been conscripted. One wrote:

> What a great game he has played! ... No one seems able to fill his place, but we have his prototype Liebknecht doing exactly the same thing in Germany. I don't forget, nor can I realise how much you must miss him ... I know how anxious Maxton is about Jimmy [MacDougall] and I know too that Maxton is haggard and ill looking, but they are out and that is the main thing ... one thing I am convinced of is that John is the biggest man in the country. His name is written large in the history of our movement and he is coming out a bigger and greater man than he went in.[4]

The energy of the Russian Revolution seemed to re-animate the socialists of Clydeside and to restore faith in the return of Maclean. The largest May Day procession Glasgow had ever seen took place, with between 70,000 and 80,000 marching to Glasgow Green where 16 speaker's platforms were built.[5] Impassioned speeches offered solidarity to the Russian workers and demanded Maclean's release, and the crowds spread out around the People's Palace and up to the High Court. The *Daily Record* commented that 'Labour Sunday' had been celebrated on Clydeside by some 212 organisations with international speakers including 'a Jew, a Lett, a Russian and a Lithuanian'.

The following resolution was moved from each platform and carried unanimously:

> That this meeting declares for the overthrow of the capitalist system of production for profit, and the establishment of a cooperative Commonwealth based on production for use as the only solution for the poverty and unemployed problem; and, further, that this meeting of the workers assembled on Glasgow Green sends its fraternal greetings to the workers of the world, pledging to use every endeavour to effect the emancipation of labour from the domination of capitalism and landlordism, and in the interest of labour, hereby declare in favour of the first day in May being held as a general holiday.[6]

The socialist *Daily Herald* reported that, including the spectators who lined the streets, nearly a quarter of a million people took part in the demonstration and 'if the Russians hear of the great meeting that took place in Caledonia at the weekend they will be over-joyed to hear how their blow for freedom has encouraged and enthused the people of Scotland.'[7] The paper added that soldiers in uniform wore red flowers of internationalism and that, 'like the soldiers in Petrograd, the men in khaki in Glasgow on Sunday were the friends of the common people and the enemy of oppression.'[8]

On May Day itself in Glasgow the Red Sunday School, one of many socialist children's groups led by the likes of Tom Anderson, drafted its commandments:

1. Thou shalt inscribe on your banner: 'Workers of all lands unite. You have nothing to lose but your chains: you have a world to win.'
2. Thou shalt not be a patriot for a patriot is an international blackleg. Your duty to yourself and your class demands that you be a citizen of the world.
3. Thou shalt not usurp the right of any man or woman, nor shall you claim for yourself any natural advantage over your fellows; for every man and woman has an equal right to an equal share in the product of their collective labour.
4. Thou shalt not take part in any bourgeois war, for all modern wars are the result of the clash of economic interests, and your duty as an internationalist is to wage class war against all such wars.
5. Thou shalt teach Revolution, for revolution means the abolition of the present Political State, and the end of Capitalism, and the raising in their place an Industrial Republic ....[9]

The extent to which the war had radicalised Glasgow was remarkable. With continuing meetings and marches, and Socialist Sunday Schools throughout the city, the workers' movement in Glasgow had organised Labour Day celebrations to rival those of any city in the world. In less than a decade, Glasgow had been transformed from a liberal bastion to a hotbed of radicalism. On 14 May, a meeting in a packed St Andrew's Hall celebrating the Russian Revolution garnered so much interest that a further 3,000 workers were addressed on the streets outside.[10] As at the May Day rally, the speeches were in Yiddish and Lithuanian as well as in English, and Helen Crawfurd and Bob Smillie both addressed the crowd outside, while Dr Charles Sarolea told the 4,500 people assembled inside the hall that the Hohenzollerns and Hapsburgs would follow the Romanovs.[11] He stopped short of mentioning the British royal family. The *Daily Herald* hailed the Glasgow meeting in support of the Petrograd Soviet as 'the fraternisation of the two great cities of the twentieth century revolution'.[12] Maclean, meanwhile, remained in his cell, cut off from the news, and gleaning what information of the Russian Revolution he could from the war reports read out to the prisoners.

The militants on Clydeside kept up the pressure against the war and for improved working conditions throughout May 1917, though the majority of workers were by no means in favour of revolution, and instead called for reform. On 28 May, the *Daily Record* ran an article under the heading 'Triple Protest': 'Assembling at Parkhead, Springburn, Partick and Govan, large processions marched yesterday afternoon to Glasgow Green where they joined forces at the monument to participate in a demonstration …The Appearance of a number of Russian Sailors on one of the lorries was a novel feature of the demonstration.'[13]

Nan Milton writes that this demonstration was 100,000 people strong and that it was organised to call for Maclean's freedom.[14] This was not reported, but we can speculate that a pro-government paper such as the *Daily Record* erred on the side of caution when it came to the numbers, as well as the demands of the demonstration. Certainly it made the news up and down the country, with the Liverpool *Daily Post* reporting it in a piece entitled 'Glasgow's Ungracious Workmen'.[15] The sympathetic *Daily Herald* described 30,000 men marching to Glasgow Green under a great crimson flag, with 100 uniformed Russian sailors in their midst. It also reported that, at a meeting of Lithuanian socialists in Glasgow that evening, two Russian sailors had taken to the podium to condemn the British government for its detention of Maclean and Petroff.[16] The meeting between the labour movement and the Russians was a success, and on 30 May, the *Daily*

Record ran pictures of 'Sailors of Emancipated Russia' visiting Rouken Glen Park with what were described as 'their new friends'.[17]

When Lenin arrived in Petrograd that spring on the famous train from Helsinki, he went to the balcony of Kshesinskaya Mansion, the Bolshevik headquarters, and told the crowd that the Communist struggle was the same in Glasgow and Berlin. A leader of the Red Sailors, Raskolnikov, reported that Lenin said to the crowd 'Germany [is] in ferment. In Britain the Government holds John Maclean in prison.'[18] At this moment, Lenin was an isolated figure, leader of a fringe political party who at that time doubted his drive for revolution, but nevertheless figures such as Maclean in Scotland and Liebknecht in Germany offered for him a model of how true communists should behave towards their warring governments. Just as the Russian Revolution was electrifying Glasgow, word of unrest on the Clyde was inspiring the Russian workers who listened to Lenin's first speech in a free Russia. Walter Kendall notes that

> John Maclean, a lonely man in a Scottish prison suddenly became a revolutionary symbol of international significance. The First All Russian Congress of Workmen and Soldiers Deputies meeting in June cabled 'Greetings to the brave fighter for the international proletariat, Comrade Maclean, and express their hopes that a new rise of international solidarity will bring him liberty.'[19]

The telegram from the Petrograd Soviet caused some confusion in Glasgow, where it was delivered in error to the Liberal MP Sir Donald Maclean,[20] who contacted the Independent Labour Party leader Ramsay Macdonald explaining the mistake:

> Dear Ramsay, I enclose a telegram which reached me on Friday or Saturday last. After strenuous efforts to persuade myself that the compliment was meant for me I am regretfully driven to the conclusion that it is meant for another member of the clan. I would be much obliged if you would forward the message to him, with my best wishes for his release.[21]

Maclean, meanwhile, had been more than a year in jail, with 22 months left of his sentence. Still in Perth Prison Hospital, his health remained poor.[22]

In early June, a conference of more than a thousand socialists in Leeds called for Maclean to be freed.[23] Momentum was growing, and it is possible that at this point the government felt that a concession to Clydeside might be helpful. Certainly the Cabinet saw releasing Maclean as 'an act of expediency'.[24] Around this time, the socialist politician and editor of the *Daily Herald*, George Lansbury, wrote to the new Prime Minister Lloyd George asking for Maclean's release, and undertaking to support his recuperation in the South of England. The Prime Minister's office raised the issue of Maclean's release with the Scotland Office in mid-June.[25]

Pressure continued to mount, and in late June, the British Socialist Party's magazine *The Call* published an article saying that 'it will be a standing shame and disgrace on the workers ... if the ruling class is thus permitted to wreak its vengeance on John Maclean and remove him permanently from its path.'[26] The public campaign eventually had its effect and, on 25 June, the Secretary for Scotland announced in Parliament that given the effects of imprisonment on Maclean's health and the fact that more than half the sentence had been served, he was justified in sanctioning the prisoner's early release.[27]

Maclean was moved to a cell in Glasgow four days later, with well-wishers welcoming him back by singing the 'Red Flag' outside. On the last day of June 1917, he was finally released on the condition that he report to a police station each week.

A telegram from George Lansbury to Agnes Maclean on 3 July read: 'I wrote to Lloyd George directly and offered to go bail and bring John south. I got a reply saying he would look into the matter and heard no more till I saw the announcement of his release. I think the Russians secured it.'[28]

Whether it was Russia, Glasgow, or London which had secured John's release, it must have been a huge relief to Agnes that her husband, now thin and looking far older than his 38 years, was out of prison.

On the same day as Maclean's release, Prime Minister Lloyd George visited Glasgow, receiving the Freedom of the city, and was

booed and catcalled by the crowds.[29] The *Daily Herald* reported that
a red flag was flown from a window along the premier's route to
St Andrew's Hall. Willie Gallacher recalls the incident: 'At the top
window of a block of flats overlooking the west entrance to the hall
used on this occasion, an old stalwart of the movement, Mrs. Reid,
her white hair crowning a face alight with the flame of revolt against
the mad slaughter of the war, was waving a great red flag.'[30]

Maclean spent a fortnight in Glasgow at Auldhouse Road with his
wife and young daughters and in July he published a letter in the
Scottish Co-operator magazine, thanking:

> all the co-operators and other friends that have congratulated me
> on my release ... Not only had I to endure barbarous cruelty myself,
> but I saw conscientious objectors, who likewise are suffering ... I
> might state that my doctor has assured me that I am only suffering
> from a slight nervous strain and a general catarrh and that all I
> require is good food, fresh air and a rest.[31]

The slight nervous strain that he mentions is an allusion to what some
have taken to be Maclean's breakdown in jail. Whether he genuinely
felt that fresh air and rest would cure him, or whether this letter is
more of his cheery bravado, is hard to say. Either way, Maclean headed
to Hastings with Agnes as the guest of George Lansbury for that rest.
Meanwhile, the Labour MP George Barnes arranged the cancella-
tion of Maclean's call-up papers, with the government's agreement.
Having released him to avert unrest on the Clyde, they did not want
to have to send him straight back to jail as a conscientious objector.
The authorities also allowed Maclean the privilege of writing a letter
to the police each week stating his whereabouts, rather than having to
report to them directly.[32] Though he remained thin, Maclean's health
improved in Hastings. He told the *Glasgow Post*, 'I am quite unrepentant, and more revolutionary than ever' and showed the reporter the
five shillings' gratuity he had earned in prison and told him he was
going to make it into a brooch for Agnes.[33]

On 14 July, Maclean wrote another open letter, this time to the
membership of the British Socialist Party, marking his release:

I regret that the holiday feeling, added to an ingrained antipathy to work, will debar me from replying to all the good souls who have written and telegraphed to me on my return to life (for prison is death). I also thank all those who offered us accommodation for a holiday here and there over the British Isles, but as my wife left it to Comrade George Lansbury to get us lodgings anywhere on the English Channel we feel sorry we are unable to accept the host of invitations.

In my lone cell I resolved that, on my return to civil life, I would appeal to the workers to demand the release of conscientious objectors, especially those detained in ordinary prisons, on the grounds of the harsh treatment meted out to them. I know what they are suffering, from what I saw in Perth Prison ...

At the same time I particularly appeal to everyone on behalf of Comrade Peter Petroff and his wife ... I ask our Russian comrades (who, by the way, along with the Irish rebels, were largely responsible for my own liberation) to cease negotiations with the British Government until both are set free.

Although my medical adviser, after a careful examination, states that I am only suffering from a slight nervous strain and a general catarrh, I mean to holiday it till the start of the Economics Class on the first Sunday of October ... Brainy bodies here are as convinced as I am that I was singled out because of the tremendous influence of the class prior to and during the war, and therefore I feel justified in continuing the policy of laying stress on the class ...

We Marxists do not need to be afraid of our principles, for this brutal, bloody war has laid bare to the dullest of intellects hosts of facts as evidence of the correctness of view of those who accept Marxism in its completeness ....

Yours, hotter than ever,
JOHN MACLEAN[34]

In this letter, Maclean touches on the key tenets of his politics, and shows subtly what has changed for him. The new concern for prisoner welfare would remain with him for life, testament to the damage done to him in jail – despite his continuous suggestion that it was 'just a little catarrh'. And there is a new insistence in the primacy of the economics classes; the working class must receive the education it needs to seize power. At the same time, credit is given to Irish and Russian rebels who Maclean now sees as spearheading the international movement that he has long believed in.

Maclean continued his stay in England, and travelled to London next, where he intended to speak at a meeting called to establish Workers and Soldiers Soviets in the UK. The meeting was disrupted by an angry crowd who rioted before Maclean could speak – he was convinced the rioters were in the pay of the Government.[35] This may not have been quite accurate, but the then head of the CID, Sir Basil Thompson, wrote in his diary before the meeting: 'They will have a rude awakening tomorrow, as I have arranged with the *Daily Express* to publish the place of their meeting and a strong opposition may be expected.'[36]

Whilst in London, Maclean met with Chicherin, by now an anti-war agitator increasingly close to Lenin, and they discussed the Russian situation and its relevance to global Marxism.[37] Fresh violence by the Russian provisional government against protesters in Petrograd, known as the 'July Days', was sparking the interest of international socialists, and it was becoming apparent that a further revolution may be approaching. Chicherin was arrested a few days later,[38] and Maclean wrote to both Chicherin and Petroff in jail, though the letters were withheld by the authorities.[39]

At the end of the summer, Maclean returned to Glasgow. Jean was now 6 years old, and Nan was 4. Nan, like her father and grandfather, suffered from respiratory complaints. But the family as a whole were healthy, there was money left in the fund for their support, and Agnes was glad to have John home. Maclean resumed his economics classes, hoping that his income from the Scottish Labour College would replace his former salary for elementary teaching. With 500 now enrolled in Glasgow[40] and a further 100 attending a separate class in Govan, as well as smaller weekly meetings across the Southside, the East End and Greenock, Maclean ran eight classes a week in this period for more than 1,000 pupils, whilst MacDougall taught a further 300 in the mining towns south and east of Glasgow.[41] It is arguable that Marxism took hold in Glasgow, Lanarkshire and Fife to a far greater degree than elsewhere in Britain in no small part as a consequence of this remarkable programme of education. Certainly it is hard to overstate the number of workers in Scotland who received an education in Marxism either directly or indirectly from Maclean. An article in the *Sunday Times* in the 1970s remarked that it was still easy to find old miners across Scotland who had been taught by Maclean.[42]

At the same time, MacDougall was working in the Lanarkshire mines, and organising a Miners' Reform Committee. In August, a one-day strike was held against the war and the rising cost of living; the first major anti-war strike in a key industry. Maclean hailed it with enthusiasm as an example of workers striking over a broad class issue:

> Last Thursday the whole of the miners in Lanarkshire ... did not dig coal, but made a hefty dig at the paunch of the profiteers and their flunkey Government. More than fifty thousand were engaged in this most healthy exercise. After processing, they assembled at thirteen places of meeting to call on the Government immediately to reduce prices. Smillie himself hinted to the whole working class that, if the Government did not take the hint, they ought to 'take action.'
>
> ... Comrades, let Thursday inspire us to beat Russia in the revolutionary race.[43]

As well as his excitement over the miners' action and the success of his economics classes, Maclean was also busy organising his Russian Political Refugees' Defence Committee. As the anarchist Guy Aldred put it, 'As others had laboured for his freedom, so Maclean now laboured for others.'[44] A letter from Peter to Irma Petroff shows that Maclean's work was not unrecognised by the prisoners:

> I am sure you were happy to read Trotsky's peremptory demand for our release but it will cheer you still more to hear that our British comrades are straining their energies to attain this end ... from Scotland it is reported in the Labour Press 'In spite of the very cold weather and the disapproval of the authorities a huge crowd of workers turned out on Glasgow Green on Sunday last.

The meeting was organised by the Clyde Workers' Committee and resolutions were unanimously passed demanding the release of Mr Peter Petroff and Mrs Irma Petroff and Chicherin.'[45]

After his initial difficulty in communicating with Petroff, Maclean was able to smuggle letters to him during this time via the Kentish Town BSP, and kept him informed both of the continuing campaign for his release and also the programme of economics classes: 'Marxism is growing rapidly now in Scotland and nothing can hold it back ... We are all well at home. Bowhill especially sends greetings. remember me to Mrs P, whose treatment is becoming widely known here. I'll write to her too.'[46]

With his organisation in the classrooms and the mines reaching new levels, Maclean was for the first time being discussed as a parliamentary candidate, specifically as an opponent to the Labour MP George Barnes in the Gorbals. The BSP, Maclean's party, was at the time affiliated to the Labour Party and would permit him to run as their candidate. The *Daily Record* reported that Maclean had received a nomination locally but that the labour movement was unlikely to support an opponent of Mr Barnes, who though unpopular was nevertheless the sitting Labour MP. [47]

At the same time, the Clyde Workers' Committee was resurrected with the aim of fighting the reduction of wages relative to the price of goods, with Gallacher again as its chair. An iron-moulders' strike which began in Kirkintilloch and spread to Glasgow and Kilmarnock ended with pay rises for the workers.[48]

This working-class and anti-war activity on the Clyde was further emboldened when the bourgeois provisional government in Russia was swept away by the October Revolution. Lenin, Trotsky and the Bolsheviks seized power. In a bloodless revolution, the Bolsheviks had taken control of Russia on a platform of bread, peace and land for all. The radical socialist regime immediately brought in a decree of peace, the emancipation of women, sweeping land reform, the decriminalisation of homosexuality and abortion, a minimum wage, an eight-hour working day, and worker control in the factories and farms. The incredible idealism and liberation that the early days of Bolshevism heralded are hard to imagine now after its terrible later failings, but in October 1917, workers around the world celebrated the great victory, not least in Glasgow. Tom Anderson wrote that when the news of the revolution broke he was with Maclean, who simply took his hand and held it silently for some moments, too overcome by emotion to speak and finally saying, 'Comrade Tom, we are going to live to see The Day.'[49] Maclean's allies, who in 1914 had been almost lone voices in international socialism, struggling to end the capitalist war, now ruled Russia. The world revolution to which Maclean had devoted his life had begun. The first steps towards ending the war had been taken. Here at last was evidence that the ruling class could be beaten, in Glasgow as in Moscow.

On 25 January 1918, an article by Preobrazhensky appeared in *Pravda*. It described the Third Congress of Soviets, and extended a hand of friendship directly to the Clyde: 'They were not present but the spirits of Liebknecht, Adler and Maclean soared among us; they were chosen as honorary chairmen of the congress, along with Lenin and Trotsky, and they will remain with us in spirit and silently guide the work of the Third all Russian Congress of Soviets.'[50]

The *Call* remarked that 'The workers on the Clyde particularly are proud of the distinction and recognise in the action of the Russian workers in electing Maclean an invisible but none the less real connection between Petrograd and Glasgow.'[51]

With the Bolsheviks in power, and looking to him for inspiration, Maclean must have felt that he was on the brink of all he had fought for. The workers were proving in Russia that they were able to bring about an end to war. Scotland was playing its part as a centre of internationalism and socialism. His sacrifice in jail seemed, as he had hoped, to have galvanised his supporters and to have given him an international platform from which to lead the working class to power. After four years of war, Glasgow was more alive than ever before to ideas of revolution.

9

Scotland's Bolshevik

In January 1918, Maclean was appointed by Lenin as the Soviet Consul in Scotland. It was reported in the press that the journalist John Reed would serve as the Bolsheviks' representative in New York and that the schoolteacher John Maclean was to fulfil the same role in Glasgow.[1]

The Foreign Office was thrown into some confusion by the appointment as they, unlike the domestic branches of Government, did not know who Maclean was. The Foreign Minister did, however, note that 'the choice of the Clyde for the appointment of a Bolshevik Consul was significant' and contacted the Home Office asking for more information. The response they received, informing them that Maclean was a Marxist educator and a convict, increased the Foreign Office's concern, and they replied to the Home Office recommending that the appointment be objected to, adding that the police in Glasgow should be asked to watch Maclean. The Home Office was able to reassure their colleagues that Maclean was already being closely observed.[2]

On 5 January 1918, the Bolshevik diplomat Maxim Litvinoff contacted Maclean in 'N.B.', i.e. North Britain:

Dear Comrade Maclean,

I am writing to the Russian Consul in Glasgow (I am not sure that there exists such a person) informing him of your appointment and ordering him to hand over to you the Consulate. He may refuse to do so, in which case you will open a new Consulate and make it public through the press. Your position may be difficult somehow, but you will have my full support. It is most important to keep me informed (and through me the Russian Soviets) of the

Labour Movement in N.B. I am writing in all haste, as I wish not to miss the occasion. It is not very safe to write very fast.

With best wishes, Maxim Litvinoff[3]

Maclean's appointment as Consul was both a symbolic gesture towards Maclean and the movement on the Clyde and also a practical position from which to pass information between Scotland and Russia, and to serve the thousands of Russians living in Scotland.[4] Maclean at once took the post seriously. He was particularly focused on provision for the dependents of those Scottish Russians who had been conscripted into the Russian Army before the Bolshevik Revolution. In Bellshill alone, there were two hundred dependent Russian families whose husbands and fathers had been sent by the British Government to fight on the Eastern Front. Maclean also, characteristically, wrote to the Secretary of State for Scotland to say that he would no longer be reporting to the police as the conditions of his parole demanded, as 'it is meaningless in view of my public position as Russian Consul in Glasgow and is derogatory to the great Russian Republic.'[5] It is clear that Maclean felt emboldened by his appointment and was prepared for further confrontations with the British state.

The Scottish Soviet Consulate was opened at 12 South Portland Street in the Gorbals. A meeting of Russian and British workers at St Mungo's Hall in Govan celebrated Maclean's appointment,[6] and demonstrations were held on Glasgow Green welcoming Maclean's recognition by Lenin and pledging support to the Soviet Government. The pro-government *Daily Record* reported:

It would be foolish either to ignore or exaggerate the unrest of organised labour in the West of Scotland. The situation is serious, but it is by no means hopeless; and it is the duty of every citizen to avoid wild words and the bitterness, which only add fuel to the rebel fires ... Few people who are not in touch with the labour and socialist movement realise the extent of the propaganda that is being carried on through demonstrations, public meetings, meetings at the factory gates, study circles, Socialist Sunday schools, and economic classes. Take one little instance. A meeting was held at Nelson's Monument on Glasgow Green on the 27th of January. It was ostensibly a demonstration to send a message of encouragement to Russia; in reality the speakers covered every point of the revolutionary programme. The audience numbered from 7,000 to 10,000.[7]

Maclean's new position gave him an even greater platform, and this fact did not go unnoticed by the authorities. On 22 March, police raided Maclean's Consulate building and arrested his colleague, the Glasgow-based Russian socialist Louis Shammes, whose connection to Maclean had already attracted the attention of MI5.[8] Shammes, or Shamus as he was also known, was sent to Barlinnie Prison to await deportation to Russia. This was a serious blow to Maclean, who could ill afford to lose a Russian-speaking member of staff. Maclean now became responsible for Shammes's family as well as his own.[9] Miss Sarafin of the Lithuanian Women's Organisation took over as Maclean's assistant.[10]

A further setback came when Maclean was deprived of funds to support his consular activities. Politburo member Kamenev was detained in Aberdeen and a diplomatic bag with a £5,000 cheque from the Bolsheviks was confiscated by the authorities.[11] Nevertheless, Maclean tried to fulfil his consular duties on behalf of Scotland's Russians, saying in May 1918: 'I also pointed out that the British government had sent Russian subjects back to Russia to fight, and had given their wives 12s 6d per week and 2s 6d for each child.[12] These women and children of the Russian community have died as a consequence of the meagre supplies given to them by the British government.'[13]

At this time, relations became frayed between Maclean and Litvinoff, as they struggled to communicate. Litvinoff, the Ambassador in London to whom Maclean reported, wrote repeatedly asking for information and received no reply. Maclean similarly had letters to Litvinoff ignored. Finally, Litvinoff received a pile of returned letters from the Glasgow Central Post Office, all marked 'Consul not recognized by HM Government'. He sent a wire to Maclean who immediately wrote in protest to the postmaster at Glasgow, asking that he stop interfering on political grounds and remain neutral.[14] Surprisingly, the letter had its effect, and a cheque for £50 from

Litvinoff was delivered to Maclean's consulate.[15] Maclean wrote to the *Call* advising correspondents of the postal issues:

> Dear Comrade, — Allow me to inform readers that all letters sent to me with the words 'Russian Consulate' on them are being returned to the senders by the Postmaster, Glasgow, because the Government does not recognise the Bolshevik Government ... I cannot assume responsibility for failure to acknowledge moneys sent but not received. One cheque sent by Mrs. D.B. Montefiore I have not received. This I learnt only by accidentally meeting her.[16]

Dora Montefiore was the famous poet, socialist and suffragette who in 1906 had barricaded herself in her home and refused to pay taxes until women were given the vote. With the financial and moral support of famous socialists such as Montefiore both at home and abroad, Maclean became increasingly bold in his propaganda, encouraging Scottish workers to follow the example of their Russian comrades and to begin the revolution at home. He advocated the planning of a local insurrection to take control of Glasgow, particularly its press and city council, and build stronger connections with socialists in London and the English coalfields. In Fife and elsewhere, Maclean encouraged workers to ready themselves to take control of factories, mines and railways. At a time when the Independent Labour Party, pacifists and religious leaders were responding to the heavy losses on the Western Front with a call for a negotiated peace, Maclean was saying, 'I want peace, but it must be a peace with revolution in it.'[17]

The British security services continued to follow Maclean and now began openly taking notes at his meetings. In Maclean's file, the Officer in Command of the Army in Scotland draws attention to the fact that, whilst agitators such as Maxton, McManus and Gallacher were engaged only in the industrial sphere, Maclean and MacDougall posed a broader political threat, openly criticising the war, encouraging revolt, and exerting a dangerous influence on the Fife and Lanarkshire coalfields as well as Glasgow 'where indications of unrest continually prevail'.[18]

Maclean spent much of his time speaking in support of a Bolshevik revolution across Scotland. At meetings up and down the country, he spread news of the Communist revolution, and encouraged Marxist education. He hoped that the British State could be 'kept busy at home,' and so prevented from sabotaging the revolution in Russia.

After the Bolsheviks pulled the Russian Army out of the war against Germany, the British Army began – along with the French, the Italians and the Americans – to fight a civil war against the Bolsheviks in Russia, uniting with the White Russian forces who favoured the re-establishment of the Tsarist autocracy. British forces, on Churchill's orders, used tens of thousands of shells containing a toxic gas called diphenylaminechloroarsine against the Bolsheviks and supplied 30,000 troops and millions of pounds worth of equipment to the White Russians.[19] Maclean hoped that his campaign for revolution at home could have the dual effect of making Scottish workers more ready to assume control should a revolution arise, whilst in the meantime preoccupying the British Government and diverting resources away from the British Army's involvement in the Russian civil war.[20]

It was at this time that Maclean fell out with David Kirkwood, the Clyde Workers' Committee member at Parkhead Forge. Since 1916, Maclean had been critical of what he increasingly saw as the overly anxious and liberal CWC. He believed that the Workers' Committee should not merely support its members in calling for improved working conditions and pay, but that it should also work to encourage anti-war sentiment and to spread revolutionary propaganda. Maclean was disgusted to learn that Kirkwood had been boasting of the raised levels of production at his factory, motivating the workers with the promise of future reward. Maclean declared that any suggestion of better conditions after the war was a lie: conditions would mean that the capitalists would continue to enforce in peacetime every privation that they had imposed during the war. He went on to argue that it was the duty of the workers to ca' canny – or go slow – reducing output and exerting their power over the ruling class and the government. Maclean argued that if the workers increased output, then they would only be made to work harder in peacetime to prepare for 'the war after the war', which capitalism made inevitable. This became the basis of his pamphlet *The War after The War*.[21] Maclean's disagreement with Kirkwood was part of a larger challenge that he made, asking the CWC to link the sectional struggles they were fighting with a genuine opposition to the war, and to connect the horror of the war thoroughly to the horror of capitalism.[22]

The War after the War laid out a simple economics lesson to highlight two things: that the workers are being exploited, and that their exploitation will lead to further imperialist wars. Building from the labour value of a shoe, and going on to argue that workers who cannot afford to eat properly are not even getting the value of their labour back, Maclean's short economics pamphlet established the need for a socialist republic. He states that increased wages and conditions may improve the lot of some workers and increase their productivity, but that this 'enlightened capitalism' still involves the worker being robbed of ever greater profits, and can act only as a brake on the establishment of Socialism. The pamphlet concluded that the capitalist drive for growth, for more production, for more profits, must inevitably lead to a need for new markets, and that this need for new markets must lead to war. Maclean's argument is that the only way to establish peace is to abolish capitalism.[23]

John continued touring the country, addressing ever larger audiences in Britain's industrial centres. In early April, Maclean spoke to miners in County Durham. A member of the crowd, Leo Kelly, reported that:

> John spoke without interruption for two hours before an enormous crowd. He made a great impression upon all ... There were five policemen there and a man taking a verbatim report of the speech. Maclean trounced the police spy and denounced policemen who were not in a union as a set of worthless 'scabs.' That night John spoke in the same place before two thousand people. John delivered the most inspiring address I ever heard him give. He dealt with Ireland and Russia. His impassioned accounts of poor Jim Connolly impressed the crowd. He accused Asquith of being a murderer, and declared the mantle of Jesus Christ had descended and fallen upon the Bolsheviks.[24]

It was clear that Maclean was only growing bolder, a communist evangelical, speaking to crowds of thousands, unafraid of policemen and politicians. In both the Scotland Office and in the military, discussions continued about the threat Maclean posed to public order. The military command advised that, if Maclean could not be re-arrested for breach of his parole, then new charges should be brought against him. The Scotland Office contacted the Foreign Office amidst concerns that Maclean had diplomatic immunity; the latter confirmed that it did not recognise him as a diplomat. At the same time, the Scotland Office also urged the Government not to normalise relations with Russia for fear that it might strengthen Maclean's hand.[25]

Maclean's popularity was growing in Glasgow and beyond, and he had just been selected as the Labour Party candidate for the Gorbals. This new prominence, combined with the constant police and security service surveillance, must have added greatly to Agnes's fear that her husband would again be taken from the family and sent to Peterhead.

Maclean nevertheless continued his campaigns in full view of the police and the secret services. And on 15 April, after just nine months of freedom, he was arrested at the Russian Consulate,[26] charged with sedition, refused bail, and taken to Duke Street Prison. The strain on his family when they heard of his re-arrest was immense. Litvinoff wrote to Agnes offering his condolences and adding that John's arrest 'will at least increase his popularity with the Russian workers'.[27]

There were eleven charges in the new indictment against Maclean. All related to contraventions of the Defence of the Realm Act under which he had been convicted two years earlier.[28] They related to speeches Maclean had made in Glasgow and Fife between January and April 1918,[29] and specific 'seditious' phrases he was accused of using included:

'tools should be downed',

'the revolution should be created',

'the Clyde district had helped win the Russian revolution',

'the revolutionary spirit on the Clyde was at present ten times as strong as it was two years ago',

'the workers on the Clyde should take control of the City Chambers, and hold the Lord Provost and other members of the council hostage, and then take control of the post offices and the banks and police stations',

'the police should be thrown in jail',

'the movement would be supported by the French Canadians and the workers in New York',

'other districts would follow the Clyde',

'the present House of Commons should be superseded by a Soviet, and he did not care whether they met in the usual place or in Buckingham Palace' and

'the workers in the munitions works should be advised to restrict their outputs.'[30]

Maclean was further accused of suggesting that the ruling class should be sent to fight in the trenches and that the workers should stay home, take their mines and factories, and raise the Red Flag like their brothers in Russia. The charge sheet also claimed that he had recommended seizing newspaper offices and food stores, and that he had argued that 'the workers should demand food from the farmers, and, if they refused, their farmhouses should be burned.' This last accusation, Willie Gallacher suggested, was evidence of the extent to which the authorities had manufactured claims against Maclean. Certainly it suggests a police spy had not fully grasped the thrust of Maclean's argument, as he was avowedly for the redistribution of farms and housing, but not for the destruction of them.[31] How far the other statements truly reflected Maclean's speeches is hard to gauge. Maclean certainly did not publish anything that encouraged seizing farms or government buildings, or taking hostages. But, given that he faced arrest for saying these things aloud, a printed record would have been unwise. It seems likely that Maclean's plans and ideas for revolution were more advanced than the written record that survives, and whilst these accounts by police spies are no doubt garbled and exaggerated, it is likely that they represent some aspects of the plans for an insurrection that Maclean was encouraging in Clydeside.[32]

During the two weeks that Maclean spent in Duke Street Jail that April, the socialist movement in Glasgow was alive with activity as it prepared for the largest May Day celebration the city had ever seen. It was to be held, for the first time, as a general strike for peace on the first day of May, with more than 50,000 workers downing tools in Glasgow's shipyards alone.[33]

The largest wartime strike ever to take place in the UK was met with hostility from large sections of the press. The *Aberdeen Press and Journal* reported that, whilst munitions and shipyard workers were 'urged to stay at their benches yesterday, large numbers took part in the May Day Celebration in Glasgow.' It also noted that a soldier was injured by demonstrators and that 'the procession was largely composed of men who appeared to be well within the military age.'[34] The *Dundee Courier* added that in Glasgow 'the spectators hissed the young socialists and shouted "go and join the army"' and 'one of the socialist banners was torn to shreds and the flagpoles were broken.'[35] The *Liverpool Echo* reported that 'A May Day procession of socialists and pacifists in Glasgow was hooted by onlookers who cried, "this is no time for holidays."'[36] The *Daily Record* ran perhaps the only positive coverage of the march from an establishment paper, with a picture of young children riding a Co-operative Society lorry, each clutching a placard that read 'each for all, all for each'; however, the comment section concluded that 'the true feeling of the city was represented on the kerb, and not on the cobbles', and praised the soldiers on leave from France who looked on in astonishment at the striking workers.[37] Despite the one-day strike being illegal, and the press reaction before and after the event painting it in a negative light, conservative estimates at the time put the number marching at above 70,000. The May Day 1918 Strike was a remarkable act of mass resistance in the city most crucial to Britain's continuation of the war.

Willie Gallacher described it as 'a demonstration that surpassed anything ever seen before. George Square, where the procession assembled, and the streets adjoining it, were packed with the gathering crowds. Column after column went marching through the square – bands playing, flags flying, never-ending shouts against the war.'[38]

The Cambridge Social History of Britain states that 100,000 people marched and adds that the police responded by raiding the Socialist Labour Party offices in Glasgow.[39] Vast quantities of socialist literature were sold, and speakers addressed large crowds from 22 platforms on Glasgow Green, before heading to Duke Street and chanting for the release of John Maclean. Cathal O'Shannon wrote in *Irish Opinion*: 'The Glasgow workers, like those in Dublin, decided to hold May Day this year on 1 May, and not the first Sunday. Glasgow and Dublin are the two cities in these countries that lead the van in the militant army of Labour, and from them, if from nowhere else, we may expect a bold lead.'[40]

Not all were so keen, and a 'Scottish Patriot' wrote to the *Daily Record*, lamenting the 'weeds' who had marched on May Day and how they reminded him of 'the weeds' who had lost Scotland her independence 300 years before, regretting further that the strike had been associated with bagpipes and 'such a highland name' as John Maclean.[41]

The next day Maclean was transferred from Duke Street Prison to Calton Jail in Edinburgh, where his trial was set for 9 May. He wrote to his wife:

> My Dearest Ag, Arrived here this morning all right. It's perhaps even colder here than in G – as usual, but I'm alright with my coat ...
>
> Convey my heartiest congratulations to W McGill and his bride ... say that I wish them long life and as much happiness as capitalism will allow ...
>
> Tell Nan I'm proud of her ... Tell Jean she must work hard to prevent Nan sneaking up on her. If they're good see what they'll get when I get the next big hug from both ... Tell Bob I'm planning out a great defeat for him at chess the next time we meet.
>
> You ought to have a little more leisure. A few afternoons in 'the glen' with the kiddies ought to do some good. With warmest love to Nan and Jean and Yourself and kindest regards to all not named. Yours, Johnnie[42]

Having reassured his family, Maclean now began writing his most famous work: 'Speech from the Dock'. With the Clyde having just shown its greatest act of opposition to the war, and with the possibility of more unrest to come, John Maclean stated before the trial that he would refuse to plead guilty or not guilty to the charges against him, rejecting the authority of the court. His attention was now focused on what would become the defining trial of his life.

10

The Accuser of Capitalism

On 8 May, forty socialists and anarchists set out from Glasgow to march through the night in protest against the arrest of John Maclean, who was due to stand trial the next day. The *Scotsman* reported that their numbers dwindled through the night and that they finished their journey by bus, suggesting that this may be 'a parable for bolshevism'.[1] But however they got there, and despite the *Scotsman*'s sneering, when the marchers arrived in Edinburgh the next day at 9 a.m. large crowds of Maclean's supporters were already being turned away from the courthouse by police.[2]

Maclean confirmed his refusal to plead and, when the Lord Justice General asked if he objected to any members of the jury, he replied that he objected to all of them, and would only accept a jury of the working class. The jury Maclean faced was again made up entirely of property-owning men.[3]

Twenty-five police witnesses gave evidence against him, as did a journalist, a mining inspector and a slater.[4] Maclean chose to be a party litigant, representing himself without the help of a lawyer. He cross-examined the witnesses, who were unable to give verbatim accounts of his speeches but instead corroborated occasional phrases. They claimed that Maclean had said 'The capitalist class don't care how many women and children are destroyed so long as they belong to the working class'[5] and that he had encouraged violent revolution. Maclean clarified some points, corrected other witnesses who had misremembered or misunderstood his statements, but did not deny making the statements for which he was standing trial.

He did not intend to use the court to prove his innocence, but, rather, his intention was to use the trial to inspire future rebellion. He intended to assert that there was a higher morality than that of

Figure 4 John Maclean outside the High Court
in Edinburgh, May 1918 (Glasgow Caledonian
University Archive Centre: Bennie Collection)

the Government's courts, and to appeal instead to the morality of the proletariat.

Hoping to be vindicated not by the courts, but by the workers, Maclean began his defence:

It has been said that they cannot fathom my motive. For the full period of my active life I have been a teacher of economics to the working classes, and my contention has always been that capitalism is rotten to its foundations, and must give place to a new society. I had a lecture, the principal heading of which was 'Thou shalt not steal; thou shalt not kill', and I pointed out that as a consequence of the robbery that goes on in all civilised countries today, our respective countries have had to keep armies, and that inevitably our armies must clash together. On that and on other grounds, I consider capitalism the most infamous, bloody and evil system that mankind has ever witnessed. My language is regarded as extravagant language, but the events of the past four years have proved my contention.

... My motives are clean. My motives are genuine. If my motives were not clean and genuine, would I have made my statements while these shorthand reporters were present? I am out for the benefit of society, not for any individual human being, but I realise this, that justice and freedom can only be obtained when society is placed on a sound economic basis. That sound economic basis is wanting today, and hence the bloodshed we are having ... I know quite well that in the reconstruction of society, the class interests of those who are on top will resist the change, and the only factor in society that can make for a clean sweep in society is the working class. Hence the class war. The whole history of society has proved that society moves forward as a consequence of an under-class overcoming the resistance of a class on top of them.[6]

According to the *Oxford English Dictionary*, Maclean here coined the term 'under-class', though he did not use it with any of the negative connotations it carries today.[7] He continued:

I wish no harm to any human being, but I, as one man, am going to exercise my freedom of speech. No human being on the face of the earth, no government is going to take from me my right to speak, my right to protest against wrong, my right to do everything that is for the benefit of mankind. I am not here, then, as the accused; I am here as the accuser of capitalism dripping with blood from head to foot.[8]

His speech was addressed as much to the hundreds of thousands who would be able to read his defence in the days after the trial, as it was to the jurors sitting across from him in court. The Clyde Workers'

Defence Propaganda Committee's preparations to print the speech were already under way.

Maclean threatened a hunger strike should he be convicted. He was positioning himself as a socialist martyr:

> I have stated in public since that I would rather be immediately put to death than condemned to a life sentence in Peterhead … Whatever is done to me now, I give notice that I take no food inside your prisons, absolutely no food, because of the treatment that was meted out to me. If food is forced upon me, and if I am forcibly fed, then my friends have got to bear in mind that if any evil happens to me, I am not responsible for the consequences, but the British government … when the government can launch millions of men into the field of battle, then perhaps the mere disposal of one man is a mere bagatelle and a trifle.[9]

He returned to the theme of the speech, the class war: 'The Lord Advocate pointed out here that I probably was a more dangerous enemy that you had got to face than in the Germans. The working class, when they rise for their own, are more dangerous to capitalists than even the German enemies at your gates.'[10]

In no way was Maclean defending himself against the charges of sedition. Instead, he was re-enacting that sedition for a larger audience: the general public, the press, and the Government.

The speech became one of the most famous ever made in Scotland, and must have been profoundly shocking to members of Edinburgh society at the trial. The *Edinburgh Evening News* reported that 'For seventy minutes his impassioned utterances rushed forth like a torrent. It was mostly irrelevant, but it was wonderful in its fluency.'[11] Maclean continued to lay out how he believed the war would end and what exactly he had been agitating for:

> From a British point of view, revolution inside Germany is good; revolution inside Britain is bad. So says this learned gentleman. He can square it if he can. I cannot square it. The conditions of Germany economically are the conditions of Britain, and there is only a very slight difference between the political structure of

Germany and that of this country at the best. And so far as we workers are concerned, we are not concerned with the political superstructure; we are concerned with the economic foundation of society, and that determines our point of view in politics and industrial action. Our Russian comrades, therefore, did the very same as the British have been doing; they appealed to the German soldiers and workers to overthrow their government.

Strikes broke forth in Italy. The strikes in January passed into Germany, more menacing strikes than have taken place inside the British Isles. An appeal was made from comrades to comrades. Many soldiers in Germany mutinied; many sailors of Germany mutinied, and these men are being shot down by their government. All hail to those working men of Germany who refused at the bidding of the capitalist to go on with this war. Their names will go down bright and shining where those of the capitalists of today and of the past will have been forgotten.

It would be a very bad thing for the workers of the world if a revolution were developed and carried through to success in Germany and no similar effort were made in this country. The German workers' enemy is the same as our enemy in this country.[12]

Maclean detailed his demand not just for peace, but also for revolution:

All the property destroyed during the war will be replaced. In the next five years there is going to be a great world trade depression and the respective governments, to stave off trouble, must turn more and more into the markets of the world to get rid of their produce, and in fifteen years' time from the close of this war—I have pointed this out at all my meetings—we are into the next war if capitalism lasts; we cannot escape it ... In view of the fact that the great powers are not prepared to stop the war until the one side or the other is broken down, it is our business as members of the working class to see that this war ceases today, not only to save the lives of the young men of the present, but also to stave off the next great war.[13]

Maclean's argument was that, if you are against war, then you must be for the revolution.

In his concluding remarks he summed up his actions and his aims, and reiterated that this speech was not for the court, but for the working class to whom he had always spoken. It is worth remembering that men were shot for treason before and after 1918 in the UK, and Maclean would not have known what sentence he would be bringing upon himself with his defiant revolutionary speech from the dock. It is also extraordinary to think of the Lord Justice General and many other members of the Edinburgh legal establishment sitting through this 70-minute speech, in which Maclean repeated the very statements which had brought about his arrest. Maclean told the court:

> I am a socialist, and have been fighting and will fight for an absolute reconstruction of society for the benefit of all. I am proud of my conduct. I have squared my conduct with my intellect, and if everyone had done so this war would not have taken place. I act square and clean for my principles. I have nothing to retract. I have nothing to be ashamed of. Your class position is against my class position. There are two classes of morality. There is the working class morality and there is the capitalist class morality. There is this antagonism as there is the antagonism between Germany and Britain. A victory for Germany is a defeat for Britain; a victory for Britain is a defeat for Germany. And it is exactly the same so far as our classes are concerned. What is moral for the one class is absolutely immoral for the other, and vice-versa. No matter what your accusations against me may be, no matter what reservations you keep at the back of your head, my appeal is to the working class. I appeal exclusively to them because they and they only can bring about the time when the whole world will be in one brotherhood, on a sound economic foundation. That, and that alone, can be the means of bringing about a re-organisation of society. That can only be obtained when the people of the world get the world, and retain the world.[14]

When the speech ended, Maclean's supporters erupted into cheers, while his detractors looked on in silence. A remarkable photograph of Maclean in court survives, though it isn't known how it was taken, or by whom. He stands upright, looking defiantly towards the judge, with uniformed police officers standing on either side of him, and his broad-brimmed hat resting on the edge of the dock.

The jury, without retiring, found Maclean guilty of all eleven charges and he was sentenced to five years' penal servitude. As he was led in handcuffs from the dock, Maclean turned to the gallery and cried 'Keep it going boys! Keep it going!'[5]

The *Scotsman* noted that 'the sentence is not one which any fair-minded person will regard as excessive', and called Maclean the 'self-appointed deliverer from oppression and starvation of a people who were not oppressed and who certainly were not starving'.[16] The trial made national news, and the 'Scotch Bolshevist' was widely accused of being an enemy agent, while the *Glasgow Herald* ran a special feature on the dangers of Bolshevism in Scotland.

At the same time, protests began against Maclean's trial and imprisonment. The National Union of Journalists met to condemn the actions of the journalist who had testified against Maclean, and the Clyde District Defence Committee was formed to campaign for Maclean and other political prisoners. The *Daily Herald* called for a 'large rally in a good cause' in June to call for Maclean's release. The Scotland Office was inundated with messages demanding he be freed.[17] Lenin wrote:

> The British Government has again started persecuting MacLean and this time not only as a Scottish schoolteacher, but also as Consul of the Federative Soviet Republic. MacLean is in prison because he acted openly as the representative of our government; we have never seen this man, he is the beloved leader of the Scottish workers, he has never belonged to our Party, but we joined with him; the Russian and Scottish workers united against the British Government.[18]

Maclean was returned to Peterhead Prison. The Government was clearly fearful of the effect on the public mood were Maclean to go ahead with his hunger strike and so granted him special privileges, including reading material and permission to have his own food brought in. However, communications between Glasgow and Peterhead to this effect were delayed and Maclean began a hunger strike regardless.[19]

Protests took place across the country and, at a Glasgow demonstration on 7 July calling for Maclean's release, violence broke out when the police attacked protestors. A large crowd had set out from George Square, led by a band playing the 'Red Flag'. According to Nan Milton, the peaceful march was ambushed by hundreds of policemen 'without any reason whatever, they drew their batons and a scene wilder than any witnessed in Glasgow for many years was enacted.'[20] Conversely, the *Yorkshire Post* reported that the protestors had tried to commandeer the trams, and drivers and passengers defended themselves with iron bars used for shifting points until the police arrived and cleared the demonstration. Twenty-one men were charged with behaving in a way likely to cause a breach of the peace. The organiser, Robert Hamilton, was also charged with being an absentee from the army.[21]

In early July, Ramsay Macdonald wrote to the Scotland Office asking that Maclean – 'who is at present enjoying your hospitality and protection'[22] – be transferred to Glasgow where he could more easily receive food from outside. However, no arrangement was made and Maclean continued to starve himself.

Dr Garrey at Peterhead Prison began force-feeding Maclean on 1 July.[23] Accounts of force-feeding in British jails describe it as an intensely painful experience. The prisoner was held down by guards while a tube was forced either through the nose or mouth, and liquid food – often milk and raw eggs – was poured down it. The experience was often likened to torture, and in 1917 the Irish Volunteer Thomas Ashe had been killed by force-feeding when liquid had been poured into his lungs rather than his stomach.[24] Maclean and his supporters would have been aware of the force-feeding endured by suffragettes such as Helen Crawfurd and Sylvia Pankhurst and would likely have read Pankhurst's description of her own experience:

> The doctors came stealing in … I felt a man's hands trying to force my mouth open. I set my teeth and tightened my lips over them with all my strength. My breath was coming so quickly that I felt

as if I should suffocate. I felt his fingers trying to press my lips apart,— getting inside,— and I felt them and a steel gag running around my gums and feeling for gaps in my teeth.

I felt I should go mad; I felt like a poor wild thing caught in a steel trap. I was tugging at my head to get it free. There were two of them holding it. There were two of them wrenching at my mouth ...

Then I felt a steel instrument pressing against my gums, cutting into the flesh, forcing its way in. Then it gradually prised my jaws apart as they turned a screw. It felt like having my teeth drawn; but I resisted—I resisted. I held my poor bleeding gums down on the steel with all my strength. Soon they were trying to force the india-rubber tube down my throat. I was struggling wildly, trying to tighten the muscles and to keep my throat closed up. They got the tube down, I suppose, though I was unconscious of anything but a mad revolt of struggling, for at last I heard them say, 'That's all'; and I vomited as the tube came up.[25]

Maclean, knowing such accounts and facing five years on the cold Buchan coast with daily force-feeding, must have feared that the effects on his health would be catastrophic. The *Edinburgh Evening News* reported at the end of October that Maclean had been force-fed for four months and that two guards watched him day and night.[26] With Soviet Russia now at peace with Germany and at war with Britain, he cannot have imagined that any diplomatic pressure could be exerted by the Bolsheviks on his behalf. In all likelihood, Maclean was willing to die for the cause, in the hope that it would inspire insurrection in Glasgow. Dr Devon agreed, writing in his medical report that if Maclean was continually force-fed it would kill him, and suggesting that he be released under the 1913 Prisoners Temporary Discharge for Ill-Health Act, also known as the 'Cat and Mouse Act'. The Undersecretary for Scotland replied that there was no reason the prisoner could not be force-fed for a year at least before there was a serious risk of death.[27]

Maclean later wrote about his treatment in prison in his usual positive style. It is hard again to read it as an honest account of his time served. He describes the daily routine:

At 5 a.m. a bell rings and every prisoner must get up, make his bed and wash. About 5.30 a.m. the orderlies serve out a big pot of porridge containing half a pound of meal and three-quarters of a pint of skimmed milk …

The general condition of food, clothing, and bedding are superior to those of multitudes outside prison, and the hours of labour are fairly short and not over-straining. Prisoners are not supposed to speak except in connection with work, but they do speak nevertheless. This is partly winked at, as it enables the authorities to use prisoners as spies to find out what others are thinking.

After one settles down the days, the weeks, the months, and the years slip in very quickly if one is a reader. As a matter of fact, one could enjoy twenty years in Peterhead better than ten in a coal mine, say.[28]

In the article, Maclean is similarly dismissive of the suffering and sickness he endured as a result of force-feeding:

This time I refused to take the food, and so was forcibly fed from July until two days before my release. There is nothing wrong with forcible feeding if you get milk, switched eggs, margarine and Bovril. One could live for years thus fed and yet be perfectly healthy. I felt very well all the time … Although the doctor developed bronchitis in my left bronchial tube, still I had a far better time on this last occasion than formerly as I pinned the doctor down to full responsibility for my condition. However he has left me with a legacy I shall keep whilst alive. If the treatment meted out to C.O.s, Sinn Feiners, and myself inspires all socialists to kill the great enemy, Capitalism, this year, then we have not suffered confinement and its consequences in vain.[29]

Agnes told a different story of her husband's health in Peterhead. She visited in October 1918 and found John a shadow of himself, thin, haggard, and with his hair entirely white. Agnes wrote to E. C. Fairchild at the British Socialist Party, letting him know Maclean's condition:

Well, John has been on hunger strike since July. He resisted the forcible feeding for a good while, but submitted to the inevitable. Now he is being fed by a stomach tube twice daily. He has aged very much and has the look of a man who is going through torture ... Seemingly anything is law in regard to John. I hope you will make the atrocity public. We must get him out of their clutches. It is nothing but slow murder.[30]

She also wrote to the Scotland Office: 'he is not in good health and it is no good trying to blind me to the fact that his health is rapidly being broken.'[31] Agnes was distressed, and it is difficult to imagine how hard it must have been to raise two daughters alone while her husband was in jail 180 miles away.

A senior prison doctor wrote: 'Suppose Maclean died from any cause in prison, he having been artificially fed, would there not be more public disturbance ... and if he were allowed to starve to death, would there not be more sympathy with him, than with those who allowed him to do so?'[32]

In fact, his hunger strike was already increasing sympathy for him. For the General Election at the end of 1918, the Labour Party in the Gorbals had selected Maclean as its candidate, to stand against its sitting MP George Barnes, who was at that time the most prominent Labour politician in the Coalition Cabinet. The local constituency party had rejected their MP as a liberal, and chose a Bolshevik in jail for sedition to stand against him, so the contest became national news. Unsurprisingly, the National Executive Committee of the Labour Party tried to challenge the decision, but in the end was forced to endorse Maclean in the election.[33]

With Maclean standing for Parliament, further questions were asked of Robert Munro, the Scottish Secretary, in the House of Commons:

King: In view of the fact that he is a probable candidate in the next general election, and that the question of his nervous condition was evaded by the right honourable gentleman, is there any intention of releasing the man who is regarded in Glasgow as a kind of martyr?

Munro: I cannot accept the second part of the question as correct, and I can see no reason at present why he should be released.

King: Does the right honourable gentleman actually mean to say that there are not thousands of men in Glasgow who regard this man as a hero and a martyr?

Munro: I am not aware of it.

Pringle: Will the right honourable gentleman allow the gentleman who is acting for Mr Maclean in his election [Willie Gallacher] to see him in prison?

Munro: I considered the request very carefully and I did not see my way to comply with it.[34]

Munro managed to stay unaware of the thousands of Glaswegians who regarded Maclean as a hero when he failed to appear at a meeting in St Andrews Hall at which he was supposed to speak. The crowd of some 4,000 people left the hall when it was announced that Munro was a no-show, and they marched instead to George Square, singing revolutionary songs and calling for Maclean's release.[35]

Among the songs sung was a new one written by the poet, lion tamer and socialist John S. Clarke. Its final lines were:

Will you suffer his destruction on the tyrants' battle ground?
Will you let the cursed wrong defeat the right?
He is one against an army, are you going to see him downed?
Are you going to let him die without a fight?
He will pay you back in plenty. It's you who stand to gain,
His lion heart is yours if he is spared,
Then workers for your own sake liberate MacLean
You could do it ay tomorrow if you dared[36]

At this time, a John Maclean Defence Committee was set up, and demonstrations were held in Glasgow, Clydebank, Leeds and Stepney Green in London, with more than 6,000 socialists meeting in Finsbury Park to demand a strike if Maclean were not set free.[37] The Labour Party Conference in November passed a unanimous resolution demanding his release.[38] In Glasgow, socialists kept up the pressure and tried to ensure that no member of the Government could speak in the city while Maclean remained in jail.[39] The *Glasgow Herald* commented that

> Mr Barnes has experienced a very rough weekend in the city of Glasgow. Discharged soldiers, trade unionists, socialists and others have all united together to make it quite impossible for him to address his constituents in a peaceable manner. We regret very much indeed that he was not allowed to enjoy perfect freedom of Speech.[40]

At the same meeting, a collection for John Maclean was raised, and the crowd jeered as it was passed across the stage without Mr Barnes contributing.[41] An election address from Churchill in Dundee was disrupted by constituents demanding Maclean's release. Churchill replied: 'You are talking of John Maclean and I shall refer to him. What I say is that if this country had been full of John Macleans we should have been conquered by the Huns. The strong forces of this country who have brought it through so many perils are not afraid of John Maclean and his backers!'[42]

All the while, Maclean's health continued to deteriorate, and Agnes wrote to the BSP, saying: 'The only alternatives in the conflict between the authorities and himself – either his death in prison, or his immediate release from prison ... From the former I believe they do not shrink, and every day brings it nearer.'[43]

In early November 1918, Agnes travelled to London to campaign for her husband's release.[44] She met with Munro and told him of the conditions she had found her husband in and how, contrary to the Minister's claims, he had been force-fed by two warders.[45] Munro responded that warders had reported Mrs Maclean complimenting her husband on his appearance when she had seen him in prison, so how worried could she really be?[46]

The *Call* published a letter stating that increasing unrest in Germany and Austria had secured the release of Liebknecht and Adler, and that the same had to be achieved in Britain for John Maclean.[47]

11

Let's Kill Capitalism This Year

While Maclean was in jail, facing daily force-feeding, the movement for workers' democracy that he had fought for was rising up across Europe. Russia was at peace with Germany, after more than 3 million deaths, the Communists had finally succeeded in ending the war on the Eastern Front. In Western Europe, rebellions took place, seeking to emulate events in Petrograd.

With discipline disintegrating in the German Army, the command planned a massive maritime offensive from Kiel, provoking a final clash with the British Navy. However, the previous year had seen a succession of mutinies throughout the German Navy, and the formation of sailors' soviets or councils had fatally undermined the ability of the Kaiser and his Imperial Chancellor to control the German armed forces. When the sailors at Kiel were ordered to attack on 3 November 1918, they revolted, seizing control of the base themselves and pointing cannons at German ships which had not joined the mutiny. Soldiers' and sailors' soviets took control of military and civil institutions across Germany and the German Revolution began. Mutineers poured into cities in convoys of commandeered trucks and, on 9 November, as they occupied the streets of Berlin, a Republic was proclaimed.[1]

These events had their own counterpoint, to a lesser extent, in the British Army. After the Etaples and Boulogne mutinies of late 1917, sedition in the military increased rapidly. In 1918, 676 British soldiers were sentenced to death for mutiny, with many more being summarily executed by their commanders. Further mutinies took place on the British mainland at Pitbright and Shoreham in 1918.[2]

In Italy, the 1917 general strike in Turin had sown the seeds of massive left-wing agitation the following year, building towards the

Biennio Rosso, the Two Red Years of 1919 and 1920 in which Italy saw thousands of strikes and occupations. Earlier, the Easter Rising in Ireland in 1916 had re-ignited the struggle for independence and, in Scotland, the Clyde and the coalfields of Fife remained sites of continuing unrest.

The German Revolution was causing concern in governments across Europe. The Director of Military Operations at the War Office, Sir Henry Wilson, wrote in his diary on 9 November:

> Cabinet meeting tonight ... Lloyd George read two telegrams from the Tiger [Clemenceau] in which he described Froch's interview with the Germans. The Tiger is afraid that Germany may collapse and Bolshevism gain control ... Lloyd George asked me if I wanted that to happen or if I did not prefer an armistice. Without hesitation I replied 'Armistice'. The whole cabinet agreed with me. Our real danger now is not the Boches but Bolshevism.[3]

Peace was declared on 11 November 1918. At the same time, socialist revolutionary movements across Europe were stronger than they had ever been. Marxists had gained positions of power in both the military and in the factories, and the very empires which the war had been fought to expand were now looking ever more fragile. The Russian, German and Austro-Hungarian monarchies had all fallen. As Lenin had predicted and as others had feared, the Great War had reduced Russia and Germany to civil war and revolution. Maclean believed that the time had come for capitalism to be finally killed off, and there was no doubt in his mind that the workers of both Petrograd and Clydeside had played a significant role in ending the war and in fomenting revolution.

Amidst the peace celebrations, the government decided that Maclean should again be released. A General Election was called for December and the Scotland Office feared that, if Maclean defeated Labour Minister George Barnes in the Gorbals and were then unable to serve his term due to his imprisonment, they might face increased unrest on the Clyde. Government agents had recently intercepted a letter from Sylvia Pankhurst to a comrade in Glasgow which ended with the words 'I expect the revolution soon, don't you?' and this was discussed in Cabinet.[4] George Barnes sent a memo to his ministerial colleagues: 'The continued agitation about John Maclean constitutes a serious danger for the Government ... I think it would be an act of grace therefore, to release [him] ... before the agitation assumes larger and more dangerous dimensions.'[5]

The Home Secretary, Lord Cave, replied that Maclean had the support of revolutionaries in Wales and London who would see his release as a triumph over the Government. But the rest of the Cabinet agreed with Barnes that clemency was still preferable.[6] And so in mid-November, Agnes Maclean received news that her husband would be released. He was granted a pardon,[7] backdated to the day that nominations for the General Election had opened.[8] The decision to pardon Maclean was a huge concession by the Government towards an entirely unrepentant revolutionary. The British Government had again changed its mind as to whether Maclean was more of a threat to them in or out of jail. The Scotland Office, even in releasing him, noted that 'if Bolshevik propaganda is largely put out in this country, Maclean will be leader.'[9]

John asked Agnes that the news be kept secret, as he did not feel up to a public demonstration. However, word had got out, and the pair were met by a crowd of socialists at Aberdeen train station on the morning of 3 December. Local papers reported that 'Maclean seemed to be quite pleased with himself and his reception',[10] but that 'those who had known him previously remarked that he was looking somewhat thinner than formerly, and that they doubted very much if he would have been able to stand the greater portion of the five years penal servitude.' Nevertheless, he was able to make what was described as a 'vigorous speech'.[11]

By the afternoon, when he reached Buchanan Street Station in Glasgow, vast crowds had gathered to greet him. The newspapers estimated that 100,000 people lined the streets, including many who had struck work.[12] James Maxton, Willie Gallagher and other leaders of the Red Clyde organisations met Maclean off the train, and a carriage was pulled by the workers through the streets with Maclean on top waving a red flag at the crowds. The suffragette and socialist Dora Montefiore wrote about the welcome for the *Call* the following week:

... the carriage in which Maclean and Mrs. Maclean were seated was drawn by dozens of willing comrades, while the 'ticket-of-leave' man waved from the box seat a huge red flag ... when the procession was halted for a minute in Jamaica Street, Maclean called for three hearty cheers for the German Social Revolution; and on these being given by thousands of voices, then called for three more cheers for the British Social Revolution, when the shouts that rent the air made a volume of sound that the capitalists of Clydeside will often remember in the near future, when they are troubled with bad dreams ...

From the trams going towards the city peeped timidly or with scared faces those who for the first time had seen flaunted to the four winds the emblem which now waves over the public buildings of Petrograd, Moscow, and Berlin. The welcome to John Maclean was a welcome of heart and of head from the younger generation to whom he has given his best intellectually in interpreting to them their historic revolutionary mission; and his best emotionally by suffering as the victim of capitalist persecution so that they, the younger generation, might have a symbol around whom to rally.

Maclean has descended into Hell, the Hell of the capitalist prison and on the third day he has risen again. His followers, who love him and trust him, have not been scattered abroad, but have gained in insight and in solidarity. His candidature for Parliament goes forward in their capable hands ... the fight will go on, and will never cease, until the Red Flag waves, not only over the City of Glasgow, but from the Clock Tower of Westminster, as a symbol that the People have entered into their inheritance.[13]

The mainstream newspapers told a similar – though less emphatic – story, adding that the procession continued to his home in Shawlands, and that there was no reason to fear for Maclean's health. The *Daily Record* printed large pictures of Maclean being greeted on the platform, and waving an enormous red flag in front of a crowd.[14]

However, when recalling the event ten years later, Dora Montefiore gave a very different account, remembering 'the agony of his wife and the sorrow of his relatives' and finding Maclean to be the 'wrung-out rags of humanity'. She added later that 'His thoughts were now disconnected, his speech was irresponsible, his mind, from solitary confinement, was absolutely self-centred. In a word, prison life had done its work on a delicately-balanced psychology, and our unfortunate comrade was now a mental wreck.'[15]

But by the time her second account was written, Dora Montefiore had parted ways politically with Maclean and she was motivated to discredit him. Her view contradicts that of Maclean's prison doctor, who wrote two months earlier that 'Mentally he was quite clear and gave no evidence of insanity.'[16]

Nevertheless, months of confinement and daily force-feeding had taken their toll on Maclean. When the springs of his carriage collapsed at Carlton Place, speeches were made, but Maclean's throat was too sore for him to speak.

Regardless of his health, Maclean's election campaign was already in full swing when he arrived back in the city. Willie Gallacher was acting as his agent, and his election address had already been circulated throughout the city. The prospect of a recently jailed Bolshevik revolutionary fighting a Cabinet minister for a seat in Parliament was an exciting one, and the press and public watched with interest. But Maclean was unwilling to make any further speeches, and did not appear in public for most of the campaign – it is a matter of debate as to whether it was his throat and respiratory complaints, or his mental health, that kept him at home. Meanwhile, the whole of Scotland was jubilant at the Allied victory and the end of the war, and the spirit of jingoism was dominant in the election, with George Barnes declaring to cheering crowds: 'I am for hanging the Kaiser.'[17]

The newspapers echoed that nationalism, and where previously the press had accused Maclean and other socialists of being German agents, they now repeated suggestions that Maclean's politics were foreign in some other way. The *Birmingham Post* carried the following article:

Now John Maclean is the head and front of whatever revolutionary movement there may be on the Clyde and the great cities in the South which are supposed to contain missionaries of his ... No Labour leader with a well-poised brain would go hunger-striking in gaol; having been so maladroit as to get himself incarcerated he would husband his strength against the time when he would be free, and not behave like a silly suffragette or a feeble-minded Conscientious Objector. That hunger-striking gives a clue to John Maclean's mentality ... That is all it is necessary to say about John Maclean – He is not a great leader of men, and should he get into Parliament now or at any time he will be an object of curiosity there, not of apprehension. But what of the movement which he personifies on the Clyde? ... These Bolshevists are in contact with Sinn Féiners. There is a large Irish element in Gorbals – Glasgow Irish next to Liverpool Irish, the least lovable sort of Irishman ... The revolutionary spirit is a foreign importation, and that it has spread to the Gorbals is to some extent due to the presence of a foreign Jewish colony there.[18]

The suggestion that teachers and Jews are behind the Marxist threat is a familiar one. A lede in *The Times* also focused on the Gorbals's 'slimy streets' and 'foreign Jews'.[19] But Maclean's closeness to the Irish and Jewish communities stood in stark contrast to the hatred that articles such as this tried to stir up. Maclean stood against anti-Semitism and the community was grateful, with the Ukrainian Relief Fund producing a button-hole badge with Maclean's face on it, and one local Jewish tailor even making a suit for Maclean as a present, having taken the measurements surreptitiously while John was giving a speech.[20]

Two days before the election, Maclean published a letter in the *Call* which was at once both a rallying cry, and a piece distancing himself from parliamentary politics. It began 'Greetings to all comrades and the mass of the working-class who forced the Cabinet to release me! ... The election in itself counts for nothing ... The real British crisis is coming, and coming quickly.' The letter emphasises that he believes that 1919 will be a crucial year in the rise of socialism, and that the conditions that will arise now the war is over will 'thrust the revolutionary section into power as on the Continent'.[21] He added that prison had not tamed him and that he had 'received the greatest honour of my life in being appointed Scottish representative of the first Socialist Republic in the world, the Russian one; and the second, in being selected as the standard-bearer of my class by the Cabinet of the British capitalist class'.[22] It seems clear that though Maclean had been released from jail to fight an election, he saw this as only a prelude to revolution.

On Friday, 13 December, the eve of polling day, Maclean made his only appearance in front of a packed St Mungo's Hall. *The Times* reported that many hundreds who could not gain admission waited outside for a glimpse of 'their hero',[23] and the *Scotsman* described the audience as being 'of the advanced socialist type', stating that when Maclean appeared he received a standing ovation of more than three minutes, with red flags waving throughout the crowd. Ahead of his speech, a talk had been given by a member of Sinn Féin, discussing the shared cause of Clydeside and Ireland[24] – a clear indication that Maclean's interest in Irish nationalism had grown over the previous years. In fact, both the Irish speaker and Maclean himself referenced Joe Robinson, the Scottish IRA leader held in Peterhead, who John may have met there. Regardless of where these increased sympathies with Ireland came from, then, as now, an introduction from Sinn Féin was not a vote winner in the more Orange neighbourhoods of South Glasgow. Just five years later, more than a third of the Gorbals vote would be won by a Unionist candidate.

Maclean spoke as a revolutionary and as a Bolshevik. He declared that it was his 'highland spirit' that had got him through jail, and that he had returned 'loyal to his class and more bitter than ever against capitalism'.[25] The focus on Irish politics and the reference to his 'highland spirit' can perhaps be seen as the seeds of a nascent nationalism emerging in Maclean's politics.

Tom Bell gives an account of the meeting with a wildly enthusiastic crowd and with thousands turned away from the rally, but he also remembers 'many people leaving the meeting while he was still speaking, obviously disturbed by the state of their friend and comrade's mind'.[26]

But if Bell's account is to be believed, it seems strange that the capitalist press of the time, which widely reported the rally, did not make any comment to the effect that Maclean seemed in any way mentally unbalanced. The *Daily Record* reported Maclean saying that 'he was out for socialism, even at the expense of John Maclean',[27] but didn't suggest that such a price looked likely to be paid.

Yet Maclean's comrades Tom Bell, Willie Gallacher and Dora Montefiore were all happy to write decades later that he was mentally ill at this point. These three comrades were all founder members, two years later, of the Communist Party, which Maclean would never join. His refusal to become a member of the party would have a defining impact on his life and legacy, particularly in the negative portrayal of him by former comrades with whom he parted ways.

In addition, Gallacher had invested huge energy in the electoral campaign, and may have been disappointed that Maclean was so uncompromising, insisting on a revolutionary programme at the clear cost of votes. Where Gallacher saw this election as an opportunity to win a seat in Parliament, Maclean regarded the election primarily as a platform for his propaganda.

The opposition, meanwhile, used Maclean's candidacy to their advantage, and an open letter from 'an ex-serviceman' was carried in newspapers around the country:

> This Labour party for which you are asked to vote is officially supporting the candidature of John Maclean, the Bolshevik Consul, who tried to breed revolution over here while you were fighting for England over yonder ... Are you going to vote for the men who by their strikes and their agitation prolonged the war and postponed the coming of victory, or for the Coalition, that carried the war to a victorious end? Are you going to vote for the men who held back the shells that might have saved the lives of some of those mates of ours who went West, or for the man who gave us the shells? We gave our blood willingly in order that Germany might be beaten. Are we going to give our votes to the men who aided and comforted Germany here? The Bolsheviks – or Barnes? That is the real issue, though you are far removed from Glasgow, for you cannot have a better illustration of the influence that is now dominating the Labour party than the fact that John Maclean, preacher of riot and red ruin, is supported and partially financed by it in his efforts to turn out G. N. Barnes, whose only faults are that he is a labour man and Briton, and not a revolutionary and an internationalist.[28]

Whether Maclean's candidacy hurt the Labour Party is unclear, but the result of the election nationally, announced two weeks later, was a landslide victory for Lloyd George's coalition of Conservatives and Liberals. The Labour Party managed to secure just 20 per cent of the vote across the country, though this was up from only 6 per cent in the previous General Election. Scotland returned six Labour MPs to Westminster, and John Maclean received 7,436 votes, to George Barnes' 14,247.[29] The voter turnout in the Gorbals was 53 per cent of registered voters; although some women had now been granted a vote, the vast majority were still ineligible. It must have been a considerable blow to some in Maclean's movement to see him defeated, and many may have felt that had he either remained in jail, or had more actively contested the election, he could have triumphed. However, the fact that more than 7,000 citizens voted for an explicitly revolutionary communist candidate and recent convict who had opposed the war was in itself a great achievement in what became known as 'the khaki election'.

Across the Irish Sea, the results of the election were very different. A landslide victory for Sinn Féin led to the establishment of the first Dáil Éireann – the Irish Assembly – as a consequence of the new Sinn Féin MPs' refusal to sit in Westminster. Much of the British left did not engage with the political shift in Ireland, believing it to be a purely nationalist movement and not a socialist issue. However, Maclean, who had long believed that the best support that could be offered to Soviet Russia was 'keeping Capitalism busy at home', saw the potential for a joint struggle by socialists and nationalists against the British Government in Ireland.

Maclean's particular willingness to support the Irish struggle may have also been tactical, in that he was able to see opportunities for building the socialist movement in Ireland in parallel with that in Glasgow, where nine IRA companies had already been established and armed.[30]

In late December, Maclean went to the Isle of Bute to recover from the election, staying in Tom Anderson's house in Rothesay.[31] Anderson, who had joined the ILP in 1897 and had founded one of the first Socialist Sunday Schools, still organised regular radical education and childcare in Glasgow. By 1918, he was a member of the

Socialist Labour Party and a De Leonist,[32] following the politics of the American socialist Daniel De Leon and advocating the takeover of all industry by radical Marxist trade unions. This position was one to which Maclean was sympathetic, believing that unions were powerful where they fought for broad class aims, rather than fighting narrow sectional battles for pay and conditions. De Leon was a founding member of the Industrial Workers of the World and, on 28 December, Maclean sent a letter to US President Woodrow Wilson asking for the release of IWW comrades: 'Sir, – You are here in Europe to negotiate a "Democratic Peace," as a Democrat. If so, I wish you to prove your sincerity by releasing Tom Mooney, Eugene Debs, Wm. Haywood, and all the others at present in prison as a consequence of their fight for "Working-class Democracy" since the United States participated in the war.'[33]

Maclean received no reply from the President, but whilst in Rothesay he did receive a communication from the King. The Under Secretary for Scotland wrote to confirm Maclean's free pardon. He replied:

Sir, – Would you be so kind as to inform the Secretary for Scotland that I do not accept your assertion that 'The King' has granted me a 'Free Pardon.'

Not 'The King' ... but the fighting workers of Britain have regained me my freedom, and a healthy fear of these workers has induced you and your friends to try this bluff of a 'Free Pardon.' All the time, however, you are trying to pester my wife and myself through your detestable spies, popularly called detectives. I welcome their attention, as it is a sign that you are foaming at the mouth at having to release me.

My immediate reply to that is a demand from the government, through the Scottish Office, for one hundred and fifty pounds (£150), the cost of recovery after my release last time and this from your cold-blooded treatment in those infernos, Peterhead and Perth.[34]

The letter, unsurprisingly, received no reply. The mention of spies is significant, however. Willie Gallacher wrote in his memoirs of seeing

Maclean in Rothesay, and that 'during this holiday it was apparent that Maclean was getting into a very sick condition. He was seeing spies everywhere.'[35] It seems likely that Maclean was paranoid, but this paranoia was not irrational. The government was continuing to spy on him, as it had done almost ceaselessly for four years, as shown by police records, court proceedings, military intelligence papers, and Sir Basil Thomson's regular reports to the Cabinet on Maclean's activities. Again, accounts of Maclean's mental instability come with motives and later political differences colour many accounts of his health.

By the start of 1919, John Maclean was back in Glasgow and preparing for what he expected to be a year of revolution. The government was anxious about the danger that large-scale demobilisation, increased automation and mass unemployment posed. At the same time, militant agitation within the armed forces increased. In January, 10,000 soldiers in Folkestone and 20,000 in Calais refused duty, chanting 'come on you Bolsheviks'.[36] Fifteen hundred airmen seized trucks and drove to Whitehall, and HMS *Kilbride* mutinied and raised the red flag. A few months later, five soldiers were killed and two officers injured in a riot in Rhyl.[37] This left-wing agitation within the army was a source of great hope to Maclean. He announced that his economics classes would resume at a new and larger venue – St Mungo's Hall.

In December, the *Worker* began to publish again, having been suppressed by Lloyd George in 1916, and in January the Clyde Workers' Committee met to discuss the problems of mass unemployment. It was agreed that the solution would be to enforce a 40-hour week, creating better conditions and more jobs. The working week at this time was 54 hours, with many workers on Clydeside working from 6 a.m. until 5.30 p.m. The Amalgamated Society of Engineers had proposed a 47-hour week, but the workers rejected this, with shop stewards such as Harry Hopkins insisting that 'working hours shall be so reduced as to absorb all unemployed while maintaining the present Rate of Wages.'[38] This demand for a total re-absorption of returning workers was expressly political, facilitating the demobilisation of the army whilst preserving the high employment rate on the Clyde and preventing the re-emergence of a reserve army of labour. The Clyde Workers' Committee called for an unofficial strike, with its short-term aim being the provision of work for soldiers and, its long-term aim, the strengthening of the labour movement's hand against the employers. In this way, it was able to win popular support from soldiers, whilst maintaining support from the more radical elements of the official and unofficial trade unions. A general strike across Clydeside was called in favour of a 40-hour week, with workers in all industries asked to down tools from late January onwards if the government did not impose a limit on working hours.

By 1919, the pressures on employment in post-war Glasgow were already beginning to be felt – and, at the same time, expressed. The year began auspiciously when, on Hogmanay, a two-month all-out strike by blind workers in the Glasgow Blind Asylum ended in victory for the workers and the reinstatement of victimised colleagues.[39] But a more brutal chapter was to take place three weeks later, though the autobiographies of key figures, including Gallacher and Manny Shinwell, all fail to mention it. In January 1919, Glasgow saw the first of a series of race riots which spread through Britain's ports. Maclean, in Lanarkshire at the time of the rioting, also does not mention the unrest in any surviving accounts. The Glasgow race riot began on 23 January, at the Sailors' Yard on James Watt Street. Some of the city's many black, South Asian, Arab and Chinese sailors had gathered there to find out if they would be given work that day. A group of white sailors began to harass them and the situation escalated. In her article about the riot, Jacqueline Jenkinson writes, 'More than thirty black sailors fled the sailors' yard pursued by a large crowd of white sailors. White locals joined the crowd which grew to several hundred strong. The rioters used guns, knives, batons and makeshift weapons including stones and bricks picked from the street.'[40]

The black sailors were chased to their boarding house on the Broomielaw, facing the Clyde in Central Glasgow, and there they were goaded and windows were smashed. Shots were exchanged and eventually the police arrived and took 30 of the black sailors into 'protective custody'. They were all later charged with either rioting or possession of offensive weapons. Just one of the white sailors was charged with a crime: assaulting a police officer. Three men were injured: two white sailors who received immediate medical attention, and a sailor from Sierra Leone whose 'gaping wounds' were ignored as he was thrown into a police van.[41] Manny Shinwell, a leader of the British Seafarers' Union, later to become a Labour MP and Cabinet minister, had spoken at the yard on James Watt Street just a few hours earlier. He had warned of the mass unemployment that would come with demobilisation if action were not taken to restrict foreign labour.[42]

Whether or not Shinwell incited the riot cannot be said with certainty. But his aim was quite clearly to stir up racial tensions within the workforce, and the riot that followed had the effect of making bosses reticent to hire non-white crews on Glasgow's ships, and led to the widespread deportation of black sailors.[43]

However, not all socialist leaders were so quick to exploit racist feeling, and later that year the *Workers' Dreadnought*, Sylvia Pankhurst's newspaper, condemned racist violence in ports: 'The Seamen's and Firemen's Union has placed its ban upon the employment of Negro seamen, so they are ashore and cannot get away. They are attacked and if they retaliate they are arrested! Is this fair play? The fight for work is a product of capitalism: under socialism race rivalry disappears.'[44]

There were further protests by black sailors and their wives in the pages and offices of Glasgow newspapers in the days that followed. And as well as this backdrop of racial violence, there was also shared struggle across divides, with January 1919 seeing putative general strikes in Belfast and Bombay as well as the 40-hour strike that approached on Clydeside.

The British Government, meanwhile, was facing a quickly escalating situation in Dublin, as the conflict between the nationalist government there and the British Government in London increased. At the same time, anxiety over the outcome of the revolutions in Germany and Russia continued. Glasgow's 40-Hour Strike movement built on this and its newspaper *Strike Bulletin*, which at its peak had a daily circulation of 20,000,[45] carried reports of industrial action in India, Spain and New York.

Despite his lack of comment on the Glasgow race riot, Maclean saw internationalism as the key focus in early 1919. On 23 January, he wrote in the *Call*:

We witness today what all Marxists naturally expected, the capitalist class of the world and their Governments joined together in a most vigorously active attempt to crush Bolshevism in Russia and Spartacism in Germany ... This is the class war on an international basis, a Class War that must and will be fought out to the logical conclusion—the extinction of capitalism everywhere.

The question for us in Britain is how we must act in playing our part in this world conflict. Some are suggesting a General Strike to enforce a withdrawal of British troops from Russia and, I suppose, from Germany as well. That, to some of us on the Clyde, is too idealistic ...

[We] think that we must adopt another line, and that is to save Russia by developing a revolution in Britain no later than this year ...

If capitalism lasts, then war is inevitable in five years: yes, and a war bloodier than the present war. Humanity is in a very tight corner, and so those who will be called to kill in the next war will have to make up their minds to fight capitalism to death this year.[46]

Maclean's refrain was now that 1919 must be the year of revolution. He even signed autographs at meetings with the words: 'Let's kill capitalism this year.' As a first step, he backed the 40-hour strike, though he hoped that it could be postponed so that the miners and railwaymen outwith Clydeside, and workers in industrial centres beyond Scotland, could be brought into the strike. Maclean was keen that the newly reinstated 'Triple Alliance' between the Miners' Federation of Great Britain, the National Union of Railwaymen and the National Transport Workers' Federation play a key role in the strike's victory and in escalating the conflict. It was his intention that a firm general strike based around engineers, miners and railwaymen could bring the government down in a matter of weeks. He then hoped that workers' organisations would take control of the factories and that the cooperative movement would take over the supply of food and fuel, enabling workers' representatives to assume power. The Triple Alliance, however, refused to back the strike.

Though many of the organisers of the 40-hour strike had less ambitious political aims – desiring shorter hours and greater employment security – the movement gained support from revolutionary and non-revolutionary socialists alike. The support was such that the official trade unions fell in line by mid-January and began to back the unofficial strike in Glasgow, given that they were by then powerless to stop it. Between 14 and 18 January, Maclean addressed crowds in Barrow, Leigh, Liverpool and Warrington, returning on 19 January to hold his weekly economics class in Glasgow, then heading to Lanarkshire to begin enlisting the miners into the 40-hour movement.[47] He was also interested in the growing textile strike in Perthshire in which police had attacked women and children.[48] Patrick Dollan laid out the importance of the industrial action in the now widely circulating *Strike Bulletin*:

> The 40 hour movement is making history. This is because it is the greatest effort made by the rank and file. For the first time the workers have become their own leaders. When the workers lead, and unity is maintained, victory is certain. There is one objective in the strike which is: to secure 40 hours' weeks for all workers. Everything else is irrelevant. The strikers are not fighting for themselves alone: they are fighting for every man, woman and child in the ranks of Scottish democracy.[49]

Willie Gallacher said of this time 'we were carrying on a strike when we ought to have been making a revolution.'[50] Whilst the revolutionary potential of Clydeside has been much discussed, and often overstated, there is no doubt that in January 1919, John Maclean was trying to make a revolution. Union leaders were mostly focused on organising Glasgow's engineers and shipyard workers, but Maclean was out of the city, trying to ensure that the country's transport, fuel and energy could also be hamstrung by a broad political strike. He was engaged in building Scotland's first attempt at a general strike, speaking in Bellshill, Motherwell and Shotts to miners who assured him that they would be downing tools.

The day of the strike, 27 January, arrived and the strike far surpassed the hopes of the organisers. Flying pickets of unemployed ex-servicemen moved about the city, whilst huge numbers of campaigning leaflets and posters were circulated. By the third day, between 70,000 and 100,000 men had struck across Clydeside. In Lanarkshire, the headquarters of the Miners' Union had been occupied by workers demanding that it back the strike.[51] The movement gathered pace, and the Home Secretary's Report on Revolutionary Organisations for 28 January stated that 'the outlook during the past fortnight has become rather dark. Strikes have taken place all over the country on the question of the forty-seven-hour week ... My Glasgow correspondent reports that the revolutionary movement is certainly gaining ground.'[52] The report suggested that the shortage of tobacco and beer was perhaps the most proximate cause of unrest, adding that 'if men could congregate in public houses they would not be driven to attend revolutionary meetings.'[53]

The same Cabinet paper contains an update on John Maclean's activities:

Since his release from prison this man has been making a series of revolutionary speeches in Lancashire. He appears to be convinced that the social revolution will come this year. His programme is for the miners to come out first on some economic issue; the other members of the triple alliance will follow suit; and then the unofficial workers committee movement will come in. He thinks that with the miners, the railway workers, the transport workers and the engineers on strike, and the army, navy and police either sympathetic or powerless, the government of the country can be transferred to the workers either peaceably or forcibly ...

Though Maclean is mentally unstable, there is sufficient method in his speeches to attract large audiences ... from 400 to about 1200 persons.[54]

The government believed that Maclean was unstable but, with the situation increasingly tense, they still saw him as a threat, particularly as he addressed large crowds on the subject of imminent revolution. A few days later the revolt feared by the authorities was to come closer than ever. As the strike continued on Clydeside, tens of thousands of workers were also out in Edinburgh, Newcastle, and Belfast where the shipyards, municipal buildings and newspapers had all been shut down.[55] At the same time, Maclean was making his way to Barrow and London to encourage English workers to join the action.[56]

In Glasgow, on Friday, 31 January 1919, with the strike now in its fourth day, workers gathered in George Square to demand that the Lord Provost back a 40-hour week. As well as engineers, shipwrights and miners, workers in the electricity plants were now on strike and Glasgow was unable to light its streets and homes. Some 35,000 striking workers marched into the city and filled George Square, waiting to hear the Lord Provost read out a response to their demands from the British Government. While Kirkwood, Gallacher, Shinwell and other leaders of the strike were inside the City Chambers, fighting broke out in the square and the red flag was raised. The source of the initial unrest is disputed, with some claiming that it was an unprovoked baton charge by the police, others stating that it was police trying to bring down the red flag, and still others suggesting that the disturbance was begun by workers preventing a tram from crossing the square. Tom Bell describes the trams, driven by blackleg labour, being ordered across the square in a deliberate attempt at provocation by the authorities.[57]

The *Scotsman* reported at the time that the Chief and Deputy Constables of Glasgow were, respectively, hit with rocks and stabbed.[58] However, few commentators today dispute the fact that it was a police riot, involving a violent attack on striking workers. The noise brought the strike leaders running out of the City Chambers to try to calm the crowds. As Kirkwood ran towards the workers, he was felled by a police baton and the Battle of George Square began.[59]

The strikers, largely led by ex-serviceman, tore up cobbles and iron railings and forced the police out of the square. A lorry was commandeered, and its stock of bottles pelted at the police.[60] The Sheriff began reading the Riot Act, but it was torn from his hands before he could finish. Kirkwood, Gallacher, Shinwell and Harry Hopkins were arrested along with scores of others, and fighting between workers and police spread to Glasgow Green and Townhead. Gallacher himself urged the crowds to disperse quietly but the riot continued, with tram cars smashed, shops looted as far away as Kinning Park, and windows broken in practically all districts of the city.[61] The Court of Justiciary was attacked,[62] and there were police baton charges against workers in other neighbourhoods, including Bellshill.[63] Gallacher goes on to suggest that it was a grave mistake for him to ask the workers to go home, when they should instead have been led to Maryhill Barracks to enlist the support of the soldiers stationed there, and take control of the city.[64]

The government was clearly aware of the potential for further disruption – or worse – and the soldiers at Maryhill were confined to barracks for fear that they would mutiny. Instead, soldiers from England and the Highlands were moved into the city. Tanks were stationed on the Gallowgate, and machine-gun nests were established in the city centre. At 3 p.m., the Cabinet met at 10 Downing Street. The Chief Secretary for Ireland reported that workers in Belfast had formed a soviet, the Minister of Labour reported that mounted police had charged a crowd in front of the municipal buildings in Glasgow, and the Scottish Secretary told the cabinet that 'it was a misnomer to call the situation in Glasgow a strike — it was a Bolshevist rising.'[65] It was announced that six tanks and a hundred army vehicles were on their way to Glasgow, and that 12,000 men were available to quell the Glasgow unrest. Reporters were sent to Glasgow by all the major newspapers, and a newly radicalised Siegfried Sassoon arrived in the city to meet the strikers.

The extent to which this clash between the workers and the government represented a revolutionary moment in Scotland has been much discussed. The fact that the strike leaders tried to end the riot, that John Maclean was out of the country, and that no attempt to meet up with serving soldiers was made, suggests that the Government had vastly over-reacted to what was, at its core, a labour dispute.

Whilst it is often said that the idea of a Glasgow Bolshevist uprising in 1919 is a fantasy, certainly it is true that John Maclean was in the coalfields of Lanarkshire, Fife and England, trying to join up the strikes and create that popular uprising, while other strike leaders underestimated the appetite for action among the workers. Nevertheless, the unrest was quashed, with its leaders jailed, Maclean still down south, and the pickets cowed by the large military presence. Though railwaymen in London carried on strikes over working hours, the mass action died down slowly, finally ending where it had begun, in Glasgow and Belfast.

A week later, on 7 February, a Cabinet meeting could now declare that, whilst the industrial unrest was still ongoing, it was largely under control, although the Secretary for Scotland did add that 'The release of MacLean had had unfortunate results. MacLean was again making most outrageous speeches, and would probably have to be rearrested.'[66]

By 10 February, the strikes had been called off, as a 47-hour week was agreed – a partial victory for the rank and file. Later that year, John Maclean wrote about the strike and final compromise in a pamphlet entitled *Sack Dalrymple, Sack Stevenson: Let Labour Revenge Bloody Friday*. Dalrymple and Stevenson had led the tramwaymen and the police respectively during the strike, and Maclean believed that they had between them provoked the violence. Maclean writes:

> A terrible blow was struck at the working class of Scotland on Bloody Friday, 31 January 1919. A mass movement was started on the Clyde on the Monday prior to reduce the working week to forty hours. The movement rapidly spread over the industrial belt of Scotland. A strike for a forty-four-hour week was simultaneously proceeding in Belfast, where the stoppage was almost complete … Had the strike feeling spread the whole country might have been involved, and in the temper of the people at the time the government feared a revolution such as had swept Germany into the hands of the 'right' socialists.[67]

The pamphlet criticises the municipality for using tram-drivers and policemen against workers who were protesting peacefully, stating that 'socialism means that your bread and butter are secure no matter what you think. Socialism means that you are free and entitled to speak your mind.'[68]

On 10 February, the report of the Director of Intelligence to the Cabinet declared the threat of revolution to be over:

> The strikes which were threatened a fortnight ago broke out in Glasgow and extended to London. The plan of the revolutionary minority was to use the Clyde as a touchstone for a general strike and, if the plan proved successful, to bring out the engineers and

railways all over the country, to seize the food and to achieve a revolution. The scheme failed ... partly because the government dealt firmly with the rioters.[69]

Part of the myth-making around the Battle of George Square relates to this over-anxious assessment by British spies. The plan described above was certainly not at the forefront of Gallacher's, Shinwell's, or Kirkwood's minds. It was, however, exactly the hope of John Maclean and other communists in Glasgow.

Maclean's conviction that the destruction of capitalism was possible under the conditions of 1919 can also be seen in his response to the prominent Scottish Gaelic nationalist Ruaraidh Erskine of Marr who, on behalf of the Scottish Home Rule Association, had asked Maclean to join their petition to President Wilson for recognition of Scottish autonomy and representation in the peace talks. Maclean replied:

> ... my blood revolts against the 'memorial to President Wilson' thanking him for what he has done for home rule all round. He has done nothing and will do nothing for home rule anywhere, as he is but the representative of brutally blatant capitalism in America, a Capitalism that means to crush Mexico under its 'heel of steel' as it already has the Philippine Islands and Cuba ... [it is] a socialist republic alone in which we can have real home rule.[70]

Maclean remained convinced that independence was a Marxist question and must emerge from revolution, not from the negotiating table of Versailles. On 8 February, Maclean addressed an audience at the Albert Hall in this vein for the 'Hands Off Russia' campaign. Other speakers included Sylvia Pankhurst, Countess Markievicz. and Jerome K. Jerome.[71] The *Call* reported that 'The climax ... was reached when EC Fairchild announced John Maclean. Round on round of applause greeted his rising, the whole vast gathering breaking into song ... In a fine peroration he maintained that armies and navies would never cease until production was socialized ... on the lines laid down by Russia.'[72]

The secret police report on the meeting is less glowing: 'John McLean made his usual incendiary oration. After that the crowd began to thin. A large number consisted of Yiddish speaking Russian Jews.'[73]

As a speaker, Maclean was now able to command huge audiences in London as he did in Glasgow, filled with a belief that a British Revolution was possible. In private however, the months of touring since he had been freed had taken their toll on his marriage to Agnes. In January, the Govan School Board had decided that, despite his official pardon, they would not re-employ Maclean.[74] He continued with political organising as his only profession, struggling to secure an income from wages at the Scottish Labour College and from collections at his meetings and classes. Agnes began to beg him to rest and to preserve his health and their family. He refused.

In the spring of 1919, John Maclean still saw a revolutionary potential on Clydeside and believed that his place was not at home, but on the streets and at the factory gates.

12

One Big Union

The political situation in 1919 continued to be volatile, and in February, the Home Secretary recommended the extension of wartime measures against sedition. He made specific reference to dangerous speeches encouraging worker control which John Maclean was then giving in Lancashire.[1] The tensions which had led to the 40-hour strike were still present, and the Government continued to be nervous about the pressures caused by unemployment and demobilisation.

Throughout the year, the British Army continued to fight against the Bolsheviks in the Russian Civil War, and some of the Russians and Lithuanians who Maclean had known in his capacity as Soviet Consul now fought in the Red Army against Britain and its allies. The entry in Maclean's diary for 2 March simply reads 'Blantyre – Jonas Shelpuk – Killed in Red Guard. Joined at Omsk.'[2] Though the war with Russia and the arrest of Russian Ambassador Litvinoff had meant that Maclean no longer had responsibility for the Soviet Consulate in Glasgow, he nevertheless continued to feel both a political, and a personal, connection to Russia. At the same time as marking the death of Red Guard soldiers, Maclean's diary also records the name and details of a Scottish soldier, Andrew Orr, held by the Red Army.[3] His unfailing contention that a bayonet is a weapon with a worker at either end meant that Maclean was also willing to help British soldiers.

A further call to Russia came in early 1919, when Lenin and Trotsky issued the 'Invitation to the First World Congress' of a new Communist International. The Third International, or 'Comintern' as it would come to be known, was to begin with a meeting of the world's leading communists and socialists. The document invited 39 different international groups to Russia, and John Maclean was one of only four invitees mentioned by name.[4] The Soviets invited the tendency of the British Socialist Party represented by Maclean – that is, the revolutionary tendency, as opposed to the parliamentary tendency represented by Fairchild, who had assumed the leadership of the party from Hyndman during the war. Maclean's revolutionary sympathies were reported at the time in the *Guardian*, which noted that he had held a minute's silence in Manchester for the memories of 'Jim Connolly', 'Rosa Luxemburg', 'Karl Liebknecht' and other martyrs.[5]

That Maclean was still a key figure in the eyes of the Bolsheviks was no surprise, and it would have seemed probable to them that he would emerge as leader of the Communist Party of Great Britain which the Comintern hoped to establish.[6] Maclean, however, would never travel to Russia. He applied for a passport and was denied.

But his failure to join his comrades in Russia did not reflect any loss of faith in the Soviet project. On 30 March, he spoke at the Engineers' Institute in Sheffield. He urged workers to take control of the mines and added that Bolshevism must come, but that England was backward and that 'delegates were being sent from Scotland to bring England into line.'[7] This marks one of Maclean's first suggestions that the Scottish working class were more advanced than the English, though he is not proposing that the revolution happen without England, only that a Scottish vanguard must be sent to radicalise the English.

In late April, he returned to Sheffield to attend the British Socialist Party Conference. Although there had been no representation in Moscow from Maclean or any other BSP members, the inauguration of the Third International in March 1919 resulted in calls for the formation of a Communist Party of Great Britain, and the BSP conference in Sheffield was dominated by this discussion, with the BSP seeing itself as the de facto British Communist Party. However, the party was still split over tensions between democratic and revolutionary socialism, and also over continued affiliation to the Labour Party as opposed to affiliation to Soviet Russia.[8]

A rather perplexed reporter for the *Sheffield Daily Telegraph* wrote that there was a 'curious divergence of opinion on subjects which one would have thought would have not necessitated discussion among such a body'.[9] This phrase might, indeed, sum up every aspect of the formation of the Communist Party of Great Britain.

As well as motions calling for an enquiry into the George Square violence and denouncing the continued British occupation of Ireland and Egypt, the conference discussed how the BSP might join with the ILP and the SLP to form the Communist Party of Great Britain, and what tactics such a party should pursue.[10]

The *Sheffield Daily Telegraph*'s report on the conference concluded that

> John McLean, the Clyde deportee, led the extremists with an impassioned oration appealing to brute force and complete war against the existing constitution. He preached the gospel of revolution in the Army and Navy, and carried the conference with him in spite of a more reasoned and intelligent appeal by Mr. Fairchild, of London, who advocated caution and British – not Bolshevik methods.[11]

Maclean concluded his speech with the words: 'It is entirely owing to the British Socialist Party that we have got a drift towards the revolutionary position ... The general strike will be the next stage in getting the food and the means of production into our hands. (cheers)'[12]

It is clear that at this conference Maclean was in a significant position within his party, a member of the National Executive and a celebrated speaker who had the zeitgeist of unity and revolution with him. He joked that the BSP should either seize the means of production, or at least seize Lloyd George.[13] Dora Montefiore wrote that

> ... the B.S.P., should be bent on changing the attitude of the thought of the masses from their belief in the efficacy of bourgeois democratic institutions to a new and enlarged outlook, when the class struggle, led on one side by the Duke of Northumberland and his ardent followers; and on the other side by Maclean ... shall reach such a degree of intensity that it will burst by internal pressure the formal framework of democracy.[14]

The shift by the BSP to a more revolutionary position brought it into line with the ideological and tactical stance that Maclean had held since 1917. It seemed natural that he would from this point on assume a greater role in the party. He spent the end of April on a speaking tour of England, Wales and Scotland and returned to Glasgow for May Day, which was again held on the first day of the month, a Thursday. The *Call* seemed justified in writing in early 1919 that 'he is pre-eminent as the standard bearer of revolutionary-Socialism in this country ... the audience at the end treated him to such an ovation that John must have felt his great sacrifices ... had not been in vain.'[15]

As his political star rose however, Maclean's personal life began to unravel. Nan describes the break-up of the family at this point, with her father unable to turn his back on revolution and her mother unable to understand his obsession with political change at the expense of his health and family. Agnes was desperate for John to take a rest from revolution.[16] Her role in the struggle, the part she saw for herself, was to support and care for John. This now came directly in conflict with his sole cause. The strain of government persecution, whilst watching her husband's health broken by prison, now proved too much.[17]

In 1919, she gave him an ultimatum, asking that he give up his political activity and concentrate on his family. Agnes's action proved to be disastrous for their marriage, with Maclean believing that government agents were behind her decision,[18] and that they had persuaded Agnes to engineer this choice between his isolation from family and the abandonment of his principles.

Maclean chose isolation, and Agnes and their two daughters Nan and Jean moved out of the house at Auldhouse Road. It is impossible to say whether the interpretation should be that Agnes was, as William Knox claims, 'unable to stand the pressures and insecurity of living with a man who lived only for the revolution',[19] or rather, that her patience was exhausted, as Harry McShane argues, 'because the years of poverty had been too much for her',[20] or, indeed, whether she left because of his monomania and paranoia – as later reported by both former comrades and by members of the secret police. What is certain is that the estrangement from his family would cause Maclean yet more suffering. The loss of his partner and confidante was a great blow, and it seems that much of the chaos that others observed in his life from this point on may have been due to the absence of Agnes, who had for so long supported him in his revolutionary work.[21]

Maclean continued to live at Auldhouse Road, offering the newly spare rooms to unemployed comrades. Despite the ructions in both his marriage and his party, he continued to campaign actively, organising demonstrations in support of political prisoners, and revolutionaries in Ireland, Egypt and India. In April 1919, he was in the gallery watching Shinwell and Gallacher receive their sentences for their part in the Battle of George Square. Arthur McManus recalled Maclean turning to him, white with anger, and saying 'it's all a hollow sham and a mockery, and Gallacher is going to have to pay the price.'[22] The pain that Maclean seems to have felt at the prospect of Gallacher's imprisonment speaks both to his loyalty to a man who was still a close comrade, and to Maclean's own traumatic experience of jail.

May Day that year was the biggest that Glasgow had ever seen, with 150,000 participants, widespread strikes, and many children taken out of school to participate.[23] The march was led by the Sinn Féin Pipe Band, and Irish tricolours were displayed among the many thousands of red flags. It took more than an hour to pass any given point. Arriving at Glasgow Green, the crowds found speakers from hundreds of socialist and cooperative organisations,[24] including Maclean and also Countess Markievicz, the Irish Republican and first woman MP.

From this point on, Maclean's interest in Irish Republicanism increased dramatically. Maclean was particularly excited about the plan for a Connolly Memorial Workers' College in Dublin to mirror the Scottish Labour College at which he continued to lecture, with classes now numbering thousands of students. In an appeal for funding and support for the Scottish Labour College, he wrote:

It is apparent that the priests of Capitalism (British and Irish alike) fear the spread of real education amongst the wage slaves since they understand that an educated working class will fight Capitalism with its robbery and 'continuous reign of terror' to the death.

> ... our College will be the envy of the workers of the world ...
> And once we have enough in Scotland we shall send help to Ireland
> to establish her Connolly College, bedad we will![25]

Maclean was extremely active in 1919, lecturing and speaking in towns and cities across the UK, teaching at the Labour College, serving on the National Executive of the British Socialist Party, and publishing twice as many articles as he did in any other year of his life. When the Government's Sankey Report considering the possible nationalisation of coal mines resulted in a compromise, wherein the owners would retain private control but the Government would enforce better pay and conditions, Maclean advocated rejecting the Government's compromise in the face of the strength of the trade union and socialist movements, 'now that British capitalism is faced with a situation that, we trust, will break it up for good.'[26]

At the end of May, Maclean held a demonstration on Glasgow Green calling for the American Consul in Glasgow to take action for the release of the IWW leader and socialist presidential candidate Eugene Debs. He described the demonstration in an open letter to Debs as 'the first of a series in Glasgow for the release of yourself, Mooney, Haywood, Berger, and the other hundreds of champions of the real cause of Labour lying in American, British and other prisons throughout the world.'[27] Debs kept the letter in the front of his scrapbook.[28] Maclean was by this time an international figure, as well known in the factories of Chicago as he was in Dublin. His diary is filled with the addresses of comrades and organisations in Vancouver, Chicago, Berlin, Kansas, Boston and New York.[29] And by late 1919 he was honorary president of both the Russian and Hungarian Soviets, chosen as a figurehead by their new revolutionary governments.[30]

The New York magazine the *Liberator* sent Crystal Eastman to report on the 1919 unrest on the Clyde. She described hearing Maclean speak in early July:

> 'Well, Wullie Gallacher's cam oot. And they're saying the treaty is
> signed and they are going to have peace, but they're not. Wullie
> Gallacher is not going to let them.'

Thus spoke John Maclean on Thursday, 3 July, 1919 in Paisley Town Hall, where three thousand workers had gathered to welcome the chief hero of the 40-hour strike after his three months in Edinburgh Jail.

Surrounding him (Maclean) were the chief figures in the great strike, behind him a socialist choir, girls all in white, below him rows upon rows of hard-headed scotch machinists, munitions workers and shipbuilders, all in their working clothes with caps on, typical Clyde workers, the sort of men that kept Glasgow despite all governmental blandishments, an *anti-war* city throughout the five years ...

Maclean is the cheeriest firebrand you ever saw. He is a mild mannered, smiling conspirator, with a round eyed, apple cheeked face, and white hair. 'Be cheerie comrades,' he says, 'you never can win a revolution without being cheerie.' Maclean believes in revolution now.[31]

It is interesting that it is from an American journalist that we hear Maclean speaking Scots. With no known surviving audio or video recording of Maclean and even his own written records of his speeches rendered in standard English, Eastman's account is perhaps the closest thing we have to hearing Maclean's voice. It is interesting too that, even after his two stretches in Peterhead, Eastman finds the kindly teacher, not the dour or paranoid revolutionary that some later reports recall.

In mid-July, Maclean travelled to Ireland, visiting for the first time since the Irish War of Independence had begun. He had been invited to stay by Delia Larkin, the sister of his friend Jim Larkin, the labour organiser, who was then in America.[32] Just as Maclean had taken a keen interest in Debs's imprisonment and was being updated by way of letters from Debs's family, he was also concerned with the political imprisonment of Delia and Jim's brother Peter Larkin in Australia and was keen to hear more from his family.[33] Maclean's own experience of political imprisonment, often suggested to be an isolating factor for him, made him into a formidable campaigner on behalf of other political prisoners around the world.

He arrived in Dublin in July 1919 to find the city under military occupation, with thousands of soldiers in the streets and political demonstrations banned. The first Dáil Éireann – the Irish Parliament – had already been held, and Nan remembers a photograph of its members hanging on the wall in their family home.[34] But, whilst he was an admirer of Sinn Féin, Maclean's own views on nationalism and war in Ireland were still conflicted. He arrived to find a city on the brink of war but nevertheless celebrating peace, as the Treaty of Versailles was marked with a national holiday on Saturday, 19 July: 'on Peace Saturday round the neighbourhood of College Green were thousands of policemen in plain clothes and spies galore … very few (mostly incomers like myself) witnessed the solemn farce of 15,000 soldiers with bayonets fixed, machine guns, and tanks, marching through the streets to celebrate peace.'[35]

Whilst in Dublin, Maclean met with key figures from the workers' movement. At a reception at Liberty Hall, he was welcomed by the journalist Cathall O'Shannon and the poet and painter George Russell, or Æ as he was known. Maclean liked Russell, writing that 'never have I met one in whom so nicely are blended the idealist and the realist. In him Ireland is seen at her best.'[36] It was intended that Maclean would speak at a meeting at Mansion House on the 22nd, but the police blockaded the venue and prevented it from taking place. The organisers commented: 'The Socialist Party is not inclined to complain of the Castle's interference in this case. John MacLean's suppression will supply him with actual experience of normal British rule in Ireland, and he may be relied upon to point the moral to the many thousands of British workers whom he will address in the next few weeks.'[37] Maclean added that 'an inspector obdurately refused to listen to my plea that I had come to civilize Ireland.'[38]

He instead addressed smaller meetings, praising Jim Larkin and James Connolly and talking of the importance of establishing 'One Big Union' in Ireland that would organise all workers regardless of craft or employment. He added 'Don't leave it to the officials. Make your own plans, fight your battle, and prepare for the next.'[39]

Whilst Maclean's militant Marxism and his knowledge of the Belfast Dockers' Strike and the Easter Rising were well received, many of his views met with an icy reception from the staunchly Nationalist crowds. He declared at Workers' Hall that he was for a workers' republic, not a Sinn Féin republic. At the Socialist Party of Ireland headquarters, he was continuously heckled as he explained that it was a problem that many Sinn Féin supporters were anti-communist because of their Catholicism. The frankness of the confrontations obviously impressed Maclean and he wrote that 'through these manifestations of the Irish mind at home I began to realize the spirit that 700 years of oppression had failed to subdue. Once the workers develop a similar hatred of Capitalism things are going to move on avalanche-like.'[40]

This idea is key for Maclean in his movement towards the belief that national feeling can be used as a recruiting sergeant for communism. In a way, Maclean was continuing in his lifelong orthodoxy, understanding through the call for the Third International that the Bolsheviks intended to build world Bolshevism by building national communist parties. The experience of the rebellion in Ireland encouraged him to believe that left-wing politics and anti-imperialism could be combined in a national struggle.

There are suggestions that Maclean's support for Irish autonomy went further than the record of his trip to Dublin suggests. Certainly he was awake to the revolutionary potential of Ireland at a time when very few Scottish Protestant labour leaders were. He wrote in 1920 that 'the Irish Sinn Féiners, who make no profession of socialism or communism and are at best non-socialists, are doing more to help Russia and the revolution than all we professed Marxian Bolsheviks in Britain.'[41] And he firmly believed that, after the national struggle, a spontaneous class war would break out in Ireland.

There have often been claims, not least by his daughter Nan Milton, that Maclean's links to James Connolly and the Easter Rising were stronger than the record shows, and that during the Irish War of Independence, Maclean moved from words to deeds. Seamus Reader, a young Glaswegian from a Scottish Protestant background who became one of the leaders of the Scottish Battalion of the IRA, wrote articles for *An t-Oglach* concerning Scottish involvement in the Irish struggle. He described Connolly having discussed Maclean's victimisation and determining that 'at least the Liffey would assert itself.' Reader also added that, after his spell in Peterhead, Maclean had links to the Irish Republican Brotherhood.[42] Gerry Cairns, former president of the John Maclean Society, maintains that in Peterhead Prison in 1918 Maclean would have met Joe Robinson who, along with Bernard Friel and Michael Callaghan, had been convicted of trying to smuggle munitions into Ireland. Cairns argues that Maclean's meetings in jail with Robinson and other political prisoners paved the way for connections to Sinn Féin and the IRA.[43]

The only evidence of a concrete link between Maclean and republican military action in Ireland is in the writings of Seamus Reader. He claims that in January 1919, soon after his release from Peterhead, Maclean met with members of 'A' Company of the Glasgow Irish Republican Brotherhood Military Board to discuss getting explosives from the miners to the Irish fighters. Reader remembers a meeting in Calton where it was explained to Maclean that 'we would only be interested in matters of a military nature and not to be giving us a lecture on economics or political science.'[44]

It is impossible to verify this account. Certainly Scottish workers, and miners in particular, offered concrete support for the IRA in many areas of Glasgow. At the same time, socialists such as MacManus, Crawfurd and Maclean had strong links to elements of the Irish nationalist movement in Dublin and Belfast. However it is not clear that John Maclean supported the targeting of British soldiers in what he would have seen as 'worker on worker' violence. In Dublin in July 1919, he argued that soldiers should be won round to the cause of Irish independence, writing in the *Worker* that he had 'urged that Ireland alone could never gain its own freedom, and her republic depended on the revolt and success of British Labour, and that therefore the Irish workers ought not to antagonise the soldiers of occupation in Ireland, but should try to win them over to the Irish point of view.' He recorded that he had faced 'bitter and outspoken' opposition on this point, as well as 'good natured correction' on referring to Britain as 'the Mainland'.[45]

Maclean's conception of revolution was always firmly based on winning all workers, including those within the army, over to the cause, and his views on Ireland in 1919 were still tactically moderate. But it is certainly clear that he knew and met with republican fighters in Glasgow, and his actions may have been more extreme than his writings. Certainly Maclean's views on Ireland had crystallised into a conception of anti-imperialist nationalism and he began to produce propaganda aimed at uniting Scottish and Irish workers against the British State.

On leaving Dublin, he headed to Durham to address the famous Miners' Gala, celebrated annually since 1871,[46] and soon after published an article called 'Will Capitalism Collapse?' in which he outlined how well the capitalists had managed to ride out the previous twelve months, overcoming unrest in the army and placating the miners and railwaymen in order to avoid a general strike, 'adding Persia and Afghanistan to the empire whilst excluding France from Syria, assuring the world all the time that these countries are clamouring for Britain's protective help'. He lamented that leaders of the working class had failed to be as audacious as the leaders of capitalism, and criticised those Marxists who believed that socialism was inevitable. The article concluded that

… the safety of society rests not in the hands of a few (leaders or heroes), but in those of the masses of mankind, conscious or unconscious … the moment will come (perhaps even this year) when the workers will challenge capitalism to the last fight and win through to the world society of a united human race, producing each for all and all for each.[47]

Maclean saw that capitalism was moving towards a stage of monopolisation and that the resulting 'One Big Trust', which Maclean saw as the end result of increasingly globalised capital, must be countered by 'One Big Union', in which all workers could be united.[48] His position had moved closer to the syndicalism of the Socialist Labour Party. However, he did not reject the tactics and vanguardism of Bolshevik revolution, of the orthodox trade unions, or even of the ballot box. As he told Crystal Eastman: 'I don't scorn any method. I would use all methods.'

What is notable is that by the end of 1919, Maclean's rhetoric is defined by anti-imperialism, outraged as he was by British action in Ireland and by the Amritsar Massacre, which he called 'the most cold-blooded butchery ever perpetrated by any conquering race'.[49]

That winter he published a pamphlet entitled *The Coming War with America*, published in five languages:[50]

> The recent war has shown the horrors and the futility of war, victors and victims suffering alike. It will be an unpardonable crime if organised labour permits human society to go through the same a few years hence for lack of warning on the part of socialists or for lack of heed to that warning.
>
> It is perfectly clear to us socialists at any rate that capitalism breeds antagonism leading to war and that the only way to avoid war and waste is to end capitalism. The characteristic feature of capitalism is the ownership of land and the means of production by a small class. The motive of ownership is not the material comfort and well-being of the whole community, but getting rich quick at the expense of the non-owners. It is this economic cleavage which has brought into being the class war.[51]

Maclean drew the conclusion that continued capitalism must mean continued imperialism and an eventual Second World War between the established imperialist power, Britain, and the emergent imperialist power, America. Whilst he was wrong as to the combatants, in 1918 Maclean already clearly foresaw another Great War, and the cycle of American wars which would drive major capitalist economies for the ensuing hundred years.[52] Of course, he hoped that these wars could be averted: 'The cutting out of market rivalry will lead to transatlantic co-operation, abundance and leisure for all … Choose, reader, world Bolshevism now or a few years hence another world war.'[53]

Maclean's speeches at this time were directed at stirring up unrest and revolution in Britain and its empire. In December, in a speech at Perth City Hall, Maclean claimed that 'we are in India to rob the people, we are in Egypt to rob the people. The War was founded first of all on the robbery of the English working man and the German working man.'[54] For Maclean in 1919, opposition to exploitation, empire and war were one and the same thing. All meant communist revolution. The *Scotsman* reported in November that Maclean was promoting armed struggle, telling a London meeting: '"Away with everything," he cried, "on with the class war." "Let them (his hearers) get their guns ready," he added; and if they "could not get guns" let them "get behind the guns of the soldiers and the sailors.'"[55]

A police report was filed for a similar speech given at Rosyth, where Maclean proclaimed that the army and navy would join the workers and that he was 'a revolutionary because he was in favour of peace.' The Lord Advocate decided not to prosecute.[56]

However, Maclean's revolutionary views were increasingly at odds with the new tactics of his party, the BSP, as it began to form the Communist Party of Great Britain. Within the BSP, there had been Fairchild on the one hand representing the parliamentary faction, and Maclean on the other, driving towards revolutionary socialism. But now a third figure came to the fore – a figure who intended to make the party more fully the instrument of Moscow.

Theodore Rothstein was a former Russian political exile who had long been a left-wing member of the SDF and subsequently the BSP, as well as a close friend of Lenin. With Russian money to spend on the project, he now acted as the key link between the Bolsheviks and the British left. However, his history of working as a translator in the British Foreign Office made him suspect to Maclean, who was already critical of Russian intervention in the process of left unity in Britain.

In November 1919, Maclean became further alienated from this new party leadership when the Liberal MP Cecil L'Estrange Malone defected to the BSP and became the first communist in the House of Commons. Malone had commanded seaplane squadrons during the First World War and been awarded an OBE. He had also been a member of the anti-communist Reconstructionist League.[57] When Maclean compared his own experiences during the First World War with the distinction and comfort that his new comrades had enjoyed, he could not help but doubt their commitment to the cause. Malone, who claimed to have experienced a Damascene conversion to Bolshevism on meeting Trotsky in Ukraine,[58] in particular seemed to Maclean to be fundamentally untrustworthy.

The disagreements between Maclean and his party were no doubt sharpened by his increasing sympathy with nationalist positions in Ireland and to a lesser extent in Scotland, although he continued to be the headline speaker for the BSP and, in particular, for the 'Hands Off Russia' campaign – which was to be the source of a final rift between Maclean and the party. Rothstein asked that Maclean give up his organisational and educational work in Glasgow and instead take a full-time, paid position leading the 'Hands Off Russia' campaign.[59] Harry McShane suggests that this short-sightedness by the party was insulting to Maclean and underestimated his commitment to the Scottish Labour College,[60] which now had more than 3,000 students enrolled.[61] Certainly, the offer marked the end of Maclean's trust in the party. It seems likely that Maclean again saw the possible influence of government spies in the request that he renounce his revolutionary work for a stable income.

Willie Gallacher writes in his *Last Memoirs* that at this time Rothstein was informed of Maclean's 'psychological disturbances'.[62] Whether this was by Gallacher himself or from other sources is unclear. But it seems likely that this information, combined with the various disagreements he had with Maclean, led to Rothstein ordering the 'reorganisation' of the Southside branches of the BSP and the subsequent removal of Maclean as a delegate.[63]

That same month Maclean had spoken at a Russian Revolution commemoration meeting on the same platform as the ex-Liberal defector Malone, but he refused to repeat the event in London. He wrote of Malone that 'Since I spoke with him in St Andrew's Hall, Glasgow I have denounced him as an agent of the Government.'[64]

To accuse a prominent party member of being a government agent could not be overlooked, and it is likely that with this Maclean sealed the door to any possible rapprochement with the British Socialist Party or the nascent Communist Party of Great Britain that it was forming. There is no evidence that Malone worked actively as a spy,[65] but his commitment to communism was short lived – he renounced the Communist Party ahead of the next election, but not before contacting Scotland Yard and offering to act as 'a restraining influence on the communists' in return for leniency on a legal matter.[66] Sir Basil Thompson refused the offer. Maclean was in the end only wrong to accuse Malone of being a spy because Special Branch refused to accept him as one.

Maclean's differences with the new Russian-backed leader in the BSP were becoming more evident. Whilst Maclean believed that the best internationalist action was to bring about a revolution at home, the party under Rothstein saw that the energy of 1919 was passing and that more traditional means of pressure could be applied by the 'Hands Off Russia' campaign and by affiliation with the Labour Party – as Lenin had requested. Maclean, as ever, was unhappy to be dictated to either by Moscow or by London.

Despite these concerns, or perhaps because of them, by early 1920, Maclean was extremely eager to visit the Russian Republic, but had his application repeatedly denied by the British Government.[67] Some on the left have suggested that, had Maclean made it to Russia, his later departure from the BSP could have been avoided. British communists have argued that Lenin might have convinced Maclean of the need for a British Communist Party and the importance of it having a presence in Westminster. Some Scottish communists have argued that, had Lenin spoken directly with Maclean, Lenin would have understood the Marxist underpinning of Maclean's subsequent push for a Scottish Communist Party and would have permitted it, having what would have been a radical impact on the future of both the hard left, and of nationalism in Scotland.

Perhaps a more likely outcome of any visit to Russia would have been disillusionment on the part of Maclean. Those amongst his comrades who did visit – including Sylvia Pankhurst – met with Irma and Peter Petroff, and there is little doubt that Maclean would have visited his old friends. Had he done so, he would have found them no less committed to socialism, but wholly disheartened by the Bolshevik system they saw emerging, and the dictatorship of the Party which was replacing the hopeful early days of revolution. In 1920, Irma Petroff wrote the poem 'Die gesprungene Saite' or 'The Broken Strings'.

> The girl sells herself,
> The beggar prays for bread,
> The soul is trampled
> In jail and need,
> No joyful labour

in any field –
pulls lowing cattle
to the Soviet manger.[68]

If the Petroffs, who had been for a decade Maclean's strongest link to Russia, were already able to see the failure of the revolution, then we can only speculate what effect a meeting with them might have had on Maclean. Though we can find possible parallels in Rosa Luxemburg's critique of Lenin, Maclean's commitment to workers' education, and his disgust for spying and suppression of free speech, may have produced an even more virulent left opposition to Bolshevism.

However, Maclean was unable to travel to Russia, and so did not attend the second World Congress of the Comintern that July. The division between him and the BSP – now the nascent Communist Party of Great Britain – remained, despite the *Scotsman* reporting rather wildly in April that year that Maclean had been 'nominated "President of the English Soviet Republic" by no less a personage than Lenin'.[69] At the same time, Maclean's suggestion that he contest the North Edinburgh by-election for the BSP was met with no enthusiasm by the party.[70] The BSP was freezing him out.

By May 1920, Maclean had formulated a response to his split with the party that had been his political home for two decades. He was to form a new campaigning group and re-launch the *Vanguard*. On May Day 1920, Maclean arrived on Glasgow Green and caused a sensation with his new paper. His editorial in the first issue declared:

Irishmen say that Ireland is unbeatable; we say that *The Vanguard* is irrepressible. It is appropriate that it be resurrected on May Day 1920 to hail the dawn of the world revolution that may break out any time and anywhere. We consecrate *The Vanguard* to the cause of the workers' revolution ...

Dissatisfaction with the plight of the BSP, maimed by the year's onslaught of capitalism, has compelled us to resurrect *The Vanguard* in the hope that we may concentrate the minds of the workers on the revolution to be gone through in this country as well as on the one gone through already in Russia.[71]

Once again May Day was celebrated enthusiastically in Glasgow, with an estimated 30 per cent of workers observing a one-day strike, and thousands marching through the streets behind silver bands, a group of cyclists, and a parade of lorries carrying children from the Red Sunday Schools. More than three hundred organisations took part, and the *Sunday Post* reported that the march halted the progress of a luxurious motor car, the occupants of which began waving a red handkerchief to general cheering.[72]

Amidst these scenes John Maclean unveiled his new organisation of travelling socialist campaigners – to be known as 'The Tramp Trust Unlimited'. Maclean's new group would publish the *Vanguard* and political pamphlets, whilst educating and agitating around the country. Alongside Maclean in the Tramp Trust was his life-long collaborator James MacDougall, who had been by his side since the two met as teenagers. Other members included Harry McShane, Peter Marshall and Sandy Ross. They immediately began to agitate for a minimum wage, reduced prices, a six-hour working day with unemployment eliminated by the rationing of work, and full mainte-nance for those who could not work. This 'fighting programme', as he called it, was intended by Maclean to win practical concessions for

THE TRAMP TRUST UNLIMITED.

Figure 5   The Tramp Trust Unlimited, with Peter Marshall, Sandy Ross, James MacDougall and Harry McShane (National Library of Scotland, Acc. 4335/3)

the workers whilst highlighting the impossibility of achieving these goals within a capitalist society. The Tramp Trust also campaigned forcefully for Irish independence, supporting itself with funds raised at meetings and from sales of the *Vanguard*.[73]

In May and June, Maclean wrote to Lord Curzon, the Foreign Secretary, yet again requesting permission to visit Russia, but he was denied.[74] The second World Congress of the Comintern took place in July and August and Lenin rebuked the likes of Sylvia Pankhurst and Willie Gallacher for their 'infantile disorder of Left Communism'. Lenin rejected the 'ultra-left' and syndicalist paths that these figures had pursued and instead proclaimed that the Communist Party of Great Britain would be parliamentary and would seek affiliation with the Labour Party, supporting the Labour Party 'as the rope supports a hanged man'.[75] Pankhurst and Gallacher returned to Britain ready to toe Lenin's line.

The BSP now became the Communist Party of Great Britain, with its membership including new recruits such as Tom Bell, Helen Crawfurd, Arthur MacManus and Willie Gallacher. At the same time, Pankhurst led the Communist Party (British Section of the Third International). Maclean, meanwhile, was in discussion with the Socialist Labour Party about the formation of a Scottish Communist Party.

Communist unity discussions continued, and Lenin personally asked Gallacher to persuade Maclean to visit Moscow and to take a greater role in uniting the different communist groupings. Whilst Pankhurst and Gallacher had disagreed with Lenin tactically, Maclean could not be classed as the sort of 'left-communist' that Lenin disdained. He did not reject participation in capitalist institutions such as elections and conservative trade unions. He was happy to be a member of a communist party that was both revolutionary and parliamentary. He had stood as a candidate in the General Election and had supported the BSP's affiliation with the Labour Party. However, Maclean remained unwilling to join the CPGB which he saw as in thrall to Russian money and government agents.

Gallacher, on his return from Moscow, had seen Maclean and passed on Lenin's request that he visit the Soviet leader.[76] Maclean had replied that, once he had tied up a few things at home, he would travel to see Lenin. But a few months later Gallacher heard that Maclean did not, after all, intend to visit Russia. He went to the Tramp Trust office to remonstrate with him. Gallacher recalls that 'I told him that Lenin and the other Soviet leaders were expecting him. He was immovable. He kept telling me he wasn't leaving Glasgow. Sandy Ross played the part of "yes man" … he was living off John like one or two others.'[77] Elsewhere, Gallacher suggests that Maclean was paranoid that Gallacher was a spy trying to get rid of him, or that the Tramp Trust Unlimited would not permit him to leave the country as it would bring to an end their earnings as public speakers. John was paying them each around £4 a week from the collection at meetings, equal to a skilled wage in a factory.[78] All these accounts seem unlikely given Maclean's repeated application for travel permits.

Gallacher is the primary source of information about Maclean's poor mental health, paranoia and stubbornness, and it seems perfectly plausible that Maclean's refusal to endorse the Communist Party of Great Britain was to be a key factor in Gallacher's negative portrayal of his former comrade. By the time Gallacher wrote his first book in 1936, he needed to find a way to portray Maclean as a heroic socialist during the war, but also as a figure whose post-war work and writings should be discounted. Gallacher suggests in his book that Maclean suffered from madness brought on by imprisonment during the war, and that he was under the sinister influence of his Jewish friend Petroff. A mental breakdown could be used to neatly separate the two periods of John's life. The suggestion that Maclean was mentally unstable was also endorsed in the 1930s and onwards by Tom Bell, Dora Montefiore and by other figures in the CPGB.[79] The particular bile which Gallacher reserves for Petroff seems most likely to be related to Petroff's escape from Nazi Germany in the early 1930s and his arrival in London full of criticism for both Stalin and Hitler. It is not until this moment of division with Maclean over the Tramp Trust and the CPGB that any rift between Gallacher and Maclean surfaces.

As previously discussed, it is impossible at this distance to judge the balance of Maclean's mind, and the many pressures that led to his sometimes erratic behaviour. What is clear though is that the likes of Gallacher in the CPGB and Basil Thompson, as the Director of Intelligence at the Home Office, had their own motives for spreading the idea that Maclean was mentally unstable.

Maclean tried a final time to visit Russia, applying via Thomas Cook for a passport to Sweden. He was again denied.[80] This failure to visit Lenin marked the final break between he and Gallacher, who was unable to understand why Maclean would not travel to Russia illegally. After their meeting in the Tramp Trust office, Gallacher immediately wrote to the SLP Executive informing them that John Maclean was deeply unwell and was suffering from hallucinations, and warning them not to continue their discussions with him. Gallacher suggests that his intention in doing so was to get John the rest and help that he needed. A more likely motive, however, was to eliminate a respected left opponent of the CPGB.

Maclean's Tramp Trust continued to tour widely throughout 1920, printing and distributing more than 200,000 pamphlets including 'All Hail, the Scottish Communist Republic', 'Proposed Irish Massacre', and 'The Irish Tragedy: Scotland's Disgrace'.[81] Harry McShane writes, 'Alongside our industrial campaign, we gave more importance to the Irish Struggle than any other group in Scotland.'[82]

Maclean wrote that 'Britain rules Ireland against Irish wishes with policemen armed with bombs.'[83] And Sir Basil Thompson reported to Cabinet in July 1920 that 'Glasgow extremists are making the most of "Hands off Ireland" and, as might have been expected, John Maclean is very much in the limelight. His Tramp Trust Unlimited published 100,000 leaflets entitled "Proposed Irish Massacre".'[84]

The extent to which the government agents understood Maclean's work can be called into question by their report that he was 'preaching general hatred towards Protestants'[85] – unlikely from a man who had attended the Free Church College. However, in 1920 at meetings in Motherwell, Partick and Port Glasgow, Maclean and the Tramp Trust were attacked by Orangemen opposed to their line on Ireland.[86] *Forward* reported:

> Maclean's battle cry is 'Hands off Ireland!' and he is carrying abroad the Fiery Cross of a general strike to secure the recall of Scottish troops from Ireland. Such a message stinks in the nostrils of the Motherwell Orangeman ... With the cry of 'Up Derry'

they rushed in on Maclean and his platform was wrecked. For a moment the outlook was black; then came the answer to the Orange challenge. 'Up Dublin' rang out, and with machine-like precision and discipline scores of young Irishmen formed a guard around Maclean.[87]

Maclean's strong pro-republican stance doubtless alienated those who would otherwise have been allies amongst the West of Scotland Protestants. But it was clear to him that the issue was one of economics and imperialism, and that religion was a distraction. He wrote: 'Everyone ought to know that the Belgians are Catholics and the Prussians Protestants. Does anyone really believe that Britain fought the greatest world war to protect Catholics against Protestants on the Continent, and now is preparing to turn the Emerald Isle red with Catholic blood to protect Protestants?'[88]

Both the war in Europe and the war in Ireland were, to Maclean, about markets. However, in his willingness to campaign on an issue that, in Glasgow particularly, was likely to alienate as many socialists as it might win over, Maclean's reluctance to compromise again became a tactical weakness in the eyes of many observers.

In two pieces published in 1920, 'Irish Stew' and 'Scotch Broth', he continued to connect the battle for independence over the water with his own cause at home. At the same time, the *Vanguard* published a nationalist series by Ruaraidh Erskine of Marr entitled 'Celtic Communism'. Maclean had refused Erskine's request to sign a petition calling for Scottish independence the year before, but now the two men became close and Maclean became a member of Erskine's National Committee which supported independence north of the Border.[89] Maclean wrote in the *Vanguard* that 'If the Bolshevik notion of world communism through national communism is scientifically correct, then we are justified in utilising our latent Highland and Scottish sentiments and traditions in the mighty task confronting us of transforming capitalism into communism.'[90]

Nationalism is for Maclean still a matter of pragmatism rather than an end in itself and, whilst his language was increasingly romantic, and his focus increasingly Celtic, these themes are always subordinate to Marxism. As Maclean began to embrace Scottish nationalism, there were two guiding factors: anti-imperialist struggles in Egypt, India and most of all in Ireland, and the Third International's decision to strive to build world communism based on a framework of national parties. He wrote that

> The communism of the clans must be re-established on a modern basis ... Scotland must therefore work itself into a communism embracing the whole country as a unit. The country must have but one clan, as it were – a united people working in co-operation and co-operatively, using the wealth that is created.
>
> We can safely say, then: back to communism and forward to communism.[91]

In the summer of 1920, a situation arose on the Isle of Lewis which Maclean hoped would ignite a revival of this Gaelic clan communism and unite issues of land, nation and class. Lord Leverhulme, the Sunlight Soap magnate and prominent English Liberal MP, had purchased Lewis and South Harris. He intended to turn the island into a major fishing port with modern canning and ice factories and a railway. Maclean summed it up as the occupation of Lewis by a 'Sunlight Soap dictator'.

Leverhulme was opposed to crofting on the island, which he saw as inefficient and a distraction from the viable industries of fishing and weaving. For Maclean, crofting was a way to disrupt wage-slavery and the industrial drive for surplus. The conflict on Lewis came to a head when ex-servicemen on the island who had been promised crofts in return for their service were denied the land by Leverhulme. Lewis land raids were organised as a result, with families marking out crofts on the landlord's farms and settling them. Leverhulme threatened eviction.

Maclean and Sandy Ross visited the raiders on Lewis and held meetings in Stornoway. They found much of the island was hostile to Maclean's message, republican communism being something of a novelty among the more god-fearing inhabitants of Stornoway. When Lord Leverhulme suspended all development work on the island until the raiders departed, The *Scotsman* reported that John Maclean would not dare repeat his attempt to spread the virus of Soviet Russia to the islands again.[92]

He returned to an audience that he knew better, publishing an edition of the Soviet pamphlet *Russia's Appeal to British Workers* with his own introduction in Glasgow that August[93] and then, in November, beginning to agitate among the city's unemployed with the Tramp Trust Unlimited. Increasing numbers of unskilled and women workers were unable to find employment as soldiers continued to be demobilised. McShane and Maclean led a march of unemployed men and women to the council building and secured 'use of the City Halls free for meetings of the unemployed ... and free baths as well'.[94]

From that time on, 3500 unemployed men and women met twice a week in the City Halls to hear Maclean speak on Marxist economics and anti-imperialism.[95] Under the banner '1914 Fighting – 1920 Starving', they picketed hotels and churches as well as the City Council. Maclean wrote, 'we mean to exhaust every constitutional method of safeguarding the unemployed of our class. Whatever happens after that we certainly will not be to blame.'[96] At a meeting with the Lord Provost, Maclean even suggested that, as the city had in the past found money to send the unemployed to the colonies, could they not now be sent to work in Russia where they would very gladly go.[97] And indeed where they would be gladly received: at the same time as Maclean praised Russia in Glasgow, Stalin addressed the Baku Soviet, praising the workers who gathered round John Maclean.[98]

By December 1920, the Tramp Trust found itself unable to sustain production of a newspaper, so drew closer to the Socialist Labour Party and began to write for its paper the *Socialist*, discontinuing the *Vanguard*.[99] In the final issue of the *Vanguard*, Maclean published an article entitled 'A Scottish Communist Party', in which he called for a meeting of all the revolutionary forces in Scotland, declaring that:

> We in Scotland must not let ourselves play second fiddle to any organisation with headquarters in London, no more than we would ask Dublin to bend to the will of London.
>
> Whatever co-operation may be established between the revolutionary forces in the countries at present composing the 'United'

Kingdom, that co-operation must be based on the wills of the free
national units ...

Scotland is firmer for Marxism than any other part of the British
Empire.[100]

Though the call is not expressly for national independence in this
piece, Maclean is clearly setting out his stall against the communists
in London and Gallacher, their representative in Glasgow. However,
he had gone further in September's *Vanguard*, stating:

The British Empire will soon burst under the various national
pressures. Egypt is being granted nominal independence, and this
sham concession will inspire India, S. Africa and other parts of
Africa, and Ireland to greater activity ...

Since the British Empire is the greatest obstacle to Communism
it is the business of every communist to break it up at the earliest
moment. That is our justification in urging a Communist Republic
in Scotland.[101]

Two meetings to form a Communist Party in Scotland took place
without Maclean that autumn, and attendees fell under the sway
of Gallacher and formed a Communist Labour Party, as opposed to
a Scottish Communist Party. This then appointed as its secretary a
man with a familiar name: John MacLean. This other John MacLean
was a new recruit from Bridgeton and our Maclean believed that he
had been chosen and appointed specifically to create the illusion that
his famous namesake was within the party. Whilst such a suggestion
has been described as paranoid, it is notable that it was only 'John
MacLean' whose name was listed in full on the party Executive.[102]

That same month the new party voted to join the CPGB; Gallacher
had succeeded in capturing the new body and in doing so had swept
up many of those with reservations about the CPGB.

Maclean condemned the Communist Labour Party as 'a shameful
bewilderment of honest socialists'[103] and announced that a real
Scottish Communist Party would be formed at a conference on
Christmas Day. It was against this backdrop that Gallacher wrote a
letter to the SLP executive suggesting that Maclean was suffering

from hallucinations and that he was being manipulated by his associate James Clunie. The letter was passed on to Clunie who then shared it with Maclean.

Maclean's Christmas Day meeting took place in Renfrew Street in Glasgow, with MacDougall chairing. Maclean delivered a speech focusing on the revolutionary potential of Ireland and Scotland and the need for separate communist parties within the British Isles. He then read out Gallacher's letter, and accused the writer of deliberately undermining him. A fight nearly broke out, and the meeting ended with no new party formed.[104] Maclean and Gallacher squaring up to each other at a Christmas Day meeting of socialists was reported gleefully in the capitalist press and portrayed as 'pandemonium' and a 'debacle.'[105]

Gallacher tried to underplay the disagreement in a report for the *Worker*:

> On 25th December, the day of 'peace and goodwill', there was quite a lively breeze up at Renfrew Street, which was given all prominence in the *Sunday Mail* and *Daily Record* …
>
> [Maclean] publicly accused me of being a Government Agent … Let us get this matter settled. We can't have a man going around trading on his past, and accusing everyone who disagrees with him of being a Government Agent …
>
> Clunie was taking a mean and despicable advantage of Maclean's weakness, a weakness that is notorious throughout the whole movement.[106]

Gallacher was now determined to eliminate Maclean as a threat to the Communist Party of Great Britain. The suggestion that Maclean was accusing anyone who disagreed with him of being a spy has been widely accepted. However, the figures he accused were Rothstein, Malone and – if Gallacher is to be believed – Gallacher himself. As we have seen, Maclean was right to mistrust Malone. Regarding his suspicions about Rothstein, Raymond Challinor comments in *The Origins of British Bolshevism* that, although Rothstein was not a spy, 'Pankhurst considered him "much too talkative for a conspirator" …

the authorities allowed Rothstein to function for so long because he provided them unintentionally with much useful information.'[107]

Though Maclean may have denounced Gallacher as a spy at the Christmas Day meeting, what survives in writing is that Maclean believed Gallacher was set on undermining him for his own gain – a view that ultimately proved correct.

Following the Christmas Day failure to form a Scottish Communist Party, Maclean instead joined the rump SLP.[108] The SLP paper the *Socialist* celebrated the arrival of this prestigious new recruit: 'In Comrade Maclean we find the revolutionist, the tactician, the educationalist, the organiser and administrator – in every way the one man worthy of the fearless trust of the revolutionary masses.'[109] 'Comrade Maclean is now a fighting member of the fighting SLP.'[110]

Despite these ongoing factional disputes, 1920 had been a productive year for Maclean, with larger classes than ever at the Scottish Labour College, and mass meetings held across England, Scotland, Wales and Ireland. But in organisational terms, the year had been disastrous; he had parted ways with the British Socialist Party and many former comrades over issues of tactical dispute and personal suspicion. His Tramp Trust Unlimited was in no way the foundation of a political party, and Maclean ended the year for the first time on the fringes of the left, joining a weakened Socialist Labour Party that had lost waves of its membership to the CPGB.

13

An Open Letter to Lenin

On 30 January 1921, a Unity Convention was held in Leeds. The CPGB could now claim to represent most of Britain's communists; with the notable exception of John Maclean and the Socialist Labour Party.[1] Maclean published an open letter to Lenin on the same day, warning him of the mistakes that the Comintern and its comrades were making by backing this new Communist Party of Great Britain:

> A conference is being held today ... at Leeds to form a united Communist Party as the British section of the Third International. I believe that you have too good a grasp of affairs to be very far deceived by the situation in Britain
>
> ... we learn that you are asked to believe that large numbers of workers are organised on a workshop basis ready for the signal of revolution, and that a well-organised and disciplined party will be got ready to head the way through the revolution.
>
> ... Gallacher, of course ... has led you to believe that there is a workshop movement in Scotland. That is a black lie. I have been at work gates all summer and autumn up and down the Clyde valley, and I am positive when I say that victimisation after the premature forty hours strike crushed the workshop movement. Unemployment today has struck terror into the hearts of those at work, as starvation is meant to tame the workless. No industrial movement of a radical character is possible at present outside the ranks of the miners ...
>
> I am of the belief that the workshop movement in England is as dead as it is in Scotland.[2]

Maclean's bleak assessment was that the revolutionary moment that had followed the Great War had passed, and he believed that key figures in the CPGB were deliberately misleading Lenin in order to secure their own power within the party. His mistrust for many in the new organisation can partly be accounted for by his various personal grievances against key members. But it is also true that a mix of aristocrats, adventurers, agents provocateurs and spies had joined at every level, and Maclean was anxious that Lenin should not be deceived into taking any unwise action based on misleading reports of the new party. He emphasised that 'Rothstein's attempt to buy Fairchild and myself brought on Fairchild's retiral from the party and my secret expulsion.'[3] The letter was for its British readers a protest against the Unity Convention, but it was also a letter sincerely intended to help to protect Lenin from false friends. He continued:

> Do not place reliance, then, on the United Communist Party that will be formed today, and do not rely on the workshop movement either.
>
> ... Remember that it was left to me to start the movement in 1917 for the release of Petroff and Tchitcherin, and that it was on Petroff's advice you in Russia made me Consul for Scotland. It was my fidelity to you and the cause of revolution that got me the five years' sentence in 1918.
>
> I am still carrying on, although betrayed, not by the workers, but by so-called 'comrades' ...
>
> As more and more are thrown idle and begin to starve ... you can realise that, sooner or later, a mass movement, vaster and bolder than ever before, is bound to show itself. The situation becomes all the more serious, since many wage-slaves here are Irishmen, whose country is being more and more cunningly and cruelly tortured. The rightful racial and class hatred of these men is going to make for an avalanche of opinion and feeling that are bound, sooner or later, to break through the bonds of English capitalism.[4]

Maclean's loyalty gives him hope that Lenin will come to understand the situation in Britain and he makes it clear that he remains very much within the Third International.

In the final paragraphs of the letter, we see the new colour of Maclean's politics, with Scotland and Ireland assuming far greater importance against the 'rightful racial and class hatred' of 'English Capitalism'. It is perhaps the first time in Maclean's writing that we see him place nationalist sentiment on a level with class politics and, whilst this nationalism is still wholly combined with his Marxist views, it is indicative of his new willingness to see the class struggle through the lens of two opposing 'Celtic' and 'English' races. There is an irony in the fact that much of his nationalist education had been imparted by Countess Markievicz, born in London, and Ruaraidh Erskine, born in Brighton. It would also be a mistake to say that hatred of the English was ever a motivating factor for Maclean. However, Maclean's willingness to conjure up an image of English capitalism rather than Scottish capitalism would have a profound impact on his legacy and on those who would pick up his ideas. It would also further distance him from comrades who saw such sentiments as a betrayal of Maclean's internationalism.

Although he published articles in the *Socialist*, the organ of the SLP,[5] Maclean was not bound tightly to the party and operated largely outside it. After a lifetime of party discipline, this must have felt a strange and lost time to Maclean. Agnes, Nan, and Jean had moved to the Scottish Borders and he saw them only occasionally. The organisations and branches through which many of his classes and demonstrations had been organised were now controlled by the CPGB. Maclean took in lodgers and devoted yet more of his energy to autonomous political organising. He continued, as he had for more than two decades, to tour the country, and lecture at the Labour College. His main focus continued to be the unemployed, through direct action against the workhouse and for the extension of parish relief.[6] He led noisy marches of unemployed workers into the wealthy churches of Glasgow's West End,[7] and large crowds, usually meeting at sunset on Glasgow Green, would be organised by Maclean into columns to march across the city, shouting about their hunger, and banging pots and pans as they reached the richer neighbourhoods.[8]

Maclean had become increasingly anxious about the threat of re-arrest, and on 14 April, the editorial of the *Daily Record* even remarked that:

There is a new note in the public utterances these days of Mr John Maclean and his fellow communist leaders. Impassioned exhortations to heroic deeds have given place to the cautious counsel of pacific measures … it may be that there is more to fear from such men cooing like turtle doves than breathing fire and slaughter.[9]

Though he was politically isolated, the government still viewed Maclean as a threat. Sir Basil Thompson's secret police reports to the Cabinet, which regularly mentioned Maclean in their sections on Communism, Russia and Ireland, now also began to report on his organising of the unemployed. In March 1921, the Cabinet heard that 'The number of registered and unregistered unemployed in Glasgow is now estimated at 50,000. Much bitterness is expressed regarding the summonses for rent … John Maclean's gangs are exploiting the position and opposing evictions.'[10]

In April, Maclean heard rumours that British soldiers in Bellahouston Hospital were recovering from injuries received in the Rhineland, where a British occupation force remained. Maclean believed that the fighting there was to secure the German coalfields and to guarantee a source of coal for Britain should a miner's strike break out.[11] Though Maclean now felt that revolution was a distant prospect, he hoped for a general strike that would restore confidence to the radical trade union movement, and so continued militant organising in the coalfields. The *Chicago Tribune* even reported that Scottish miners had been 'drilling and arming with a view to seizing the mines' and that 'the recognised leader of the Scottish Reds is John Maclean.'[12]

The post-war privatisation of Britain's mines took place on 31 March 1921, in the face of vigorous protests by the miners' unions. Having reassumed control of the mines, the owners lost no time in implementing significant pay cuts, with wages reduced by up to 40 per cent in some areas. A strike was called for 15 April, with the miners demanding no reduction in pay. The 'Triple Alliance' was invoked, with railway and transport workers unions pledging to come out on strike in sympathy. Although Maclean was not hopeful that a militant trade union movement still existed on the scale seen in previous years, he still wrote encouragingly of the long-expected strike:

The general strike may bring starvation, but it will be the starvation of our class and not of a fraction of our class, and it will be starvation in the struggle for existence. Such starvation, even followed by reduced wages, is better than these evils unaccompanied by a fight. Solidarity of fight and solidarity of suffering will weld our class together for the final solidarity of success.[13]

But the solidarity that Maclean hoped for faltered, and the Triple Alliance broke down, with the railway, transport and dockers' unions backing out of the alliance. The miners went on strike alone and Lloyd George famously remarked to them that he was 'not heartless enough for this kind of thing'.[14] This collapse in the Triple Alliance was a grave defeat for the unions nationally and highlighted the lack of militancy at that time among English workers generally.

In Glasgow, however, the strike in solidarity with the miners went ahead. In May, the dockers at Rothesay Dock and later across the rest of Glasgow defied their union and struck in solidarity. They were followed by their colleagues at Ayr, Ardrossan, Bo'ness, Leith and Dundee, and by Scottish railway workers who refused to transport coal for the duration of the strike.[15] Whilst the defeat of the Triple Alliance was a major setback in England, in Scotland it proved to be a disaster. Undermined by their English colleagues, striking workers in Scotland had little power and, along with the English miners, were starved back to work. The Scottish Dockers' Union was nearly bankrupted. Morale among those workers who had participated in the sympathy strikes was shattered by the eventual failure of the industrial action.

The events of 1921 marked a serious blow to the confidence of Scottish trade unions that had seen a decade of rising militancy.[16] The pressures on the unions, combined with the reduction in their members' wages, had a dramatic effect on the income of the Scottish Labour College and so of John Maclean. The unions began to struggle to fund the classes.[17] The strike had failed and its failure caused significant damage to working-class institutions.

Despite these political and financial troubles, Maclean wrote sweet and cheerful letters to his family in the Borders throughout 1921. In early May, he wrote to Nan and Jean:

What a great life you must be having ... Fancy finding nests with eggs and young ones in them! I wonder what kind of language the young birds speak? Is it the Bonchester language or the Langside one? I suppose you both will be seeing how the nests are made, and the things the birds use to make them ... You will have to make a collection of grasses, leaves and wild flowers... You should have been in Glasgow on May Day with the whole host of boys and girls who drove on lorries to Glasgow Green singing the 'Red Flag' and other songs. Sing the 'Red Flag' every day that the masters rob the workers, and that socialism is the only thing to stop the robbery. Don't worry about the ghost stories in the Bible and the silly stories about a good god who lets soldiers kill other men to please the rich robbers ....[18]

The letter is full of affection and instruction. But the notes of hurt at his separation for them are unmissable. The two nests are Bonchester Bridge near Hawick where Agnes, Nan and Jean were, and Langside in Glasgow where John lived alone.

The 4th of May 1921 saw the most dramatic incident of the Irish War of Independence to occur in Glasgow. Members of the IRA attacked a police van as it passed along High Street carrying the IRA prisoner Frank Carty. A fire-fight ensued and a police officer was killed. Carty was not liberated.[19] The Glasgow police responded with violent attacks and raids on Irish and Catholic households throughout the city.

In an article entitled 'Scottish History in the Making', Maclean discussed the IRA attack and the fear of violent reprisals. He reminded readers that the police riot of 1919 had followed the killing of a policeman in Parkhead and cautioned that 'the government was prepared to spill plenty of blood in Glasgow, in fact; prepared to give us a taste of the Paris Commune at the end of 1871.'[20] He added that he suspected agents provocateurs were seeking to provoke violence against republican and communist workers. Certainly Maclean's incredulity about the attack was justified to an extent, given that the IRA command had ordered against such direct action for fear that it would disrupt gunrunning from Glasgow. But these orders were ignored.[21] Maclean was correct in that the authorities used the attack as an excuse for a clampdown, and police raids were carried out not just on Sinn Féiners, but also on the printers of the *Socialist* and on the Scottish Labour College. He concluded his article on the episode by urging the Irishmen and the workers to 'stand steady and calm' and he criticised the blowing-up of telegraph poles at Barrhead that week, saying that his reservations about the violence were 'no plea for passive starvation, but for refusal to resort to childish displays of petty force when the government is ready to give us a deluge of blood'.[22] As in Dublin the year before, Maclean was unwilling to sanction violence and rash action for the Irish Cause.

The historian Raymond Challinor has challenged the assertion that John Maclean's belief in false flag operations and police conspiracies was a symptom of paranoia. He cited quotations from *Forward* in 1921 denouncing 'the army of agents provocateurs supplied by Scotland Yard and the capitalists', and 'Sir Basil Thompson's scoundrels, who are being paid by the taxpayer to create crime and revolution, there is more Scotland Yard money than Bolshevik money making revolution today', or 'until Sir Basil Thompson and his gang are cleared out we have an enemy in our midst that is a more deadly threat to our community than a foreign invader.' All of these quotations could be used to suggest that Maclean was suffering from paranoid delusions. However, they are all in fact the words of Ramsay MacDonald.[23] The future prime minister had far less reason than Maclean to see spies and agents provocateurs everywhere, and yet MacDonald's tone is the same as that of Maclean's. This places Maclean's conspiracy theories in the context of a wider movement that was besieged by government agents.

Maclean's article in the *Socialist* on 12 May also added that 'communists true or false' were being rounded up and charged with sedition up and down the country 'with the obvious intent ... of creating an impression that an attempt was being prepared to start a revolution.'[24] Maclean did not mention that he was among those arrested. He had been stopped days before by police after a meeting in Airdrie and charged with sedition, having told a crowd that if they gave their money to agitators rather than to bookmakers they would get a better return. He was released on bail of £50 and the trial was set for 17 May.[25] A letter that Maclean sent to Nan and Jean from just before the trial survives:

> How pleased I was to get your two letters. But what awful writing! I am pleased you are still looking for nests and watching the young ones grow … I am so busy going up and down the Clyde to meetings that I have no time to kill the weeds in the garden let alone to gather flowers. I think you had better both come back and keep the garden in tidy condition … Now I expect to be going on holiday for three months as your mother will explain, so you will not require perhaps to write to me again for a long time. So be good girls, and learn hard to be clever.[26]

After two years of freedom, Maclean now expected to return to jail. The trial took place at Airdrie Sheriff Court. Three constables testified against Maclean, claiming that he had said that the full apparatus of the government's war machine had been thrown into action to keep the middle classes fed and warm whilst forcing the miners back to work for lower wages.[27]

Maclean again defended himself, cross-examining the police officers, and announcing that he had begun a hunger strike. Harry McShane reported on Maclean's defence for the *Socialist*:

> Maclean gave an outline of the lecture which he gave at Airdrie … He said that the revolution he advocated was the coming to power of the working class. He was not in favour of fighting with navymen, as they were not to blame. He did not believe in exhorting men to violence when they had not the accoutrements of war. He had consistently warned the workers not to run their heads below batons, nor their stomachs against bayonets …
>
> The Fiscal, cross-examining, questioned Maclean about what he meant by revolution. Maclean held out both hands, one above the other; and said they represented the two classes in society, the top one being the capitalist class. He then swung his hands round to the reverse position, and said that was revolution.[28]

The Sheriff found Maclean guilty and sentenced him to three months. But Maclean's hunger strike won concessions and it was agreed that he would be treated as a political prisoner and would be allowed his own clothes, food, books and newspapers, as well as a letter and two visits a week.[29] McShane and others took care of Maclean's affairs, and many of Maclean's students visited him in jail.[30]

In June, the secretary of the Scottish Labour College wrote to Agnes to say that whilst in jail Maclean had requested that half his salary be used to pay a replacement teacher, MacDougall, and that the other half be sent to Agnes and the girls.[31] However, the income of the Scottish Labour College had fallen by nearly half due to the miners' strike and wider cuts to wages, and the Labour College was therefore unable to pay.[32]

Maclean was released on 17 August and went directly to the Central Police Court where he appeared as a defence witness for Harry McShane, who had been arrested for selling literature on Glasgow Green praising the German socialist martyr Karl Liebknecht. Maclean's defence was that he himself had done little else but sell socialist literature on Glasgow Green for the last 23 years, mostly in front of police officers, and so ought to know that it was not a crime. Nevertheless, McShane was fined five shillings.[33]

By this time, money was extremely scarce for Maclean and his comrades. Income from the Scottish Labour College had dried up, and his earnings from speaking tours and pamphlets was low due to the general reduction in living standards and to Maclean's spell in prison. Johns' home at 42 Auldhouse Road was now fully mortgaged, and McShane remembers that Maclean was eating pease brose – a mixture of ground yellow peas and hot water – for most meals.[34]

Despite barely feeding himself, Maclean gathered the money to stand with McShane for election to the Municipal Council and Maclean continued his organising work, with his focus continuing to move away from the factory gates of the working class's wealthier elements and into the slums of the poorest. The change in Maclean's own position and privilege at this time may have been a factor in this shift, but it was at the same time tactical: during wartime Maclean had seen that it was the munitions workers who had the most power. Now, in peacetime, he saw those with the least to lose and the most to gain as his natural constituency. McShane remarks also that 'it was through the unemployed movement that the socialist movement came closest to the women in the Twenties and Thirties.'[35] Parish relief and other support was particularly hard to access for single women and Maclean made this, along with the support of widows, his main concern. The Tramp Trust fought evictions and, as McShane wrote, 'the movement was closer to women because it was closer to the streets.' It is hard to imagine that Maclean did this without thinking of his own wife and two daughters whom he was unable to support; Agnes had by now taken work again as a nurse. He wrote playful notes to his daughters – 'send me some raspberry jam by aeroplane!'[36] – and reminded them that the government only hated their father because 'he fights for Cinderella and all like her.'[37]

On 13 September, Maclean gave a speech at Dunmore Street in the Gorbals. Amidst the four-storey tenements of one of the most notorious slums in Europe, he told the crowd: 'as long as I am a free man, I will say the same – that, if you cannot get food in a constitutional way, I say, take it!'[38] A week later, these words were reprinted in hundreds of newspapers across Britain and America, when both Maclean and MacDougall were arrested. Maclean's trial was set for 25 October, bail was refused,[39] and he began a hunger strike in protest.[40] The governor of Duke Street Jail applied to the local Parish Council for Poor Relief on Maclean's behalf, but the request was refused. The assessor had simply written the word 'Socialist' in red at the top of the application – presumably not as a recommendation.[41]

From Duke Street Prison, Maclean released his Kinning Park Election Address. His programme was revolutionary in the literal sense although, as ever, it contained steps towards its ultimate goal which were designed to offer practical support to those suffering most under the current system:

> To defeat me the police have thrust me into prison. For at least a dozen times the Lord Provost got the police to keep me out of the City Chambers during council sittings whilst I was on deputation duty from the unemployed. The police even prevented me from leading the shelterless into Glasgow Cathedral. Kingston and K.P. have therefore to decide whether policemen are going to run the

political life of the city. I ask both wards to vote me out of prison, Harry McShane and myself into the Council, and the homeless into houses.[42]

Maclean's address then detailed measures including state work for the unemployed, shelter for the homeless, no rent to be paid by the unemployed, municipal restaurants providing cheap food for workers and free food for strikers and the unemployed, a right to a three-bedroom council house for every family, 'municipal theatres, music halls, picture houses, and other forms of amusement for the people', and a new Glasgow municipality extended to 'embrace the Clyde Valley and so include Lanarkshire, Renfrewshire, Dumbarton-shire, and perhaps a bit of Stirlingshire and Ayrshire'.

He called for more powerful local government which would oversee housing, employment and leisure. Over the next half-century, many of the points in his programme would be adopted. The address ended, however, with the assertion that even these reforms could not be enough:

> Even supposing we had this programme carried out, we are far from The Goal of Labour: the social or common ownership of everything managed by the chosen representatives of the workers. Only when the world is run by the workers of the world for their own benefit, and not for the benefit of a landlord-Capitalist-Class, will security of livelihood and peace between the nations be obtained. That is Communism. That is why we are Communists. To convert Capitalism into Communism is a Revolution. In that sense we call ourselves Revolutionist.

Maclean stood against a Labour candidate, or 'Pink Labour' as he referred to them, in contrast to his own Red Labour. The only notable omission from his election material is any mention of Ireland. Unusually for Maclean, he may here have acknowledged the need for a compromise on principles in the face of a largely Orange electorate in Kinning Park. Regardless, Maclean failed to get elected, polling 2,421 votes and coming in second place.

On 18 October 1921, James MacDougall was found guilty and sentenced to 60 days in prison. After the damage to his mental and physical health caused by his imprisonment in 1916, this second spell in jail would mark the end of MacDougall's active political career, although he remained a loyal friend to Maclean and his family.

A week later, Maclean was tried at Glasgow Sheriff Court, again for making seditious speeches. This, his fifth prosecution, was the first time that the jury was not all-male, with four women included in the panel.[43] Again, the court was packed and crowds marched outside. Maclean was accused of seditious speech, of telling the poor to take bread, of calling the Lord Provost a murderer for allowing the hungry to starve, and of saying that people in Scotland must be as brave as the Irish, and vote – or if necessary fight[44] – their oppressors out of power.[45]

Despite enduring force-feeding for 14 days before his trial,[46] Maclean again defended himself, this time throughout a ten-hour trial. He began by arguing that he should be entitled to a jury of the unemployed to hear his case,[47] and continued by stating that the accounts of his speeches given by police spies were garbled, but that when it came to the accusation that he had told hungry men and women, surrounded by food, that they should not allow themselves to starve, he would not deny it. He addressed the jury saying: 'All I am out for is food for my class, and I am not afraid to say it ... I am glad of this prosecution today because it has brought out that John Maclean is not prepared to let human beings die of starvation.'[48] He added 'I for one am out for a Scottish Workers' Republic.'[49]

The jury found him guilty of making seditious statements likely to incite popular disaffection and resistance to authority, but also found that he did not intend to incite violence.[50] He was sentenced to twelve months which he served in Barlinnie Prison. To the relief of the prison authorities, he ended his hunger strike upon conviction.[51] The *Worker* published an editorial protesting the sentence: 'Twelve Months! Was ever such a monstrous sentence passed on any man for such a trivial offence? ... Maclean is in prison because he is a menace to the privileged class who hold power in society today.'[52]

The government again received a 'large number of resolutions from Labour bodies demanding his release' and the Prime Minister contacted the Scotland Office asking if leniency might be shown, but the view was taken that Maclean should serve his full sentence.[53]

As before, Maclean was treated as a political prisoner and was able to wear civilian clothes, and again he had his own books brought in. These included textbooks on industrial history and economics, and also on calculus, zoology, chemistry, physiology and German grammar. Maclean's thirst for knowledge was undimmed and it is clear that he intended to use his imprisonment as a period of study. While in jail, he was also able to get to know his fellow inmate Guy Aldred, the leader of the Glasgow Anarchist Group.[54] His closest friend out of jail was James Clunie, who wrote and visited regularly. Maclean's letters to Clunie are conversational and often concerned with the well-being of friends as well as the imprisonment of Jim Larkin and Eugene Debs in America:

> I trust when you write the Petroffs you'll extend my heartiest greetings to them. I trust they are well and busy. You might extend to them from me a hearty welcome to Glasgow as my guest should circumstances allow them to visit Glasgow again.
>
> At present I'm wading through Marshall's *Principles* once more. How weak, how insipid alongside Marx's *Capital*. Still I enjoy it because I oppose Marshall at every turn. It's like reading the leaders in the *Glasgow Herald*.
>
> As I have now only three months to go at the limit till my release, I am looking forward to a long talk with you on many subjects ... I am reading Einstein's popular little book on relativity.[55]

While in jail, Maclean devoured books and magazines about science, philosophy and psychology, often writing to Clunie with thoughts and connections between the different disciplines. At the same time, Maclean's main conversant within Barlinnie was the Reverend William Fulton. Although Maclean had renounced his faith nearly thirty years before, he had never lost his interest in Christianity, writing not long before that 'the only way to end all the trouble is by the establishment of Socialism (Christ having failed).'[56] His speeches throughout his life had deployed religious imagery. In what would be his final stretch in prison, Maclean attended religious services and spoke regularly with the chaplain. Nan Milton dismisses her father's connection with the chaplain as simply a way to 'break the monotony of prison life',[57] but Fulton suggests that it was a meaningful connection:

I was allowed to walk round the exercise ground in company with John. He proved the best of company, could talk freely on any subject, or about the books he was then reading. I could say he had around fifty books in his cell, but at that time he was intent on psychology. This had, he said, been neglected in his earlier education ... I found him genuinely interested in hearing of my experience as a soldier during the war ... he of course was a pronounced pacifist but this brought us closer together ... John's religion for prison purposes was classified as 'Quaker,' and he received visits from a worthy friend of mine who professed this faith. There were no Quaker services but I persuaded him to come to our weekly prison service – as otherwise he was confined to his cell from Saturday until Monday exercise periods. I told him of course that neither my colleague (who he heartily disliked) nor I could pass on anything likely to be helpful to him, but to come to the church services would at least give him a change on Sunday forenoons. He said he liked the way I put it – no catch in it! – so it was arranged for John to attend the services ...

At his request, I was allowed by the governor to visit his wife ... I was very much taken with her, a nice quiet homely woman who accepted her lot uncomplainingly ... I had a warm welcome and was able to report to John, as I know his homelife was constantly in his thoughts.[58]

There was a reconciliation between Agnes and John at this time, and she visited Glasgow regularly to check on his house and affairs while he was in prison. She also tried to bring his daughters to see him, although they were not allowed into the jail. Agnes was a committed socialist, but her politics sprang from a Christian tradition and it may be that having a minister as their intermediary was helpful to John and Agnes during these months.

Maclean continued to study, and to write to his friends. Though there was one brief recurrence of his fears around contaminated food,[59] it seems from all accounts that he was in robust health during his time in Barlinnie, albeit eager for his release. He wrote to his comrade in the Tramp Trust, Peter Marshall, a month before his release, calling him 'Pietro' and saying 'four weeks today I'll be kicked out of this temple of the scrapped gods to begin a campaign in Kinning Park!'[60] At the same time, he arranged for his autumn economics classes to be scheduled in Glasgow and Greenock.[61] As release approached, Maclean was planning local and national political campaigns, running for both council and for parliamentary seats again in the Gorbals.

He left Barlinnie Prison on 25 October 1922 and wrote to Nan and Jean the next day:

> I'm sure your mother will have told you I'm free again ... I was so very very sorry that the wicked men who kept me a prisoner wouldn't let you in to see me ... I've heard wonderful stories how you are both growing so big, and I'm just a wee bit afraid that if you don't come home soon, I won't know you! ... I was amused to read Jean's letter where she said she was going back *only* to Julius Caesar in history. That's right Jean, tell your teacher about Wells' great *History of the World*, and how your father took you back two hundred thousand years before Julius Caesar was born at all ... I'll write again soon, but you have both to write me a right good letter each, or I'll come through and gobble you up like the angry ogre.

The letter, like many he wrote to them, asks emotively and perhaps insensitively for the girls to come home, a message no doubt intended as much for Agnes as for Nan and Jean.

In November 1922, his first month of liberty that year, Maclean contested two elections. He published several pamphlets explaining his position and campaigned as a republican communist. His address was uncompromising: 'I stand in the Gorbals and before the world as a Bolshevik, alias a Communist, alias a Revolutionist, alias a Marxian. My symbol is the Red Flag, and it I shall always keep it floating on high.'[62]

He detailed his life's work and the force that the government had used to crush him, as well as the need to support Gandhi in India and Zaghlul in Egypt, and to break up the Empire in Ireland and in South Africa. In this context, he advocated a nationalist and a communist line, saying 'I wish a Scottish workers' republic, but Scottish workers to be joined in one big industrial union with their British comrades against industrial capitalism.'[63] The address concluded:

I'll support any fight for palliatives honestly started by the workers, until our day arrives.

If you understand the above fully you'll see that no detailed programme is necessary in this address.

If you cannot agree with me then vote for George Buchanan, the representative of the Labour Party. On no account vote for anyone else. Yours for the world revolution.[64]

The address is quintessentially Maclean. Internationalist, communist and revolutionary, and yet willing to make practical concessions to the point of advising which moderate to elect. As ever, Maclean intended his campaign to be a chance for education and emancipation, with little thought as to the likelihood of winning.

Maclean wrote to his daughters again just before the vote:

I'm busy in the Gorbals, and expect by Wednesday, the election day, to have about lost my voice. If you come through in the New Year, you'll have to use the dumb language of finger signs ...

I've bought the first number of Cassell's *Book of Knowledge* for you, and if your heads are not swollen up like balloons when you've swallowed all the numbers, then I'll be a Dutchman!

Both must read *Robinson Crusoe*, *Swiss Family Robinson*, *Gulliver's Travels*, *Pilgrim's Progress*, novels by Walter Scott, Dickens and Thackeray. You won't understand the novels very well at first, but the more you stick to your reading, the easier it will become, and the more pleasure you will get from it ... write down all new words, look up their meaning and pronunciation, and then try and use them in conversation at home, and letters in school ... your ambition must be to use your knowledge for the *benefit* of others, not to beat them ... you must also read poetry from Shakespeare, Milton, Burns, Tennyson etc.[65]

Election day arrived on 15 November and Maclean came in second again in the Kinning Park council election with an increased vote share of 4,287. In the Gorbals Parliamentary election, he polled 4,027 votes, a significant fall from the last election, but still not the result of a fringe candidate. In fact, Maclean reasoned that if he could rely on 4,000 revolutionaries in the Gorbals, he could estimate there were 100,000 in the Clyde Valley.[66] Part of the drop in votes in the Gorbals may be explained by the fact that in this election he was standing not just against the discredited National Labour Candidate as before, but also against George Buchanan, a popular ILP member and a socialist who would go on to hold the seat for 26 years. The result in the Gorbals, with Independent Labour in first place, National Labour in second place and a communist coming third, would be reflected across the city, with the Labour Party doubling its share of the vote in Scotland and the ILP taking ten of Glasgow's constituencies. Motherwell elected Britain's first Communist MP, and the Communist Party also came within 800 votes of taking Greenock. These new Red Clydeside MPs included David Kirkwood, Emanuel Shinwell, James Maxton and John Wheatley, all of whom Maclean had taught and worked with in the previous years of agitation. Under the banner of either the CPGB or the Labour Party, Maclean might have been among them.

The new MPs were sent off to Westminster from St Enoch station by a demonstration of more than 100,000 singing the 'Red Flag'. But they arrived in Westminster to find themselves toothless before the machinery of Parliament. Davie Kirkwood – hated by Maclean as a pro-war reformist – mourned the fact that Red Clydeside's MPs were able to achieve so little.

In 1922, the Tramp Trust Unlimited had been dissolved, with its members abroad or in jail. With the key figures out of the way, the agitation had stopped. McShane decided to join the Communist Party and this marked the end of his connection to Maclean. In early 1923, a particularly bitter encounter with the CPGB resulted in their taking control of Maclean's beloved Scottish Labour College and forcing him out.[67] Although it had some success in parliamentary elections, the Communist Party was still struggling to establish itself as the sole party of the radical left in Glasgow, and control of the Labour College was seen as key to achieving this goal.

While in jail Maclean had lost both his campaigning organisation and control of the Labour College that he had worked so hard to create. Britain's foremost revolutionary was now on the outside of a left that had its sights set on Parliament.

14

All Hail the Scottish Workers' Republic

Maclean wrote a long letter to his family just before Christmas 1922:

Fancy your father at a dance on Thursday night ... You should have seen your father do the fox trot and other wild beast trots. It was more amusing than the zoo ...

I've been so busy going to unemployed meetings and classes at night that I've had no time to read, let alone write, and dancing has left me so tired that I think I'll go off to Robinson Crusoe's Island and sleep for twenty years like old Rip Van Winkle whose story is told by a wonderful Yankee writer called Washington Irving.

I think I would waken with a beard so long that I could tie it round my waist like a belt and then round my head like a turban!

... I'm sending you each ten shillings. What a fabulous sum of money for little girls (beg pardon, big young ladies) to spend all at once! You'll be going to Edinburgh to buy up the city, for Hawick will be too small.

If I'm not getting a turkey to eat at least I'll be as fat as a turkey, for I'm going to Mr Ross's for my Xmas dinner and then to the football match as we did long years before you chicks (beg pardon, big young ladies!) were born at all ...

When Socialism comes there will be presents for all, books for all, concerts for all, dances for all and happy homes for all. Now that's too serious for Xmas, so I will stop.[1]

Maclean's letters to his children show him as the irrepressible educator. But he was now unable to find paid work as a teacher, either of children or of the working class. He appealed again in January to be reinstated by the Glasgow School Board, writing – perhaps unwisely – on paper headed 'John Maclean – Consul of the Russian Republic'. The Director of Education refused him. [2]

If Maclean was unable to find work it seemed there was no possibility of his succeeding in reuniting his family. He returned to the only other kind of employment he had known: work for a revolutionary party. On 23 February 1923, Maclean founded the Scottish Workers' Republican Party. The membership was mainly composed of defectors from the SLP, although Maclean wrote to the *Socialist* offering his continued support for the paper despite his new party's Left Nationalist line.[3]

To what extent the Scottish Workers' Republican Party offered a coherent programme or an ability to build beyond the Clyde Valley is doubtful, but the party is notable as being the first to support Scottish independence. Maclean stood for the SWRP in the Thirtieth Ward in Glasgow as a 'Red Labour candidate,' stating that 'pink labourism is of no use to the workers.'[4]

He had begun to see the Labour Party as his major enemy and he now campaigned against it, seeing it as a force for preserving capitalism. Though there may have been a place for a party to the left of Labour, Maclean's republicanism and nationalism, although less strident and less romantic in tone than they had been in 1920 and 1921, were perhaps an electoral and organisational hindrance to him. The perception of the SWRP as a party on the fringes was reinforced by the party's rivals. *Forward* commented 'if mere talking could bring us nearer the Scottish Commonwealth the Socialist Workers Republican Party are the fellows to get us there at record speed. If facility for the use of "dams" and "bloodies" and other choice epithets could do it, they would have us there already.'[5]

McShane wrote that 'it had some queer people that I didn't like – they had never been to John's economics classes, they knew nothing about socialism or revolutionary work.'[6] Certainly Maclean was isolated. Of his former allies, only Peter Marshall joined the party, the rest having already been swept up into the ILP or the CPGB. And the calibre of the membership of the SWRP was questionable to some, with even Maclean commenting of one of its own electoral candidates: 'he was very weak in brain and character ... we simply kept him off the platform.'[7]

Nevertheless, the SWRP had the membership and resources to stand in every council election across multiple wards, and prominent figures including Countess Markievicz[8] and Sylvia Pankhurst spoke at its rallies.[9] Even Maclean's fiercest detractors did not deny that he was still able to draw huge crowds.

The SWRP's weekly meetings of the unemployed took place at the Govan Cross Picture Palace on Helen Street. The thousand-seat converted ice-rink would play host to Maclean and other speakers every Sunday night by arrangement with the manager James Hamilton. When the owner found out what his cinema was being used for, he fired Hamilton and banned the meetings.[10] The SWRP began a nightly picket of the cinema until Hamilton was reinstated. Direct action such as this and the picketing of evictions were the main activities for Maclean and his party throughout 1923. Maclean also campaigned for justice for Bernard Murdoch, who he believed had been murdered by Glasgow police.[11]

On 12 April, Maclean was arrested at the Picture House picket and charged with causing an obstruction.[12] The case was heard at Govan Police Court,[13] where he was read amended charges of 'having used words and behaviours likely to cause a breach of the peace' by standing on a table in the street and causing large crowds to gather.[14] The trial resulted in a guilty verdict and a fine which Maclean refused to pay. Curiously, when a policeman arrived to arrest him for non-payment a week later, Maclean decided to take a trip to Ireland instead, and no further action was taken.[15]

It would seem that the authorities no longer viewed Maclean as a credible threat. Despite the fact that the SWRP continued to campaign and contest elections for nearly two decades, it is remembered as little more than a footnote in Scottish socialism, and was often more concerned with beating 'the pinks' of the Labour party than with any actual prospect of victory.[16] The widest press coverage the party received was for disrupting Communist and Labour Party meetings.[17]

By this time, Maclean was heavily in debt. McShane wrote that 'John was weak, living on one or two pounds a week, without enough for food or warm clothing, he was desperately anxious for the mass movement of workers to break out.'[18] He saw his old comrade one last time when John Maclean led a demonstration to his door to stop McShane's eviction. The two men did not speak.[19]

Maclean visited Ireland several times during 1923, and this may to some extent account for the more muted nationalist language of his writings after 1922. Gone is explicit talk of Celtic communism and the Scottish race. Gone too is the focus on 'English capitalists' – though the combination of anti-imperialism and proto-socialism that led to these positions is still distinct. He told Nan and Jean: 'The French are as good as the Germans or any other people (except we Scots of course, ha! ha! ha!) ... your business as socialists is to remember that all the people of the world are as good as any other.'[20]

Nationalism brought with it new risks and, in these last years, Maclean warned regularly against the 'British Fascisti'.[21] It is possible also that developments in Ireland had disillusioned him. The Irish Free State had been formed in 1922 and fell far short of the hopes of many republicans, including Maclean. The Free State did not include six of the counties in Ulster, and left Ireland still a dominion of the British Empire. The bloody civil war that followed horrified Maclean, who had always believed that the working class should never take up arms against itself. In June 1923, he visited Ireland again, just after the civil war had ended in a truce. He described the trip, and the Irish war for independence, in a letter to Nan and Jean:

> I took a trip last Monday to Dublin, and came back on Thursday night ... When we landed on the River Liffey at the North Wall we made tracks for the headquarters of the Irish Transport Workers Union called Liberty Hall, a hall that was blown down by cannon shot at Easter 1916, when a friend of mine, James Connolly, started a revolution to keep Ireland out of the war ... After Connolly was wounded he surrendered, and the dirty English Government had him shot, along with other brave Irishmen. This aroused Irishmen all over the world against England, called by us John Bull ... but John sent soldiers, called because of their dress 'Black and Tans,' and killed many Irishmen. The Irish killed many in return and destroyed buildings owned by the English.

... As we walked up O'Connell Street we saw other vast ruins of huge hotels blown down by the Free State soldiers fighting the Republicans inside ... Here were Irishmen, who had stood should to shoulder against England, now killing one another whilst England looked on and laughed. Just a year ago this fighting started on the 29th of June, when the Free Staters blew down a building as large as Glasgow's Municipal Buildings, called the Four Courts. From then till May Day bridges and buildings have been destroyed all over Ireland.

On May Day, Jim Larkin returned to Ireland from the United States ... on that day De Valera, leader of the Republicans called for a truce.

... On the way to his [Jim Larkin's] house, strange to say, we met his brother Pete, Jack Carney, and another man married to his sister, Delia Larkin. We soon got to the house and were welcomed by Jim and Delia. I hadn't seen Jim for ten years, as he was in [the] USA, and whilst there he had been kept in prison over two years. They all invited us to stay, so there we stayed.

... Jim Larkin is the greatest man in Ireland and is out for an Irish Workers' Republic as I'm out for a Scottish Workers' Republic.[22]

Maclean's explanation for his 12- and 10-year-old daughters was more sympathetic to the two sides in the Irish Civil War than he had been at other times. In 1922, he had written to Cosgrove, the leader of the Free State, acknowledging 'the tight corner into which John Bull's Government had placed the Irish "Free" State' and asking him to show mercy and not execute republican prisoners, stating that 'Further executions will reduce you and your colleagues to ... the blood-stained tool of John Bull Imperialism.'[23] And in 1920, he had written 'if Ulstermen cannot tolerate an Irish Republic, let them take a taste of emigration.'[24] But by 1923, whilst Maclean still had faith in an Irish Workers' Republic, his appetite for utilising nationalism to further that cause seemed to have diminished, though this may have been simply a practical rather than an ideological shift.

Maclean stood in council elections once again on his return to Scotland, contesting the Townhead ward unsuccessfully in July. Over the following months, the internal row about Tariff Reform took down the Conservative government – split as it was between free trade and an imperial trading bloc. A General Election was called, and Maclean began to prepare for the SWRP's campaign. Optimistic as ever, he wrote to Clunie, 'The Capitalist reactionaries for the moment are swinging politically into power, but the next swing will be more decidedly to the "Left" (red), and then may rapidly evolve a situation calling us into power.'[25]

The CPGB was less positive about Maclean's electoral campaign, describing the SWRP candidates as 'a pack of political ragamuffins whose only qualification appears to be a brass face ... Every Labour defeat they cause will hearten the baby-starvers.'[26] When Sylvia Pankhurst spoke at a packed SWRP rally at Glasgow City Halls, the *Worker* simply said, 'She's a clever wumman is Sylvia Pankhurst, but she's jist a female John Maclean.'[27]

Pankhurst was worried by the Maclean she met in 1923, writing that he spoke outside in all weathers, and survived on pease brose.[28] But the *Worker* was right about Pankhurst's sympathies with Maclean. By 1923 she too had broken with the CPGB, which had sought to control both her and her newspaper the *Workers' Dreadnought*. Maclean and Pankhurst were alike in various respects: two heroes of the anti-war movement, admired by Lenin as true communists, and dismissed by the CPGB as unstable irrelevancies. Maclean's line was nevertheless unwavering in that he supported the Bolsheviks generally though he opposed their interventions in British communism: 'In spite of my keen desire to go to Russia, in spite of my equally keen desire to help Lenin and the other comrades, I am not prepared to let Moscow dictate to Glasgow. The Communist Party has sold itself to Moscow, with disastrous results both to Russia and to the British revolutionary movement.'[29]

Maclean continued to write cheerily to his wife and daughters, however, saying in July:

The Glasgow Fair Holidays are now gone and past for another year and your father spent his at home for the first time in his history I think. I had staying with me a Negro called Neil Johnston all the week, but we spent it very quietly ... Neil Johnston comes from the Barbados Islands away in the West Indies and he was telling me all about life there … He learnt English, Spanish, Portuguese, German … Dutch, Danish, Flemish, and French. Now you chicks must learn from the black man and study languages so that you may be able to move around.[30]

In August, Agnes visited Glasgow and she and John spent time together. John wrote to her at the end of August:

When I asked you to come home with the girls I had the idea that it wouldn't be only for the holiday but for good. Before you came at all I had a presentiment that you had a longing to return once more and I think that was confirmed by the look in your face as the train steamed out of the station. When at Lizzie's I tried to study your face, and I felt it was that of a broken person. Had your separation from home improved your appearance and spirits I would have been content to leave things alone but your appearance has left me far from comfortable to put it mildly. When you were here I was afraid to ask you to stay as I had no source of income to guarantee a passable existence … I have revolved the matter several times over and have come to the conclusion now to leave it to you definitely to decide on your course of action whether you will stay at Bonchester or return home.[31]

Agnes replied at once:

This is a real red letter day and a turning point surely in our lives! I have been waiting for such a letter to come for some time now and so I must have had a presentiment that you had a longing for me to come back home. Am I right? I take it that you would not have asked me unless your trust in me is firm once more. I have been through hell these last four years because you lost faith in me. It has been very hard. I never realised how sweet home was until I lost it or how comforting – I can't find a better word – hubby was until I lost him. Need I say more? As you say, finance will be a difficulty. I am afraid for that part of it but have faith that you will get a position suited to your ability.[32]

John replied:

> Good god you have never been out of my thoughts since I got your
> letter ... At the station when you were leaving, I had it on my
> tongue to ask you to stay, but somehow I couldn't get the words. I
> could have cut my tongue out when I realised on parting that you
> wished to be at home ... Need I write more? Come a thousand
> times come by the first bus and train, and I trust I'll give you a
> welcome warmer than words.[33]

However, Agnes and the children did not return for some months,
as finances and child care remained obstacles. She visited again in
September and Maclean wrote to her that 'last weekend was the
best I've had for four years at least.' But still Agnes stayed in Hawick.
Over the following months, the same old conflicts emerged between
them as she begged him to take a break from politics and not stand in
the December election: 'It is your duty to stand by me and leave the
election alone for this time. Let your friends know that your wife's
health will not stand the excitement of an election. That will not
damn you but the very opposite.'[34]

Maclean's devotion to the class struggle and firm hope of revolution
continued to destroy his family. His inability to step back and to rest,
and his blindness to his own poor health, are qualities that at other
times allowed him tremendous reserves of energy, but in November
1923 they were to bring only suffering. That autumn he wrote the
only downhearted letter that survives in all of his correspondence:

> Excuse my delay in replying to your last one, but the wretched
> weather, a worse throat, and an almost empty pocket just about
> make one sink into one's self and cut entirely with the rest of the
> world ... if the winter proceeds as it appears to do then it is going
> to be a very hopeless one with no sure promise you'll be back here
> at Xmas, much as I'd wish so.[35]

A few days later, the Glasgow School Board again rejected Maclean's
petition to be reinstated as an elementary school teacher.[36] Concerned
letters followed, and Agnes was furious that John had turned down a

job at the Labour College. He refused the role when the college made it a condition that he give up all political agitation.

Nevertheless, she could not wait any longer to return to him: 'I will come back to you this weekend Johnnie, but Jean and Nan will follow on later if we can get the wherewithal to feed them. Fancy, coming home at long last.'[37]

On 17 November 1923, Agnes returned to the family home at 42 Auldhouse Road. But John continued to campaign. The *Scotsman* declared that 'with the big foreign element in the constituency John Maclean may unexpectedly find himself in Westminster.'[38] On 23 November, he issued his manifesto:

For the wage-earning class there is but one alternative to a capitalist war for world markets. The root of all trouble in society at present is the inevitable robbery of the workers by the propertied class, simply because it is the propertied class. To end that robbery would be to end the social troubles of modern society. The way to end that robbery is the transfer of the land and the means of production and transport from the present possessors to the community. Community ownership is Communism. The transfer is a Social Revolution, not the bloodshed that may or may not accompany the transfer.[39]

Maclean argued that a Social Revolution was possible sooner in Scotland than in England, and that a Parliament should be formed in Glasgow to prevent Scottish youth being sent to die in another 'English' war. He concluded: 'Every vote cast for me is for World Peace and Eternal Economic Security for the Human Family.'[40]

But all the while his health was failing fast, and his chronic throat and lung complaints worsened. At a speech at the Oatlands Cinema on Glasgow's Southside on 25 November, Maclean suffered a coughing fit on stage and had to be taken home. That night his condition worsened and he developed a fever.

Agnes had been back at home with her husband for less than two weeks when he died of pneumonia on the morning of St Andrew's Day, 30 November 1923.[41]

In her final letters to John, Agnes had written: 'I am not on with you standing as a candidate in your present condition. Again it is wasting your health when it should be given to your wife and bairns. No one would be better pleased than me to help for the common good. But you can't help effectively when the home is not right.'[42]

In his final letter to Agnes, John had written: 'If I go down, I must go down with my flag at the mast-top. Nothing on earth can shift me from that. Now there's the tragedy for you, as clearly and bluntly as I can put it.'[43]

They could not have known that tragedy would come so quickly. A decade of persecution by the state, imprisonment and poverty had finally stopped Maclean in his mission to liberate humanity. Unable to turn away from his quest for revolution, and incapable of allowing himself to rest and recover with his family, he died aged just 44, at home with his wife.

15

The John Maclean March

Maclean's funeral, the largest Glasgow has ever seen, was presided over by his friend Tom Anderson. The pall-bearers included the Labour MPs George Buchanan and James Maxton.[1]

The ceremony was explicitly socialist, and Anderson wrote that 'Comrade Lee' made the oration:[2] Lee was a radical pro-Bolshevik church minister from Glasgow's East End.[3] The service nevertheless was a secular one,[4] and the vast outdoor gathering resembled one of Maclean's many meetings in life more than it did a church service. The crowd stood in the cold and sang the 'Internationale', the 'Red Flag', and 'A Rebel Song'. The small cemetery at Eastwood was full to bursting as Maclean was lowered into the ground by the Auldhouse Burn that makes its way into the Clyde, just as the many thousands of mourners marched back across the city to the towns and districts throughout Clydeside where John Maclean's memory was celebrated.

A memorial fund was established to provide for Agnes, Nan and Jean. Workers gave lavishly and concerts and meetings in Maclean's honour were held to raise funds.[5] The final total was £1713 2*s* 7*d*,[6] or more than £70,000 in today's money.

Obituaries were carried locally and internationally by both the capitalist and the socialist press. George Lansbury wrote that

> It was love of his fellow-men, affection for little children which drove him on ... Only a few days before his death even when he himself was bodily sick he went to a slum home to see a sick child whom he found without warmth or food or a doctor. He sent for all of these paying for them with what he had in his pocket. Afterwards going to the labour rooms to borrow money for a tram fare home.

When I heard of this I remembered, as you who read this will remember the words 'Inasmuch as ye did it to the least one of these my children ye did it unto Me.' Actions such as this were part of his everyday life, and brought him love and affection from the very poor.

We whom he fought against because of our methods, can only stand by with bowed heads. Pay our tribute to one who gave himself to the service of others. Had he been able to see his way to stand in with the rest of us there is no position he could not have filled: but he followed the light of his conscience wherever it led him.[7]

Tributes poured into 42 Auldhouse Road. Among the most touching was one from Neil Johnston, Maclean's friend from Barbados who had been staying with him before Agnes returned,

He was the greatest man in Scotland, one great lump of kindness and sincerity ... I have an overcoat for the last six months which was lent to me by your Husband. Can you be so kind to let me retain it as a remembrance of him whom I shall always remember as the truest and best friend I had in Europe. You are well aware of the bias conception which is prevalent in Scotland about a Man of Colour. Some people seem to think that colour can prevent one from being refined and cultured and void of clean and noble aspirations. But your husband has proven to be a real white man by inviting me to his home in which I have spent the most peaceful happy and tranquil moments of my life ....[8]

Both Johnston and Lansbury remember Maclean as a kind and dedicated friend of the downtrodden. Lansbury also notes the stubborn righteousness that at once was his strength and his weakness. As a young man, Maclean had listed his heroes as John Ball, Socrates and Jesus; great moral forces, itinerant rebels. They all met early deaths, unwilling to compromise or bow to an authority they knew to be wrong. Maclean's death cannot be said to be wholly at the hands of the state, though the state undoubtedly played its part. He was not executed like his heroes, but he was burnt out by his refusal to compromise – with the state, the labour movement, or even his family.

Of John's six siblings only the youngest, Lizzie, survived him – a testament to the terrible conditions that forged the fighters of Red Clydeside. Those conditions of poverty, sickness and poor housing were what Maclean fought against his whole life. He was a rebel in every sense of the word, unable to toe the line in any party or organisation. But he was not a factionalist or a sectarian, and he was always able to see that the conditions that shaped the lives of the working class were the same in every party, city and nation. It is tempting to wish that he had joined the CPGB or taken a larger role in another party and lived up to his potential as a leader, but such a compromise would have never been possible. Maclean was a rebel, a disturber of the comfortable, a revolutionary. To add to the biblical analogies that surround him, Maclean was a prophet rather than a king.

In the years immediately following Maclean's death, his direct organisational legacy was slight. Each year, until the Second World War, some 500 people would march from Egglington Toll to his grave in silence on the anniversary of his death.[9] On May Day 1924, it was declared before the large crowds that 'capitalism had killed

Figure 6 John Maclean's funeral procession, including a film crew, makes its way along Auldhouse Road, 1923 (National Library of Scotland, Acc. 4335/6)

John Maclean, but not his message.'[10] Republicans and communists continued to celebrate him, and his party, the SWRP, continued to contest local elections well into the 1930s,[11] though it became increasingly a sect commemorating its fallen leader and publishing pamphlets about Maclean.[12]

But whilst the SWRP continued to oppose both the Labour and Communist Parties, the majority of working-class politics in Glasgow and Scotland remained within those two spheres. Maclean's unemployed movement and his Labour College fell into the hands of the CPGB and eventually lost momentum. The Labour Party took control of the City Council in 1933 and went on to largely disappoint its voters.

Maclean's organisational legacy may have been slight, but his political legacy has been vast. The continued prominence of socialism in the West of Scotland, the successes of the Communist Party in the Central Belt and in Fife, the campaign to support the Spanish Republic, and the distinct West of Scotland Trotskyism that emerged can all to some extent be credited to Maclean. The tens of thousands of men and women who Maclean taught went on to transform the city. The mass education that Maclean carried out over more than two decades had its real result in the radicalisation of Glasgow's working class. There are many answers to the question of why Glasgow has, for more than a hundred years, been considered a red city; from geography, to demography, housing stock, industry, the Irish diaspora, its position in the Union, education, the sharp contradictions of capitalism and religion in the city; but amongst all these factors, indisputably, is John Maclean. No other individual did more to create the idea of Glasgow as a Marxist city, and so arguably of Scotland as a progressive nation.

In the 1930s, both the Labour Party and the Communist Party vied for Maclean's legacy, though neither found it easy to synthesise his beliefs with theirs. James Maxton, the leader of the ILP, began a biography of Maclean in the 1920s but never completed it,[13] and Willie Gallacher of the CPGB published his first memoir *Revolt on the Clyde* in 1935 with the aim of capturing Maclean for the communists. Gallacher's book sought to celebrate Maclean's vital role in Red Clydeside whilst also destroying his post-war reputation and so explaining away his later criticisms of the CPGB and of Gallacher himself. Perhaps spurred on by the character assassination in Gallacher's book, Maclean's daughter and son-in-law, Nan Maclean and Tom Mercer, began a new biography in the 1930s, with access to John Maclean's papers. Tom and Nan were members of the Left Fraction, a Trotskyist group that was prominent in Glasgow. They hosted the renowned Trinidadian Marxist C. L. R. James and discussed Maclean and Scottish socialism with him.[14] After a visit in 1938, James wrote: 'It is now certain that the book belongs to the Fourth International and that J.M.'s immense prestige and tradition will be ours. To me this is a political matter of the greatest significance and is in fact a great victory for the revolutionary movement in Britain as opposed to the CP and the centrism of the ILP.'[15]

The importance that James placed on the life and work of Maclean 15 years after his death highlights the regard in which he was still held. The single copy of the finished biography was sent to C. L. R. James in London to arrange publication, but before he managed this he left the manuscript on a train. It was never recovered and Nan would spend the next three decades re-assembling the material.[16]

The first full-length biography of Maclean was, therefore, published in 1944 by Tom Bell, and held the Communist Party line that he had been a great leader who lost his mind in prison, resulting in confused nationalist ideas. But this new orthodoxy was about to be challenged by another group who wished to claim Maclean: the poets. In their pamphlet *Homage to John Maclean*, T. S. Law and Thurso Berwick wrote 'In the matter of who do we remember and how do we remember him, the poets always have the last word, something which politicians among others should always remember.'[17]

The word of the poets resounded on the twenty-fifth anniversary of Maclean's death in 1948, when two of the great figures of the Scottish renaissance, Hugh MacDiarmid and Hamish Henderson, held a Maclean commemoration. Under the auspices of the Scottish-USSR Friendship Society, the event claimed Maclean for a new tradition of left-wing Scottish culture. Readings came from Sorley Maclean, Sydney Goodsir Smith, Thurso Berwick and MacDiarmid himself, as well as performances from Hamish Henderson, the Unity Theatre, and the Young Communist League Choir. MacDiarmid remembered Henderson's opening speech:

> The common people cannot raise to its heroes the monuments which organised hypocrisy raises for 'the fallen' – the fallen of wars which are always costly and often unjustifiable. But the commons of Scotland have made for Maclean a surer and more lasting monument in their minds … a symbol of all that is best in our national tradition and the only real guarantee of our national future.[18]

MacDiarmid read his poem 'Krassivy':

> Scotland has had few men whose names
> Matter – or should matter – to intelligent people,
> But of these MacLean, next to Burns, was the greatest
> But it should be of him, to every Scotsman and Scotswoman
> To the end of time, as it was of Lenin in Russia.
> When you might talk to a woman who had been
> A young girl in 1917 and find that the name of Stalin lit no fires
> But when you asked her if she had seen Lenin
> Her eyes lighted up and her reply
> Was the Russian word which means
> Both beautiful and red.
> Lenin, she said, was 'krassivy, krassivy'.
> John MacLean too was krassivy, krassivy
> A description no other Scot has ever deserved.[19]

Thurso Berwick called the Maclean memorial event 'the first swallow of the Scottish folk revival' and – alongside the Edinburgh People's Festival – it marks the realisation of the Scottish cultural renaissance that would go on to forge so much of modern Scottish cultural and political identity.[20] Sorley Maclean's poem 'Clan Ghill-eain', highlights the leading role now given to John Maclean:

> … but he who was in Glasgow
> the battle post of the poor
> great John MacLean
> the top and hem of our story.[21]

The identification of Scottish poets and musicians with 'the Maclean line' of a radical left nationalism provided for Scottish art a crucial rejection of Moscow, Washington and London and a sense of continuity with a radical Scottish identity in a global context. MacDiarmid even founded a magazine, *Voice of Scotland*, which stated that 'our principal aim is advocacy of Independent Workers' Republicanism à la John Maclean!'[22] In Maclean, they were able to find a figurehead who was both Scottish and international. Drawing on ancient mythology, Naomi Mitchison wrote that at the core of community was the myth of the king who dies for his people, and for Scotland it was: 'John Maclean who was a king of Clydeside'.[23] Maclean was a king who had died for Scottish workers, but he was also a king crowned by Lenin himself; a martyr, uncorrupted by the totalitarianism of the 1930s and '40s, and full of the hope and passion of the first communist heroes – Luxemburg, Liebknecht, Lenin, Gramsci. Indeed, for MacDiarmid, Maclean was a link to Leninism and ideological vanguardism, and for Henderson he was a Scottish Gramscian, a cipher for the people.[24] Around these ideas of Maclean, Scottish artists built a tradition of Scottish radicalism that placed Scotland's political life on a par with that of any European nation. Maclean could provide a missing link between international communism and Scottish nationalism: a counterpoint to what MacDiarmid called 'the narrow parochialism of the Scottish bourgeoisie nationalists.'[25] Here was nationalism and populism in a romantic tradition that could be tied to Burns, Wallace and Bonnie Prince Charlie and, just as importantly, to Marx and Engels. MacDiarmid believed that 'it is only along Maclean's line that Scotland has any worthy future'[26] and in that belief he swept up many of his poetic contemporaries.

Further revivals of Maclean's legacy took place around the fiftieth anniversary of his death and the centenary of his birth, mostly led by Nan Milton (née Maclean) and the John Maclean Society. Two biographies, Milton's and Broom's, and a first and only collected writings, as well as a regular newsletter were published. There were plays by John McGrath, Freddie Anderson and Archie Hind, and more songs by the likes of Matt McGinn.[27] The John Maclean Society also oversaw the annual march, and the construction of a memorial cairn, partly funded by Scottish celebrities including Sean Connery, at Maclean's birthplace in Pollokshaws.[28] The cairn reads: 'John Maclean, Famous pioneer of working-class education, he forged the Scottish link in the golden chain of world socialism.'

But despite the claims of world socialism, Maclean has in recent times stood foremost as an icon of Scottish nationalism. To what extent he would embrace the movement as it exists today is contentious; undoubtedly his attitude toward it would be thrawn. It is hard to imagine that Maclean would see the idea of a Scotland, independent but still existing under capitalism, as any kind of ideal. He would, however, still see the breaking-up of Britain as a blow against capitalism and imperialism. Maclean's assessment that Britain would play a leading role in a capitalism that is dependent on war to drive the global economy seems no less urgent and devastating now than it did in his lifetime.

Maclean would also no doubt see the radical opportunities for land reform, nationalisation of industry, and rent controls that devolution and independence can make possible. A struggle for independence on the Maclean line, though, would necessarily be a revolutionary struggle, one that re-imagined modern Scotland entirely, working for liberation of the people not the nation. Were Maclean to take part in a campaign for independence today it seems likely that he would do so by fighting the housing crisis, unemployment and rising fascism – just as he did in the 1920s.

If the struggles of twenty-first-century Scotland may seem relatable, the figures at the forefront would be less recognisable. Though socialist leaders in Scotland have modelled themselves on Maclean, from Jimmy Reid to George Galloway and Tommy Sheridan, the lead in Scottish radical politics today comes increasingly from the young, the queer, migrants, women and people of colour. Maclean too always looked toward outsiders and the oppressed for knowledge and leadership. And whilst the left in Scotland may be fractured and small today, it is no more so than it was in 1910, a mere five years before Maclean, Barbour, Gallacher, Crawfurd and thousands of others built it to perhaps its greatest height. There is no question that Maclean would see cause for hope in the state of Scotland, as he always did.

Like most revolutionaries, Maclean's life is both heroic and tragic. His disdain for compromise and his unfaltering confidence in himself and his class were the source both of his huge influence, and of his isolation and early death. Whatever failings he may have had as an organiser and as a husband, he was undoubtedly a colossal figure as an educator and a champion of the dispossessed. His life and work provide a continuing education, not just in Marxism and Socialism, but in how moments of destruction might be turned to human liberation. He is emblematic of the way in which pedagogies of hope can keep struggles alive through the marginal gains that they win and the utopias of which they provide a glimpse. John Maclean's life provides the opportunity to live imaginatively, to see that another Glasgow, another Scotland, another world is possible.

Maclean also stands as a tragic warning of the damage that single-minded devotion to a cause can do, and of the need for loved ones, rest and self-care.

His life and work has too often been covered by political sectarianism, competing claims for his legacy insisting that his nationalism, his internationalism, his Bolshevism, or his democratic socialism be at the fore. But he is a far more complex figure than that allows, with more to offer. Much ink has been wasted discussing what Maclean's political positions might be today, what bile he might have in store for Scottish Labour and for the SNP. How Maclean might teach and organise in the modern world we can't know. But I think what is clear is that his commitment to revolution, to the destruction of oppression and exploitation, and to the masses getting everything they can from life, would be undiminished. Where Maclean saw the Great War as the crisis of capitalism that might open the people's eyes in 1914, I think that today he would see other urgent threats as the clearest way to draw out the evils of exploitation and expansion. Just as in 1918 he told people that peace was impossible without socialist revolution, in 2018 I believe Maclean would be telling us that you are either against capitalism, or you are for the end of the world. His famous rallying cry – 'we are out for life and all that life can give us' – reminds us that then, as now, the struggle is for our very existence.

Notes

Chapter 1

1. Anderson, Tom, *Comrade John Maclean* (Glasgow: The Proletarian Press, 1938) p. 46.
2. *The Scotsman*, 4 December 1923, p. 5.
3. Ripley and McHugh put the figure at 10,000. Timothy Neat puts it at 30,000. Contemporary accounts vary from a few hundred to 20,000.
4. Thatcher, Ian, D., 'John MacLean: Soviet Versions', *History*, Vol. 77, No. 251 (October 1992), pp. 421–9.
5. Young, James D., *John Maclean Clydeside Socialist* (Glasgow: Clydeside Press, 1992) p. 242.
6. Henderson, Hamish, 'Freedom Come All Ye' in *Collected Poems and Songs*, edited by Raymond Ross (Edinburgh: Curly Snake Publishing, 2000).
7. Crawford, Robert, *Robert Burns and Cultural Authority* (Iowa City: University of Iowa Press, 1997) p. 96.
8. MacDiarmid, Hugh, 'John Maclean 1879–1923' in *Selected Poetry* (New York: New Directions Publishing, 2006).
9. Aldred, Guy, *John Maclean* (Glasgow: Bakunin Press, 1940) p. 16.
10. *Workers' Dreadnought*, 8 December 1923.
11. Morgan, Edwin, 'On John Maclean' in *Collected Poems* (Manchester: Carcanet, 1996).

Chapter 2

1. The Gàidhealtachd is the Gaelic-speaking area of Scotland, particularly the Highlands and Western Isles.
2. Milton, Nan, *John Maclean* (London: Pluto, 1979) p. 15.
3. Marx, Karl, *Capital*, Volume 1 (London: Laurence & Wishart, 1970) p. 730.
4. Milton, *John Maclean*, p. 15.
5. Anderson, Tom, *Comrade John Maclean* (Glasgow: The Proletarian Press, 1938) p. 3.
6. Milton, *John Maclean*, p. 15.
7. Broom, John, *John Maclean* (Loanhead: MacDonald, 1973) p. 17.

8. Cairns, Gerry, *The Red and The Green a Portrait of John Maclean* (Dublin: Connolly Books, 2017) p. 14.

9. Milton, Nan, *John Maclean* (London: Pluto, 1979) pp. 15–17.

10. Anderson, *Comrade John Maclean*, p. 14.

11. Anderson, *Comrade John Maclean*, p. 4.

12. McShane, Harry, *Remembering John Maclean* (Glasgow: John Maclean Society, 1973) p. 2.

13. James Clunie Papers, National Library of Scotland, Acc. 4334/1.

14. Crawford, Robert, *On Glasgow and Edinburgh* (Cambridge, MA: Harvard University Press, 2013).

15. Fyfe, Peter, 'What the People Sleep Upon', a paper delivered at the Congress of the Sanitary Institute in the Glasgow University, 1904.

16. Muir, Edwin, *A Scottish Journey* (Edinburgh: Mainstream Publishing, 1996) p. 104.

17. John Maclean Papers, National Library of Scotland Acc. 4251/9.

18. Maxton would be a lifelong friend, with Maclean even keeping his friend's card from 1922 tucked inside the cover of his 1919 pocket diary.

19. MacLean, John, in *Vanguard*, December 1915.

20. Anderson, *Comrade John Maclean*, p. 3.

21. Milton, *John Maclean*, p. 19.

22. Ibid. p. 20.

23. Glasgow City Archives, Mitchell Library.

24. Anderson, *Comrade John Maclean*, p. 14.

25. John Maclean Papers, National Library of Scotland Acc. 4251/9.

26. Ripley, B. J., and McHugh, J., *John Maclean* (Manchester: Manchester University Press, 1989) p. 13.

27. John Maclean Papers, National Library of Scotland Acc. 4251/9.

28. Milton, *John Maclean*, p. 21.

29. John Maclean Papers, National Library of Scotland Acc. 4251/8.

30. Bell, Tom, *John Maclean: A Fighter for Freedom* (Glasgow: Communist Party, Scottish Committee: 1944) pp. 2–3. The same statement appears in Maclean's 1918 Gorbals Election Address.

31. *Pollokshaws News*, 8 December 1923.

Chapter 3

1. Milton, Nan, *John Maclean* (London: Pluto, 1979) p. 22.

2. Ripley, B. J., and McHugh, J., *John Maclean* (Manchester: Manchester University Press, 1989) p. 14.

3. Marx, Karl, and Engels, Frederick, *Collected Works*, Volume 47 (Michigan: International Publishers, 1995) p. 576.

4. Bell, Tom, *John Maclean: A Fighter for Freedom* (Glasgow: Communist Party, Scottish Committee: 1944) p. 10.

5. Anderson, Tom, *Comrade John Maclean* (Glasgow: The Proletarian Press, 1938) p. 12.

6. From conversations with Ellice Milton and Denis Maclean Wilson.

7. John Maclean Papers, National Library of Scotland Acc. 4251/8.

8. *The Socialist*, January 1924.

9. Maclean, John, in *Justice*, 9 July 1914.

10. Anderson, *Comrade John Maclean*, p. 14.

11. Pankhurst, Sylvia, *The Home Front* (London: Hutchinson & Co., 1932) p. 263.

12. *Justice*, 14 July 1907.

13. Ripley and McHugh, *John Maclean*, p. 19.

14. Clinton, Alan, *The Trade Union Rank and File: Trade Union Councils in Britain 1900–1940* (Manchester: Manchester University Press, 1986).

15. *The Scotsman*, 28 January 1909, p. 8.

16. *The Scotsman*, 11 February 1905, p. 8.

17. Peters, James Nicholas, 'Anti-Socialism in British Politics c. 1900–22: The Emergence of a Counter-Ideology', PhD Thesis, Nuffield College Oxford.

18. *Socialism or Freedom*, 1906, Available at Glasgow Digital Library https://sites.scran.ac.uk/redclyde/redclyde/rc150.htm; accessed 15 May 2018.

19. Barberis, Peter, McHugh, John, and Tyldesley, Mike, *Encyclopaedia of British and Irish Political Organizations: Parties, Groups and Movements of the 20th Century* (London: A&C Black, 2000) p. 279.

20. Maclean, John, *In the Rapids of Revolution* (London: Allison & Busby, 1979) p. 68.

21. John Maclean Papers, National Library of Scotland Acc. 4251/9.

22. Pankhurst, *The Home Front*, pp. 263–5.

23. Crawfurd, Helen, 'Unpublished Autobiography', edited by Fiona and Beryl Jack and available in the Glasgow Women's Library, p. 28.

24. 'Notes of Lectures on Economics by John Maclean', in Glasgow Caledonian University Archive Centre.

25. 'Miss Cameron's Lecture Notes from John Maclean's Classes', Glasgow Archive, Mitchell Library.

26. Royden Harrison, quoted in Young, James, D., *John Maclean Clydeside Socialist* (Glasgow: Clydeside Press, 1992) p. 132.

27. The pamphlet's title is a reference to Upton Sinclair's book *The Jungle*. This is confirmed in a letter from John Maclean to Roy Butchart written on 23 September 1922. The letter is held in Glasgow Caledonian University Archive Centre.

28. Maclean, John, *The Greenock Jungle* (1907).

29. Nevin, Donal, *James Larkin: Lion of the Fold: The Life and Works of the Irish Labour Leader* (Gill & Macmillan Ltd, 2006) p. 23.

30. *Justice*, 24 August 1907, p. 4.

31. Ibid.

32. Darlington, Ralph, *Syndicalism and the Transition to Communism: An International Comparative Analysis* (Farnham: Ashgate Publishing, 2013) p. 117.

33. John Maclean Papers, National Library of Scotland Acc. 4251/8.

34. Morgan, Kevin, 'In and Out of the Swamp: The Unpublished Autobiography of Peter Petroff', *Scottish Labour History* (48, 2013) pp. 23–51.

35. Knox, W. W., *A History of the Scottish People 1840–1940*, https://www.scran.ac.uk/scotland/pdf/SP2_10Economy.pdf; accessed 15 May 2018.

36. Milton, *John Maclean*, p. 39.

37. Ibid., p. 48.

38. Lindsay, David, *The Crawford Papers: The Journals of David Lindsay, Twenty-seventh Earl of Crawford and Tenth Earl of Balcarres (1871–1940), During the Years 1892 to 1940* (Manchester: Manchester University Press, 1984) p. 114.

39. *Dundee Evening Telegraph*, 10 September 1908, p. 3.

40. *Greenock Telegraph*, 7 September 1908, p. 4.

41. Ibid.

42. Ibid.

Chapter 4

1. Milton, Nan, *John Maclean* (London: Pluto, 1979) pp. 46–47.

2. Ibid., p. 43.

3. John Maclean Papers, National Library of Scotland Acc. 4251/5.

4. Ibid.

5. Ibid.

6. The *Ravensheugh* fared less well than Maclean. It sank four miles off Skerryvore in October 1911. Nine men survived, and ten were drowned when one of the two lifeboats failed to launch: Crawford, Ian, and Moir, Peter, *Argyll Shipwrecks* (Wemyss Bay: Moir Crawford, 1994) pp. 188–9.

7. Broom, John, *John Maclean* (Loanhead: MacDonald, 1973) p. 35.

8. Avrich, Paul, *The Modern School Movement: Anarchism and Education in the United States* (Princeton: Princeton University Press, 2014) p. 32.

9. Eastwood and Govan School Boards Minutes in the Glasgow Archive, The Mitchell Library.

10. From an article in *Forward*, quoted in Milton, Nan, *John Maclean* (London: Pluto, 1979) p. 41.

11. Broom, *John Maclean*, p. 36.

12. Bell, Tom, *John Maclean: A Fighter for Freedom* (Glasgow: Communist Party, Scottish Committee: 1944) p. 19.

13. Broom, *John Maclean*, p. 32.

14. The receipt for furniture can be seen at Glasgow Museum Resources Centre.

15. Milton, *John Maclean*, p. 48.

16. Connolly, James, and Ó Cathasaigh, Aindrias, ed., *The Lost Writings* (London: Pluto Press, 1997) p. 230n.

17. Maclean, John, *In the Rapids of Revolution* (London: Allison & Busby, 1979) p. 62.

18. Maclean, John, in *Forward*, 30 July 1910.

19. *San Franscisco Call*, 7 May 1910, p. 1.

20. Broom, *John Maclean*, p. 39.

21. Milton, *John Maclean*, pp. 49–50.

22. Young, James, D., *John Maclean Clydeside Socialist* (Glasgow: Clydeside Press, 1992) p. 109.

23. John Maclean Papers, National Library of Scotland Acc. 4251/9.

24. Ibid.

25. Craig, Maggie, *When the Clyde Ran Red* (Edinburgh: Mainstream Publishing: 2011) pp. 19–25.

26. Ibid., p. 65.

27. Ballantine, Ishbel, *The Singer Strike, Clydebank, 1911* (Clydebank: Glasgow Labour History Workshop, 1989).

28. Craig, Maggie, *When the Clyde Ran Red* (Edinburgh: Mainstream Publishing: 2011) p. 48.

29. Maclean, John, in *Justice*, 1 April 1911.

30. Maclean, John in *Justice*, 15 April 1911, p. 5.

31. Ibid.

32. Maclean, John, in *Justice*, 4 January 1913.

33. Maclean, John, in *Justice*, 11 November 1911, p. 5.

34. Maclean, *In the Rapids of Revolution*, p. 62.

35. From an article in *Forward*, quoted in Milton, *John Maclean*, pp. 70–1.

36. House bill for 42 Auldhouse Road, Newlands, 1 September 1913, by John Maclean, cost £130.15/-. In Glasgow Museum Resources Centre.

37. From a conversation with Denis Maclean Wilson.

38. Ripley, B. J., and McHugh, J., *John Maclean* (Manchester: Manchester University Press, 1989) p. 48.

39. Manifesto of the International Socialist Congress at Basel, 24–25 November 1912.

40. Merridale, Catherine, *Lenin on the Train* (London: Penguin, 2017) p. 81.

41. Milton, *John Maclean*, p. 78.

Notes

Chapter 5

1. Milton, Nan, *John Maclean* (London: Pluto, 1979) p. 79.
2. Ripley, B. J., and McHugh, J., *John Maclean* (Manchester: Manchester University Press, 1989) p. 71.
3. *Glasgow Herald*, 23 March 2014.
4. Craig, Maggie, *When the Clyde Ran Red* (Edinburgh: Mainstream Publishing: 2011) pp. 89–90.
5. National Archive, HO 45/10690.
6. Milton, *John Maclean*, p. 80.
7. Gallacher, Willie, *Revolt on the Clyde* (London: Laurence & Wishart, 1990) p. 21.
8. *Justice*, 17 September 1914.
9. Maclean, John in *Justice*, 17 September 1914.
10. Gallacher, *Revolt on the Clyde*, p. 18.
11. Fletcher, Anthony, *Life, Death, and Growing Up on the Western Front* (New Haven, CT: Yale University Press, 2013) p. 36.
12. Milton, *John Maclean*, pp. 82–4.
13. John Maclean Papers, National Library of Scotland Acc. 4251/9.
14. Wrigley, Chris, *Arthur Henderson* (Cardiff: GPC Books, 1990) p. 77.
15. Ibid.
16. Hulett, Alistair, *Red Clyde* (CD) (Australia: Red Rattler, 2002).
17. Hardach, Gerd, *The First World War, 1914–1918* (Oakland: University of California Press, 1981) p. 208.
18. Gallacher, *Revolt on the Clyde*, pp. 33–9.
19. Ibid.
20. *New York Call*, 2 March 1915.
21. Gallacher, *Revolt on the Clyde*, p. 33.
22. Field, Gordon Lawrence, *The First World War* (Exeter: Wheaton of Exeter, 1966) p. 20.
23. Luxemburg, Rosa, *The Rosa Luxemburg Reader* (New York: NYU Press, 2004) p. 313.
24. Bell, Tom, *John Maclean: A Fighter for Freedom* (Glasgow: Communist Party, Scottish Committee, 1944) p. 30.
25. Milton, *John Maclean*, p. 87.
26. Maclean, John in *Forward*, 8 April 1915, p. 2.
27. Maclean John in *Forward*, 18 May 1915.
28. National Archive, MUN 5/19/221.1/2.
29. Maclean, John, in *Vanguard*, November, 1915, p. 5.
30. https://sites.scran.ac.uk/redclyde/redclyde/rceve9.htm; accessed 14 May 2018.
31. Broom, John, *John Maclean* (Loanhead: MacDonald, 1973) p. 58.

32. Ibid.
33. Maclean, John, *The War after the War* (London: Socialist Reproduction, 1974) p. xxiv.
34. Byres, Michael, 'Clyde Workers' Committee', https://sites.scran.ac.uk/redclyde/redclyde/docs/rcgrocwc.htm; accessed 14 May 2018.
35. Young, James, D., *John Maclean Clydeside Socialist* (Glasgow: Clydeside Press, 1992) p. 131.
36. Bell, *John Maclean: A Fighter for Freedom*, p. 24.
37. John Maclean Papers, National Library of Scotland, Acc. 4251/1.
38. Minutes of Govan School Board Dec. 1914–Dec. 1915, in the Glasgow Archive of the Mitchell Library.
39. Maclean, John, in *Forward*, 3 May 1915.
40. STUC Report, 1916.
41. Milton, *John Maclean*, pp. 102–3.
42. Bell, *John Maclean: A Fighter for Freedom*, p. 50.
43. Crawfurd, Helen, 'Unpublished Biography', Edited by Fiona and Beryl Jack and available in the Glasgow Women's Library, Chapter 14.
44. Craig, Maggie, *When the Clyde Ran Red* (Edinburgh: Mainstream Publishing: 2011) p. 112.
45. Melling, Joseph, *Rent Strikes: People's Struggle for Housing in West Scotland* (Edinburgh: Polygon, 1983) photo.
46. Rodger, Richard, ed., *Scottish Housing in the 20th Century* (Leicester: Leicester University Press, 1989) pp. 79–80.
47. Broom, *John Maclean*, p. 59.
48. *Glasgow Herald*, 15 October 1915.
49. Milton, *John Maclean*, p. 99.
50. Maclean, John in *Vanguard*, October 1915.
51. Milton, *John Maclean*, p. 100.
52. Bell, *John Maclean: A Fighter for Freedom*, pp. 44–5.
53. Ibid.
54. Ibid.
55. John Maclean Papers, National Library of Scotland, Acc. 4251/2.
56. Bell, *John Maclean: A Fighter for Freedom*, p. 46.
57. Petroff, Peter, 'Unpublished Autobiography', Chapter 13 (available in the International Institute of Social History, Amsterdam) p. 14.
58. John Maclean Papers, National Library of Scotland, Acc 4251/1.
59. Thatcher, Ian D., Representations of Scotland in Nashe Slovo during World War One: A Brief Note, *The Scottish Historical Review*, Vol. 78, No. 206, Part 2 (Oct., 1999) pp. 242–3.
60. National Records of Scotland, HH 16/123.
61. Milton, *John Maclean*, pp. 101–2.
62. Ripley and McHugh, *John Maclean*, p. 89.

63. Maclean, John, in *Vanguard*, October 1915.
64. *Journal of the Scottish Labour History Society*, Issues 7–15 (Glasgow: Scottish Labour History Society, 1973) p. 59.
65. Milton, *John Maclean*, p. 102.
66. Ibid.
67. Gallacher, Willie, *Revolt on the Clyde* (London: Laurence & Wishart, 1990) p. 55.
68. Ibid. pp. 55–6.
69. John Maclean Papers, in National Library of Scotland, Acc. 4251/1.
70. Pankhurst, Sylvia, *The Home Front* (London: Hutchinson & Co., 1932) p. 262.
71. Milton, *John Maclean*, p. 103.
72. Gallacher, *Revolt on the Clyde*, p. 57.
73. Ripley and McHugh, *John Maclean*, p. 79.
74. Milton, *John Maclean*, p. 104.
75. Taudevin, A. J., *Mrs Barbour's Daughters* (London: Oberon Books, 2015) passim. In 2018, after a long campaign by local socialists and trade unionists, a statue of Mary Barbour was erected in Govan.
76. *Vanguard*, December 1915 (unattributed in the original, but said to be by John Maclean in *The Rapids of Revolution*).
77. Milton, *John Maclean*, p. 104.
78. Connolly, James, in *Workers' Republic*, 20 November 1915.
79. *Appeal to Reason*, 22 January 1916, p. 4.
80. John Maclean Papers, National Library of Scotland, Acc. 4251/2.
81. Maclean, John in *Vanguard*, November 1915, p. 5.
82. McShane, Harry, quoted in Sherry, Dave, *John Maclean: Red Clydesider* (London: Bookmarks Publications, 2014) p. 57.

Chapter 6

1. *Daily Herald*, 4 December 1915, p. 22.
2. Ripley, B. J., and McHugh, J., *John Maclean* (Manchester: Manchester University Press, 1989) p. 86.
3. Petroff, Peter, 'Unpublished Autobiography', Chapter 13 (available in the International Institute of Social History, Amsterdam) pp. 1–2.
4. Gallacher, Willie, *Revolt on the Clyde* (London: Laurence & Wishart, 1990) p. 59.
5. Morgan, Kevin, 'In and Out of the Swamp: The Unpublished Autobiography of Peter Petroff', *Scottish Labour History* (48, 2013) p. 11.
6. Anon. but attributed to H. M. Hyndman, *Justice*, 23 December 1915, p. 4.
7. Maclean, John, letter in *Justice*, 30 December 1915, p. 7.

8. Petroff, 'Unpublished Autobiography', Chapter 13, pp. 34–5.

9. *The Scotsman*, 1 March 1916, p. 8.

10. Ripley and McHugh, *John Maclean*, p. 87.

11. Maclean, John, in *Justice*, December 1915.

12. Petroff, 'Unpublished Autobiography', Chapter 13, pp. 22–3.

13. MacDougall, James, in *Vanguard*, November 1915, p. 7.

14. Petroff, 'Unpublished Autobiography', Chapter 13, p. 19.

15. Broom, John, *John Maclean* (Loanhead: MacDonald, 1973) p. 67.

16. *Vanguard*, December 1915, p. 5.

17. *Daily Herald*, 4 December 1915, p. 22.

18. Central Munitions Labour Supply Committee, Memo number 22nd (October 1915).

19. p. 108.

20. Petroff, 'Unpublished Autobiography', Chapter 13, p. 11.

21. Milton, *John Maclean*, p. 114.

22. Craig, Maggie, *When the Clyde Ran Red* (Edinburgh: Mainstream Publishing: 2011) p. 126.

23. HMSO, *Official History of the Ministry of Munitions Volume IV: The Supply and Control of Labour 1915–1916*.

24. Ibid.

25. Milton, *John Maclean*, p. 114.

26. Petroff, 'Unpublished Autobiography', Chapter 13, pp. 15–16.

27. Ibid.

28. Hattersley, Roy, *David Lloyd George: The Great Outsider* (London: Hachette, 2010).

29. Gallacher, *Revolt on the Clyde*, p. 98.

30. *Forward*, 1 January 1916.

31. Petroff, 'Unpublished Autobiography', Chapter 13, p. 27.

32. Craig, *When the Clyde Ran Red*, p. 130.

33. Milton, *John Maclean*, pp. 115–16.

34. Gallacher, *Revolt on the Clyde*, p. 115.

35. Milton, *John Maclean*, p. 115.

36. Hattersley, *David Lloyd George: The Great Outsider*.

37. Ripley and McHugh, *John Maclean*, p. 93.

38. An irony of this arrest is that it would lead to Petroff's deportation to Russia and to his playing a key role in the Brest Litovsk treaty – a far greater danger to the British war effort than he posed in Glasgow or Fife.

39. National Archives, HO/144/2158/322428.

40. National Records of Scotland, AD 15/16/18.

41. Milton, *John Maclean*, pp. 116–17.

42. Petroff, 'Unpublished Autobiography', Chapter 13, p. 37.

43. Ibid.

44. Ripley and McHugh, *John Maclean*, p. 94.

45. Maclean, John, and MacDougall, James, *A Labour College For Scotland*, https://www.marxists.org/archive/maclean/works/1916-collage.htm; accessed 14 May 2018.

46. Ripley and McHugh, *John Maclean*, p. 94.

47. *The Worker*, 29 January 1916, p. 5.

48. Gallacher, *Revolt on the Clyde*, p. 117.

49. Petroff, 'Unpublished Autobiography', Chapter 13, p. 17.

50. Milton, *John Maclean*, p. 121.

51. National Records of Scotland, AD 15/16/18.

52. Ibid.

53. Broom, *John Maclean*, p. 75.

54. Milton, *John Maclean*, p. 121.

55. Briggs, Asa, and Saville, John (eds), *Essays in Labour History 1886–1923* (London: Springer, 1971) p. 155.

56. *Scotsman*, 13 July 2005.

Chapter 7

1. Milton, Nan, *John Maclean* (London: Pluto Press, 1979) p. 122.

2. Ibid.

3. Ibid.

4. National Records of Scotland, AD 15/16/18.

5. John Maclean Papers, National Library Of Scotland, Acc. 4251/2.

6. Bell, Tom, *John Maclean: A Fighter for Freedom* (Glasgow: Communist Party, Scottish Committee: 1944) pp. 59–60.

7. Broom, John, *John Maclean* (Loanhead: MacDonald, 1973) p. 77.

8. John Maclean Papers, National Library Of Scotland, Acc. 4251/3.

9. John Maclean Papers, National Library of Scotland, Acc. 4251/2.

10. Milton, *John Maclean*, pp. 123–4.

11. *Dundee Courier*, 13 April 1916, p. 4.

12. *Daily Record*, 13 April 1916, p. 4.

13. *The Scotsman*, 13 April 1916, p. 8.

14. Albert Ward's account of Maclean's speech as quoted in Petroff, Peter, 'Unpublished Autobiography', Chapter 13 (available in the International Institute of Social History, Amsterdam) p. 49.

15. Ibid.

16. *The Call*, 6 September 1917, p. 5.

17. *Daily Record*, 13 April 1916, p. 4.

18. *Fife Free Press & Kirkaldy Guardian*, 15 April 1916, p. 4.

19. *Labour Leader*, 20 April 1916.

20. *Dundee Courier*, 13 April 1916, p. 4.

21. *Aberdeen Press and Journal*, 27 April 1916, p. 3.

22. *The Scotsman*, 13 April 1916, p. 4.

23. Trotsky, Leon, in *Nashe Slovo*, 4 July 1916.

24. Young, James D., 'John Maclean, Socialism, and the Easter Rising', in *Saothar*, Vol. 16 (1991), pp. 23–33.

25. National Records of Scotland, AD 15/16/18.

26. Young, *John Maclean Clydeside Socialist*, p. 170.

27. Johnston, Tom, in *Forward*, 6 May 1916.

28. Gallacher, Willie, *Revolt on the Clyde* (London: Laurence & Wishart, 1990) p. 119.

29. Knox, William, *James Maxton* (Manchester: Manchester University Press, 1987) p. 24.

30. Gallacher, *Revolt on the Clyde*, p. 122.

31. Milton, *John Maclean*, p. 126.

32. Knox, *James Maxton*, p. 25.

33. Craig, Maggie, *When the Clyde Ran Red* (Edinburgh: Mainstream Publishing: 2011) p. 143.

34. Broom, *John Maclean*, p. 82.

35. Chicherin, Georgy, in *Nashe Slovo*, 16 May 1916, translated by Maria Artamonova, http://www.scotland-russia.llc.ed.ac.uk/wp-content/uploads/2017/01/The-Scottish-Labour-Movement-Nashe-Slovo-1916.pdf; accessed 18 May 2018.

36. Gallacher, *Revolt on the Clyde*, p. 122.

37. *Daily Record*, 20 October 2013.

38. National Records of Scotland, HH16/124.

39. Maclean, John, in *The Red Dawn*, Vol. I, No. 1, March 1919, pp. 8–9.

40. *The Scotsman*, 17 August 1916, p. 7.

41. Milton, *John Maclean*, p. 132.

42. Ibid.

43. Ibid., p. 133.

44. John Maclean Papers, National Library of Scotland, Acc. 4251/2.

45. Milton, *John Maclean*, p. 134.

46. John Maclean Papers, National Library of Scotland, Acc. 4251/2.

47. Lenin, V. I., *Collected Works*, Volume 24, April–June 1917 (Moscow: Progress Publishers, 1974) p. 79.

48. Lenin, V. I., *Collected Works*, Volume 25, June - September 1917 (Moscow: Progress Publishers, 1974) p. 25.

49. Ibid., p. 274. Gramsci also praises Maclean along these lines in the final issue of *L'Ordine Nuovo*, 1 March 1925.

50. Broom, *John Maclean*, pp. 88–9.

51. Milton, *John Maclean*, p. 135.

52. John Maclean Papers, National Library Of Scotland, Acc. 4251/2.

53. National Records of Scotland, HH16/126.

54. National Records of Scotland, HH16/123/26385/20.

55. National Records of Scotland, HH16/123/26385/20.

56. National Records of Scotland, HH16/123/26385/20.

57. National Records of Scotland, HH16/123/26385/47.

58. *The Call*, 12 December 1918, p. 6. Among those things 'tabulated and indexed' are years of doctors' records concerning Maclean's eating, conversation, and sexual habits. The intensity of surveillance that Maclean faced in prison is testified to by the great many files from that time available in the National Records for Scotland.

Chapter 8

1. Gallacher, Willie, *Revolt on the Clyde* (London: Laurence & Wishart, 1990) pp. 136–7.

2. Ibid.

3. *The Call*, 12 April 1917.

4. John Maclean Papers, National Library Of Scotland, Acc. 4251/2.

5. *Hamilton Advertiser*, 12 May 1917, p. 3.

6. *Daily Record*, 7 May 1917, p. 3.

7. *Daily Herald*, 12 May 1917, p. 10.

8. Ibid.

9. Weinbren, Daniel, *Generating Socialism: Recollections of Life in the Labour Party* (Stroud: Sutton, 1997) p. 32.

10. *Daily Record*, 14 May 1917, p. 3.

11. *Hamilton Advertiser*, 12 May 1917, p. 3.

12. *Daily Herald*, 19 May 1917, p. 10.

13. *Daily Record*, 28 May 1917, p. 3.

14. Milton, Nan, *John Maclean* (London: Pluto Press, 1979) p. 138.

15. *Liverpool Daily Post*, 29 May 1917, p. 8.

16. *Daily Herald*, 2 June 1917, p. 6.

17. *Daily Record*, 30 May 1917, p. 1.

18. F. F. Raskolnikov, quoted in Young, James D., *John MacLean: Clydeside Socialist* (Glasgow: Clydeside Press, 1992), p. 172.

19. Kendall, Walter, *Russian Emigration and British Marxist Socialism*, https://www.cambridge.org/core/services/aop-cambridge-core/content/view/S0020859000002364; accessed 9 October 2017.

20. Donald Maclean's son, Donald Duart Maclean, along with Guy Burgess, defected to the Soviet Union in the 1950s.

21. John Maclean Papers, National Library Of Scotland, Acc. 4251/2.

22. *Daily Herald*, 19 May 1917, p. 3.

23. Milton, *John Maclean*, p. 138.

24. National Records of Scotland, HH 16/126/26385/20.

25. Ripley, B. J., and McHugh, J., *John Maclean* (Manchester: Manchester University Press, 1989) p. 101.

26. *The Call*, 7 June 1917.

27. *Dundee Courier*, 26 June 1917, p. 3.

28. Broom, John, *John Maclean* (Loanhead: MacDonald, 1973) p. 92.

29. Ibid.

30. Gallacher, Willie, *Revolt on the Clyde* (London: Laurence & Wishart, 1990) p. 154.

31. *The Scottish Co-operator*, 13 July 1917.

32. Ripley and McHugh, *John Maclean*, pp. 102–3.

33. *Glasgow Post*, 1 July 1917.

34. Maclean, John, in *The Call*, 19 July 1917, p. 4.

35. Broom, *John Maclean*, p. 94.

36. Thomson, Sir Basil, *The Scene Changes* (London: Collins, 1939), p. 383.

37. Ripley and McHugh, *John Maclean*, p. 104.

38. Sheĭnis, Zinoviĭ, *Maxim Litvinov* (Moscow: Progress Publishers, 1990) p. 93.

39. Ibid.

40. Milton, *John Maclean*, p. 159.

41. Broom, *John Maclean*, p. 95.

42. *Sunday Times Magazine*, 25 November 1979, pp. 72–86.

43. Maclean, John, in *The Call*, 9 August 1917, p. 3.

44. Aldred, Guy, *John Maclean* (Glasgow: Bakunin Press, 1940) p. 21.

45. National Archives, HO 144/17487.

46. National Archives, HO 144/17487.

47. *Daily Record*, 15 October 1917, p. 3.

48. Gallacher, *Revolt on the Clyde*, pp. 170–1.

49. Anderson, Tom, *Comrade John Maclean MA* (Glasgow: Proletarian Press, 1938).

50. Gorinov, Mikhail, M., *The Preobrazhensky Papers: Archival Documents and Materials. Volume I: 1886–1920* (Leiden: Brill, 2014) p. 314.

51. Broom, *John Maclean*, p. 97.

Chapter 9

1. *The Scotsman,* 30 January 1918, p. 3.

2. National Archives, FO 371/329520491.

3. Broom, John, *John Maclean* (Loanhead: MacDonald, 1973) p. 97.

4. http://www.bbc.co.uk/legacies/immig_emig/scotland/strathclyde/article_1.shtml; accessed 18 May 2018.

5. National Archives, *Revolutionary Agitation in Glasgow and Clydeside with special reference to the cases of John Maclean and other*, CAB 24/44/38.

6. *John Maclean Papers*, National Library of Scotland, Acc. 4251/2.

7. *Daily Record*, 31 January 1918, p. 2.

8. National Records of Scotland, HH 16/1/128/26385/39.

9. Milton, Nan, *John Maclean* (London: Pluto Press, 1979) p. 157.

10. In the Maclean Papers at the National Library of Scotland are a letter from Maclean to Sarafin asking for money, a clipping of a press report of an event at which Maclean and Sarafin spoke, and a letter from Maxim Litvinoff on Consular business addressed to Miss Sarafin.

11. Wheeler-Bennet, John W., *Brest-Litovsk: The Forgotten Peace, March 1918* (London: W.W. Norton and Company, 1971) p. 284.

12. Equivalent to around £30 a week at 2018 prices.

13. Speech from the Dock, At the High Court, Edinburgh, 9 May 1918.

14. Milton, *John Maclean*, p. 157.

15. John Maclean Papers, National Library of Scotland, Acc. 4251/4.

16. Maclean, John, in *The Call*, 18 April 1918, p. 5.

17. Bell, Tom, *John Maclean: A Fighter for Freedom* (Glasgow: Communist Party, Scottish Committee: 1944) p. 68.

18. National Archives, HH.16/130/26385/42 and *Revolutionary Agitation in Glasgow and Clydeside with special reference to the cases of John Maclean and other*, CAB 24/44/38.

19. *Guardian*, 1 September 2013.

20. Milton, *John Maclean*, pp. 157–9.

21. Broom, *John Maclean*, pp. 99–100.

22. Howell, David, *A Lost Left* (Manchester: Manchester University Press, 1986) p. 177.

23. Maclean, John, *The War After the War* (Bristol: Bristol Radical History Group, 2017).

24. Broom, *John Maclean*, p. 100.

25. National Archives, HH 16/130/26385/42 and Parliamentary Archives, LG F/1/7/15.

26. Broom, *John Maclean*, p. 101.

27. John Maclean Papers, National Library of Scotland, Acc.4251/4.

28. Bell, *John Maclean: A Fighter for Freedom*, p. 70.

29. *Dundee Evening Telegraph*, 9 May 1918, p. 2.

30. John Maclean Papers, National Library Of Scotland, Acc. 4251/3.

31. Bell, *John Maclean: A Fighter for Freedom*, pp. 70–1.

32. John Maclean Papers, National Library Of Scotland, Acc. 4251/3.

33. Foster, John, 'Strike Action and Working-Class Politics on Clydeside 1914–1919', *International Review of Social History*, Vol. XXXV (1990), pp. 33–70.

34. *Aberdeen Press and Journal*, 2 May 1918, p. 3.

35. *Dundee Courier*, 2 May 1918, p. 3.

36. *Liverpool Echo*, 2 May 1918, p. 2.

37. *Daily Record*, 2 May 1918, p. 4.

38. Gallacher, Willie, *Revolt on the Clyde* (London: Laurence & Wishart, 1990) p. 196.

39. Thompson, F. M. L., *The Cambridge Social History of Britain, 1750–1950*, Volume 1 (Cambridge: Cambridge University Press, 1992) p. 237.

40. Quoted in Young, James, D., *The May Day Celebrations in Scotland*, http://www.workerscity.org/the_reckoning/james_d_young.html; accessed 13 January 2018.

41. *Daily Record*, 3 May 1918, p. 2.

42. John Maclean Papers, National Library of Scotland, Acc. 4251/3.

Chapter 10

1. *The Scotsman*, 10 May 1918, p. 4.

2. *Dundee Evening Telegraph*, 9 May 1918, p. 2.

3. National Records of Scotland, AD 15/18/19.

4. *Dundee Evening Telegraph*, 9 May 1918, p. 2.

5. *The Scotsman*, 10 May 1918, p. 6.

6. Maclean, John, Speech for the Dock at Edinburgh High Court, May 1918, in Maclean, John, *In the Rapids of Revolution* (London: Alison & Busby, 1978) pp. 100–15.

7. Welshman, John, *Underclass: A History of the Excluded Since 1880* (London: Bloomsbury, 2006; 2013), p. 164.

8. Maclean, Speech for the Dock, *In the Rapids of Revolution*, pp. 100–15.

9. Ibid.

10. Ibid.

11. *Edinburgh Evening News*, 10 May 1918, p. 2.

12. Maclean, Speech for the Dock, *In the Rapids of Revolution*, pp. 100–15.

13. Ibid.

14. Ibid.

15. *Dundee Evening Telegraph*, 9 May 1918, p. 2.

16. *The Scotsman*, 10 May 1918, p. 4.

17. Milton, Nan, *John Maclean* (London: Pluto Press, 1979) pp. 175–6.

18. Lenin, V. I., *Collected Works*, Volume 27, February–July 1918 (Moscow: Progress Publishers, 1974) p. 483.

19. Ripley, B. J., and McHugh, J., *John Maclean* (Manchester: Manchester University Press, 1989) p. 108.

20. Milton, *John Maclean*, pp. 176–7.

21. *Yorkshire Post*, 8 July 1918, p. 6.

22. John Maclean Papers, National Library of Scotland, Acc. 4251/2.

23. Ripley and McHugh, *John Maclean*, p. 108.

24. Miller, Ian, *A History of Force Feeding, Hunger Strikes, Prisons and Medical Ethics, 1909–1974* (London: Palgrave MacMillan, 2016) passim.

25. Pankhurst, Sylvia, in *McClure's Magazine*, August 1913.

26. *Edinburgh Evening News*, 31 October 1918, p. 3.

27. National Records of Scotland, HH 16/126.

28. Maclean, John, in *The Red Dawn*, Vol. I. No 1, March 1919, pp. 8–9.

29. Ibid.

30. Maclean, *In the Rapids of Revolution*, p. 115.

31. National Records of Scotland, HH16/136/26385.

32. National Records of Scotland, HH16/125.

33. Ripley and McHugh, *John Maclean*, p. 110.

34. *The Scotsman*, 7 November 1918, p. 5.

35. Broom, John, *John Maclean* (Loanhead: MacDonald, 1973) p. 112.

36. Clarke, John S., 'The Man In Peterhead' (Glasgow: Women's Section of the Glasgow District Council of the British Socialist Party, 1918).

37. *Sheffield Daily Telegraph*, 25 November 1918, p. 5.

38. *Daily Herald*, 23 November 1918, p. 8.

39. Gallacher, Willie, *Revolt on the Clyde* (London: Laurence & Wishart, 1990) pp. 204–5.

40. *Glasgow Herald*, 24 August 1918.

41. *Derry Journal*, 21 August 1918, p. 2.

42. *Liverpool Daily Post*, 27 November, 1918, p. 5.

43. Broom, *John Maclean*, pp. 110–11.

44. *Edinburgh Evening News*, Friday 15 November 1918, p. 3.

45. *Daily Herald*, 23 November 1918, p. 2.

46. John Maclean Papers, National Library of Scotland, Acc. 4251/3.

47. *The Call*, 14 November 1918.

Chapter 11

1. Kuhn, Gabriel, *All Power to the Councils! A Documentary History of the German Revolution of 1918–1919* (Oakland, CA: PM Press, 2012) passim.

2. Rothstein, Andrew, *The Soldiers' Strikes of 1919* (New York: Springer, 1980) passim.

3. Callwell, Sir C. E., *Field Marshal Sir Henry Wilson, His Life and Diaries*, Volume 2 (London: Cassell and Company, 1927) p. 148.

4. *Fortnightly Report on Revolutionary Organisations in the United Kingdom and Morale Abroad*, 2 December 1918, CAB 24/71/25.

5. Cabinet Paper Memo by George Barnes, National Archives, CAB 24/70 15/C/21.

6. Cabinet minutes 28 November 1918, National Archives, CAB 23/42/10.

7. Cabinet Paper Memo by Robert Munro, National Archives, CAB 24/71/101.

8. National Records of Scotland, HH 16/126/26385/71.

9. National Records of Scotland, HH 16/126.

10. *Aberdeen Evening Express*, 3 December 1918, p. 3.

11. *Aberdeen Press and Journal*, 3 December 1918, p. 2.

12. *Edinburgh Evening News*, 4 December 1918, p. 3.

13. Montefiore, Dora in *The Call*, 12 December 1918, p. 6.

14. *Daily Record*, 4 December 1918, p. 12.

15. Montefiore, Dora, *From a Victorian to a Modern* (London: E. Archer, 1927) p. 201.

16. National Records of Scotland, HH 16/125.

17. *Sunday Post*, 1 December 1918, p. 1.

18. *Birmingham Daily Post*, 11 December 1918, p. 4.

19. *The Times*, 28 November 1918.

20. Henderson, Hamish, and Finlay, Alec, eds, *The Armstrong Nose* (Edinburgh: Polygon, 1996) p. 271.

21. *The Call*, 12 December 1918, p. 6.

22. Ibid.

23. *The Times*, 14 December 1919, p. 26.

24. *The Scotsman*, 14 December 1918, p. 8.

25. Ibid.

26. Bell, Tom, *John Maclean: A Fighter for Freedom* (Glasgow: Communist Party, Scottish Committee, 1944), p. 79.

27. *Daily Record*, 14 December 1918, p. 9.

28. *Yorkshire Evening Post*, 13 December 1918, p. 8.

29. James MacDougall contested the neighbouring constituency of Glasgow Tradeston for the British Socialist Party and came second with 19 per cent of the vote.

30. Foster, Gavin, 'Scotsmen Stand by Ireland', *History Ireland*, Vol. 16, No. 1 (January–February, 2008), p. 35.

31. Gallacher, William, *Revolt on the Clyde* (London: Laurence & Wishart, 1990) pp. 213–14.

32. Hubler, Angela, E., *Little Red Readings: Historical Materialist Perspectives on Children's Literature* (Jackson: University Press of Mississippi, 2014) notes to introduction.

33. *The Call*, 29 December 1918, p. 1.

34. *The Call*, 2 February 1919, p. 2.

35. Gallacher, *Revolt on the Clyde*, pp. 213–14.

36. Sherry, Dave, *Russia 1917: Workers' Revolution and the Festival of the Oppressed* (London: Bookmarks Publications, 2017) p. 172.

37. Winslow, Barbara, *Sylvia Pankhurst, Sexual Politics and Political Activism* (London: Routledge, 2013) p. 123.

38. Griffin, Paul (2015) 'The Spatial Politics of Red Clydeside: Historical Labour Geographies and Radical Connections', Glasgow University PhD thesis, http://theses.gla.ac.uk/6583/accessed 18 May 2018.

39. Alland, Sandra, in Page, Ra (ed.), *Protest* (Manchester: Comma Press, 2017) pp. 125–47.

40. Jenkinson, Jacqueline, *Black Sailors on Red Clydeside: Rioting, Reactionary Trade Unionism and Conflicting Notions of 'Britishness' Following the First World War*, Stirling University, p. 5, http://storre.stir.ac.uk/bitstream/1893/1069/1/TCBHamendedversion.pdf; accessed 18 May 2018.

41. Ibid.

42. *Evening Times*, 23 January 1919, p. 1.

43. Jenkinson, *Black Sailors on Red Clydeside*, p. 38.

44. *Workers' Dreadnought*, 21 June 1919.

45. McKay, J., 'Biography of William Gallacher' (unpublished), Glasgow Caledonian University Research Collections, William Gallacher Memorial Library, 1993, p. 100.

46. *The Call*, 23 January 1919.

47. John Maclean's Diary for 1919, Glasgow University Archive Centre.

48. Ibid.

49. *Strike Bulletin*, 31 January 1919, p. 1.

50. Gallacher, *Revolt on the Clyde*, p. 221.

51. Cameron, Jim, *Red Flag Over the Clyde* (Glasgow: Militant Labour, 1994).

52. *Fortnightly Report on Revolutionary Organisations in the United Kingdom and Morale Abroad*, 28 January 1919, CAB 24/74/13.

53. Ibid.

54. Ibid.

55. *Illustrated London News*, 8 February 1919, p. 13.

56. Milton, Nan, *John Maclean* (London: Pluto Press, 1979) p. 190.

57. Bell, Tom, *John Maclean: A Fighter for Freedom* (Glasgow: Communist Party, Scottish Committee, 1944), p. 85.

58. *The Scotsman*, 1 February 1919, p. 7.

59. Milton, *John Maclean*, p. 191.

60. *The Age* (Melbourne, Australia), 4 February 1919, p. 5.

61. *Dundee Courier*, 1 February 1919, p. 3.

62. *The Scotsman*, 1 February 1919, p. 7.

63. *Exeter and Plymouth Gazette*, 1 February 1919, p. 1 (under the headline: 'Clyde Bolsheviks Break Loose').

64. Gallacher, *Revolt on the Clyde*, pp. 230–3.

65. War Cabinet Minutes, 31 January 1919, CAB 23/9.
66. War Cabinet Minutes, 7 February 1919, CAB 23/9.
67. Maclean, John, *Sack Dalrymple, Sack Stevenson* (Glasgow: 1919).
68. Ibid.
69. *Fortnightly Report on Revolutionary Organisations in the United Kingdom and Morale Abroad*, 8 February 1919, CAB 24/75/16.
70. *Aberdeen Press and Journal*, 29 January 1919, p. 5.
71. *Detroit Free Press*, 23 March 1919, p. 51.
72. Milton, *John Maclean*, p. 192.
73. *Fortnightly Report on Revolutionary Organisations in the United Kingdom and Morale Abroad*, 8 February 1919, CAB 24/75/16.
74. *Aberdeen Press and Journal*, 23 January 1919, p. 3.

Chapter 12

1. *Prosecution of Seditious Speakers*, 5 February 1919, CAB 24/74/56.
2. John Maclean's Diary for 1919, Glasgow University Archive Centre.
3. Ibid.
4. Trotsky, Leon, *The First Five Years of the Communist International*, Vol. 1 (London: New Park, 1973) Appendix 4, https://www.marxistsfr.org/archive/trotsky/1924/ffyci-1/app04.htm;accessed 18 May 2018.
5. *The Guardian*, 3 February 1919, p. 8.
6. *The Worker*, 2 October 1920.
7. *Fortnightly Report on Revolutionary Organisations in the United Kingdom and Morale Abroad*, 7 April 1919, CAB 24/77/93.
8. Milton, Nan, *John Maclean* (London: Pluto Press, 1979) pp. 201–2.
9. *Sheffield Daily Telegraph*, 22 April 1919, p. 3.
10. *Pall Mall Gazette*, 21 April 1919, p. 2.
11. *Sheffield Daily Telegraph*, 21 April 1919, p. 2.
12. *Western Morning News*, 22 April 1919, p. 6.
13. *The Guardian*, 21 April 1919, p. 7.
14. *The Call*, 24 July 1919, p. 2.
15. *The Call*, 23 January 1919.
16. Milton, *John Maclean*, p. 197.
17. Ibid.
18. Maclean, John, *In The Rapids of Revolution* (London: Alison & Busby, 1978) p. 235.
19. Knox, W. (ed.), *Scottish Labour Leaders, 1918–39* (Edinburgh: Mainstream Publishing, 1984) p. 190.
20. McShane, Harry and Smith, Joan, *No Mean Fighter* (London: Pluto Press, 1978) p. 151.
21. From a conversation with Dr Tessa Cook.

22. Broom, John, *John Maclean* (Loanhead: MacDonald, 1973) pp. 122–3.

23. Ibid., p. 124.

24. *Edinburgh Evening News*, 1 May 1919, p. 5.

25. Maclean, John, in *The Worker*, 5 July 1919, p. 1.

26. *The Call*, 27 March 1919, p. 5.

27. Broom, *John Maclean*, p. 125.

28. Debs, Eugene Victor, unpublished scrapbook, Book One, Volume One, 31 July 1920, in the Tamiment Institute, New York.

29. John Maclean's Diary for 1919, Glasgow Caledonian University Archive Centre.

30. *The Voice of Labour – Official Organ of the Irish Transport and General Workers Union*, 2 August 1919, p. 5.

31. *The Liberator*, Volume 2 Issue 10, October 1919, pp. 28–33.

32. Broom, *John Maclean*, p. 125.

33. Milton, *John Maclean*, p. 207.

34. Ibid., p. 196.

35. Ibid., p. 208.

36. Ibid., pp. 209–10.

37. *The Voice of Labour*, 2 August 1919, p. 5.

38. Broom, *John Maclean*, p. 126.

39. *The Voice of Labour*, 2 August 1919, p. 5.

40. Milton, *John Maclean*, p. 209.

41. Maclean, John, in *The Vanguard*, August 1920, p. 1.

42. Milton, Nan, 'John Maclean and Ireland', *Socialist Scotland/ Alba Soisealac*, Winter 1979, pp. 8–9.

43. Cairns, Gerry, *The Red and the Green, A Portrait of John Maclean* (Glasgow: Connolly Books, 2017) p. 120.

44. Reader, Seamus, from unpublished memoirs quoted in Cairns, *The Red and the Green*, pp. 124–5.

45. Maclean, *In the Rapids of Revolution*, pp. 161–2.

46. *The Voice of Labour*, 2 August 1919, p. 5.

47. Maclean, *In the Rapids of Revolution*, p. 196.

48. Maclean, John, Introduction to Hay, John M., *The Beardmore Vickers Octopus* (Glasgow: Socialist Information and Research Bureau, Glasgow) p. 1 – the Glasgow Socialist Information and Research Bureau was a small organisation with its offices on St Vincent Street in Glasgow. It was partially funded by Maxim Litvinoff.

49. Maclean, John, *Ireland's Tragedy, Scotland's Disgrace* (Glasgow: John Maclean Society, 1970) p. 8.

50. *The Globe*, 15 October 1919, p. 6.

51. Maclean, *In the Rapids of Revolution*, pp. 182–90.

52. In the years after the publication of this pamphlet, Maclean began to see war between the United States and Japan in the Pacific as a keener threat, as he details in a letter to Roy Butchart written on 23 September 1922. The letter is held in Glasgow Caledonian University Archive Centre.

53. Ibid.

54. *Dundee Courier*, 11 December 1919 p. 6.

55. *The Scotsman*, 14 November 1919, p. 6.

56. National Records of Scotland, HH 16/126.

57. Ripley, B. J., & McHugh, J., *John Maclean* (Manchester: Manchester University Press, 1989) p. 127.

58. Malone, Cecil L'Estrange, *The Russian Republic* (New York: Harcourt, Brace & Howe, 1920) passim.

59. Ripley and McHugh, *John Maclean*, p. 124.

60. McShane and Smith, *No Mean Fighter*, pp. 122–3.

61. *The Times*, 14 January 1921, p. 11.

62. Gallacher, William, *Last Memoirs*, (London: Lawrence and Wishart, 1966) p. 141.

63. Ripley and McHugh, *John Maclean*, p. 125.

64. Maclean, John, in *The Vanguard*, June 1920.

65. Ripley and McHugh, *John Maclean*, p. 127.

66. Report on Revolutionary Organisations in the United Kingdom, 13 January 1921, CAB24/118/CP2452.

67. National Records of Scotland, HH 16/126.

68. Petroff, Irma, 'Die gesprungene Saite', translated by Henry Bell from the German in Peter Petroff's unpublished autobiography, Chapter 24, pp. 4–5, available in The Social Institute, Amsterdam.

69. *The Scotsman*, 21 April 1920, p. 2.

70. *Dundee Evening Telegraph*, 23 March 1920, p. 5.

71. *The Vanguard*, May 1920.

72. *Sunday Post*, 2 May 1920, p. 3.

73. McShane and Smith, *No Mean Fighter*, p. 115.

74. Broom, *John Maclean*, p. 128.

75. Lenin, *Collected Works*, Volume 31, April–December 1920 (Moscow: Progress Publishers, 1974) p. 88.

76. Gallacher, *Last Memoirs*, pp. 214–16.

77. Gallacher, William, letter to the author in Broom, John, *John Maclean*, (Loanhead: MacDonald, 1973) p. 128.

78. McShane and Smith, *No Mean Fighter*, p. 115.

79. Pitt, Bob, *John Maclean and the CPGB* (London: Pitt Publications, 1995).

80. Milton, *John Maclean*, p. 241.

81. McShane and Smith, *No Mean Fighter*, pp. 115–20.

82. Ibid.

83. Maclean, John, *The Irish Tragedy: Scotland's Disgrace*, Pamphlet, 1920.

84. *Report on Revolutionary Organisations in the United Kingdom*, 8 July 1920, CAB 24/108/92.

85. *Report on Revolutionary Organisations in the United Kingdom*, 1 July 1920, CAB 24/108/66.

86. McShane and Smith, *No Mean Fighter*, p. 117.

87. Broom, *John Maclean*, p. 131.

88. Maclean, John, *The Irish Tragedy: Scotland's Disgrace*, Pamphlet, 1920.

89. *Scottish Review*, Issue 42, 1919.

90. Maclean, John, in *The Vanguard*, September 1920.

91. Maclean, John, *All Hail the Scottish Communist Republic*, 1920.

92. *The Scotsman*, 25 September 1920.

93. *Russia's Appeal to British Workers*, with a preface by John Maclean (Glasgow: 1920).

94. McShane and Smith, *No Mean Fighter*, p. 121.

95. *The Socialist*, January 30, 1921.

96. *The Vanguard*, November 1920.

97. *The Scotsman*, 22 October 1920, p. 3.

98. Stalin, Joseph, *Three Years of Proletarian Dictatorship; Report Delivered at a Celebration Meeting of the Baku Soviet*, November 6, 1920.

99. McShane and Smith, *No Mean Fighter*, p. 123.

100. Maclean, John, in *The Vanguard*, December 1920.

101. Maclean, John, in *The Vanguard*, September 1920.

102. Ripley and McHugh, *John Maclean*, p. 133.

103. Maclean, John in *Vanguard*, December 1920.

104. Milton, *John Maclean*, p. 257.

105. *Daily Record*, 26 December 1920.

106. *The Worker*, 8 January 1921.

107. Challinor, Raymond, *The Origins of British Bolshevism* (London: Croom Helm, 1977) p. 247.

108. Harry McShane disputes this, saying that the Tramp Trust Unlimited continued independently. It may be true that Maclean joined the SLP and the Trust stayed autonomous. Or it is possible that McShane, who shortly afterwards joined the CPGB, wished to brush over a brief association with their rival.

109. *The Socialist*, 13 January 1921.

110. *The Socialist*, 24 February 1921.

Chapter 13

1. *The Communist*, 5 February 1921.

2. Maclean, John, in *The Socialist*, 30 January 1921.

3. Ibid.

4. Ibid.

5. *Dundee Evening Telegraph*, 18 January 1921, p. 6.

6. Milton, Nan, *John Maclean* (London: Pluto Press, 1979) p. 261.

7. MacDougall, Ian, *Voices from the Hunger Marches* (Edinburgh: Polygon, 1991) p. 16.

8. Milton, *John Maclean*, p. 263.

9. *Daily Record*, 14 April 1921.

10. Report on Revolutionary Organisations in the United Kingdom, 23 March 1921, CAB 24/121/65.

11. Report on Revolutionary Organisations in the United Kingdom, 21 April 1921, CAB 24/122/59.

12. *Chicago Tribune* (Chicago, Illinois), 24 September 1920, p. 2.

13. Maclean, John, in *The Socialist*, 27 January 1921.

14. Renshaw, Patrick, *Nine Days that Shook Britain: The 1926 General Strike* (Garden City, NY: Anchor Press, 1976) p. 71.

15. Kenefick, William, *Red Scotland!: The Rise and Fall of the Radical Left, c. 1872 to 1932* (Edinburgh: Edinburgh University Press, 2007) pp. 188–9.

16. Ibid.

17. McShane, Harry and Smith, Joan, *No Mean Fighter* (London: Pluto Press, 1978) p. 127.

18. John Maclean Papers, in National Library Of Scotland, Acc 4251/5.

19. Noonan, Gerry, *The IRA in Britain, 1919–1923* (Oxford: Oxford University Press, 2014) p. 147.

20. Maclean, John, in *The Socialist*, 12 May 1921.

21. Noonan, *The IRA in Britain, 1919–1923*, p. 147.

22. Maclean, John, in *The Socialist*, 12 May 1921.

23. Challinor, Raymond, 'Letters', in *History Workshop Journal*, Volume 22, Issue 1, 1 October 1986, pp. 220–1.

24. Maclean, John, in *The Socialist*, 12 May 1921.

25. *Daily Herald*, 16 May 1921, p. 5.

26. John Maclean Papers, in National Library Of Scotland, Acc 4251/5.

27. Aldred, Guy, *John Maclean* (Glasgow: Bakunin Press, 1940) p. 46.

28. Harry McShane in *The Socialist*, May 1921.

29. Milton, *John Maclean*, p. 269.

30. John Maclean Papers, in National Library Of Scotland, Acc 4251/3.

31. Ibid.

32. Milton, *John Maclean*, pp. 269–70.

33. Broom, John, *John Maclean* (Loanhead: MacDonald, 1973) p. 141.

34. McShane and Smith, *No Mean Fighter*, p. 130.

35. Ibid., p. 131.

36. John Maclean Papers, in National Library Of Scotland, Acc 4251/5.

37. John Maclean Papers, National Library of Scotland Acc. 4251/9.

38. Bell, Tom, *John Maclean: A Fighter for Freedom* (Glasgow: Communist Party, Scottish Committee: 1944) p. 117, and scores of American newspapers, see, for example, *The Topeka State Journal* (Kansas), 22 September 1921, p. 4.

39. National Records of Scotland, HH 16/122/26385.

40. *Daily Herald*, 4 October 1921, p. 5.

41. Glasgow Poor Relief application, 29 September 1921, available in the archives of the Mitchell Library.

42. Maclean, John, *To the Electors of Kinning Park Ward*, from Duke Street Prison, 12 October 1921.

43. *Dundee Evening Telegraph*, 26 October 1921, p. 5.

44. National Records of Scotland, HH 16/122.

45. *The Scotsman*, 14 October 1921, p. 5.

46. *Daily Herald*, Tuesday 11 October 1921, p. 2.

47. *Daily Herald*, 26 October 1921, p. 2.

48. John Maclean Papers, in National Library Of Scotland, Acc 4251/3.

49. Aldred, *John Maclean*, p. 48.

50. *Western Gazette*, 28 October 1921.

51. National Records of Scotland, HH 16/122/26385.

52. *The Worker*, 12 November 1921.

53. National Records of Scotland, HH 16/122/26385.

54. Aldred, *John Maclean*, p. 48.

55. James Clunie Papers, in National Library of Scotland 4334/1.

56. MacLean, John, *Vanguard*, December 1915.

57. Milton, *John Maclean*, p. 275.

58. Broom, *John Maclean*, pp. 147–8.

59. Ibid.

60. John Maclean Papers, in National Library Of Scotland, Acc 4251/3.

61. Bell, *John Maclean: A Fighter for Freedom*, p. 120.

62. Maclean, John, Election Address, November 1922.

63. Ibid.

64. Ibid.

65. John Maclean Papers, in National Library Of Scotland, Acc 4251/5.

66. Maclean, John, in *The Socialist*, December 1922.

67. Ripley and McHugh, *John Maclean*, p. 151.

Chapter 14

1. John Maclean Papers, in National Library Of Scotland, Acc. 4251/5.

2. John Maclean Papers, in National Library Of Scotland, Acc. 4251/1.

3. Challinor, R. C., *The Origins of British Bolshevism* (London: Croom Helm, 1977) p. 274.
4. Maclean, John, Election Address, February 1923.
5. *Forward*, 25 August 1923.
6. McShane, Harry and Smith, Joan, *No Mean Fighter* (London: Pluto Press, 1978) pp. 151–2.
7. James Clunie Papers, in National Library of Scotland 4334/1.
8. Ripley, B. J., and McHugh, J., *John Maclean* (Manchester: Manchester University Press, 1989) p. 154.
9. Shipway, Mark, *Anti-Parliamentary Communism: The Movement for Workers' Councils in Britain 1917–1956* (London: Springer, 2016) p. 17.
10. Ripley and McHugh, *John Maclean*, p. 153.
11. *The Socialist*, January 1924, p. 1.
12. *Edinburgh Evening News*, 13 April 1923, p. 5.
13. Procurator Fiscal's Criminal Complaint, Papers of Brenda Bennie (John Maclean Papers), Glasgow Caledonian University Archive Centre.
14. *Aberdeen Press and Journal*, 16 April 1923, p. 8.
15. Broom, John, *John Maclean* (Loanhead: MacDonald, 1973) p. 158.
16. James Clunie Papers, in National Library of Scotland 4334/1.
17. *Aberdeen Press and Journal*, 25 October 1923, p. 8.
18. McShane and Smith, *No Mean Fighter*, pp. 151.
19. Ibid.
20. John Maclean Papers, in National Library Of Scotland, Acc. 4251/5.
21. John Maclean Election Leaflet, November 1923, Glasgow Archive, the Mitchell Library.
22. John Maclean Papers, in National Library Of Scotland, Acc. 4251/5.
23. Foster, Gavin, '"Scotsmen, stand by Ireland": John Maclean and the Irish Revolution', in *History Ireland*, Issue 1, 2008.
24. MacLean, John, *The Irish Tragedy: Scotland's Disgrace*, 1920.
25. James Clunie Papers, in National Library of Scotland 4334/1.
26. *The Worker*, 6 October 1923.
27. *The Worker*, 3 November 1923.
28. John Maclean Papers, in National Library Of Scotland, Acc. 4251/9.
29. Maclean, John, Election Address, November 1922.
30. John Maclean Papers, in National Library Of Scotland, Acc. 4251/5.
31. Ibid.
32. Ibid.
33. Ibid.
34. Ibid.
35. Ibid.
36. *Dundee Courier*, 2 November 1923, p. 5.
37. John Maclean Papers, in National Library Of Scotland, Acc. 4251/5.

38. *The Scotsman*, 26 November 1923, p. 7.

39. Maclean, John, Election Manifesto, 23 November 1923.

40. Maclean, John, Election Manifesto, 23 November 1923.

41. Broom, *John Maclean*, p. 170.

42. John Maclean Papers, in National Library Of Scotland, Acc. 4251/5.

43. Ibid.

Chapter 15

1. *The Scotsman*, 4 December 1923.

2. Anderson, Tom, *Comrade John Maclean* (Glasgow: The Proletarian Press, 1938) p. 46.

3. Cairns, Gerry, *The Red and the Green, A Portait of John Maclean* (Glasgow: Connolly Books, 2017) pp. 178–81.

4. *Glasgow Evening Times*, 3 December 1923.

5. *Falkirk Herald*, 12 April 1924, p. 1.

6. Anderson, *Comrade John Maclean*, p. 47.

7. *Daily Herald*, 15 December 1923, p. 4.

8. John Maclean Papers in National Libray of Scotland, Acc. 4251/8.

9. Anderson, *Comrade John Maclean*, inside back cover.

10. *Bellshill Speaker*, 2 May 1924, p. 5.

11. Local newspapers report the SWRP running candidates until at least 1937 when one candidate stood for two wards in Glasgow (*The Scotsman*, 23 October 1937, p. 17).

12. Aldred, Guy, *John Maclean, Martyr of the Class Struggle – The Man, His Work, and His Worth*, (Glasgow: Bakunin Press, 1932) published by the joint committee of the SWRP and the Anti Parliamentary Communist Federation.

13. The first few thousand words were completed and were at some point in possession of Hugh MacDiarmid. A few notes for the biography survive among Maxton's papers in the Mitchell Library, including the note 'ask Tom Johnstone about the police protecting Maclean in Kirkintilloch', an incident I could not find out anything more about.

14. Hogsbjerg, Christian John, 'CLR James in Imperial Britain, 1932–1938', PhD Thesis from the University of York, 2009.

15. James, C. L. R., 'Report on Activities in the Provinces' [unpublished document written for the attention of the Central Committee of the Revolutionary Socialist League dated June 1938. From 'Revolutionary Socialist League 1938–39', Tait and Watson Political Papers (MS 0559 / MS 41), University of Stirling Library Archives and Special Collections.

16. James, C. L. R., *World Revolution* (Durham, NC: Duke University Press, 2017) note to the appendix.

17. Law, T. S. and Berwick, Thurso (eds), *Homage to John Maclean* (Loanhead: John Maclean Society, 1973) p. 3.
18. Gibson, Corey, *Voice of the People* (Edinburgh: University of Edinburgh Press, 2015) p. 134.
19. Law and Berwick (eds), *Homage to John Maclean*, p. 18.
20. Gibson, *Voice of the People*, p. 135.
21. Law and Berwick (eds), *Homage to John Maclean*, p. 7.
22. Maley, Willy and O'Gallagher, Niall, 'Coming Clean about the Red and the Green: Celtic Communism in Maclean, MacDiarmid and MacLean Again', in Willy Maley and Alison O'Malley Younger (eds), *Celtic Connections: Irish Scottish Relations and the Politics of Culture* (Oxford: Peter Lang, 2012).
23. *The Scotsman*, 28 January 1949, p. 4.
24. From a conversation with Christopher Silver.
25. MacDiarmid, Hugh, *The Company I've Kept* (Oakland: University of California Press, 1967) p. 133.
26. Ibid., p. 137.
27. When Matt McGinn died, his ashes were scattered on Maclean's grave.
28. *Sunday Times Magazine*, 25 November 1979, p. 75.

Bibliography

Manuscript Sources

Cabinet Papers, National Archives
Foreign Office Papers, National Archives
The Glasgow Archive, The Mitchell Library
Glasgow Museum Resources Centre
Harry McShane Papers, National Library of Scotland
Home Office Papers, National Archives
James Clunie Papers, National Library of Scotland
John Maclean's Diary for 1919, Glasgow Caledonian University Archive Centre
John Maclean Papers, National Library of Scotland
John Maclean Papers, National Records of Scotland
John Maclean Papers, Willie Gallacher Memorial Library
Munitions Office Papers, National Archives
Papers of Brenda Bennie (John Maclean Papers), Glasgow Caledonian
    University Archive Centre
Samuel Stewart Collection, Glasgow Caledonian University Archive Centre
Scotland Office Papers, National Archives
STUC Archive, Glasgow Caledonian University Archive Centre
Tait and Watson Political Papers, Stirling University Archive

Newspapers and Periodicals

Aberdeen Evening Express
Aberdeen Press and Journal
Age
An t-Oglach
Appeal to Reason
Bellshill Speaker
Birmingham Daily Post
Call
Chicago Tribune
Communist
Cotton Factory Times
Daily Herald
Daily Record

Derry Journal
Detroit Free Press
Dundee Courier
Dundee Evening Telegraph,
Evening Times
Edinburgh Evening News
Exeter and Plymouth Gazette
Falkirk Herald
Fife Free Press & Kirkcaldy Guardian
Fight Racism, Fight Imperialism
Forward
Glasgow Echo
Glasgow Herald
Glasgow Post
Globe
Guardian
Hamilton Advertiser
Illustrated London News
Journal of the Scottish Labour History Society
Justice
Labour Leader
Liberator
Liverpool Daily Post
Liverpool Echo
L'Ordine Nuovo
McClure's Magazine
Nashe Slovo
New York Call
Pall Mall Gazette
Pollokshaws Review
Pollokshaws News
Pravda
Red Dawn
San Francisco Call
Scotsman
Scottish Cooperator
Scottish Review
Sheffield Daily Telegraph
Socialist
Strike Bulletin
Sunday Post
Sunday Times Magazine

The Times
Topeka State Journal
Vanguard
Voice of Labour
Western Gazette
Western Morning News
Worker
Workers' Dreadnought
Workers' Republic
Yorkshire Evening Post
Yorkshire Post

Books and Pamphlets

Aldred, Guy, *John Maclean, Martyr of the Class Struggle – The Man, His Work, and His Worth* (Glasgow: Bakunin Press, 1932).

Anderson, Tom, *Comrade John Maclean MA* (Glasgow: Proletarian Press, 1938).

Avrich, Paul, *The Modern School Movement: Anarchism and Education in the United States* (Princeton, NJ: Princeton University Press, 2014).

Ballantine, Ishbel, *The Singer Strike, Clydebank, 1911* (Clydebank: Glasgow Labour History Workshop, 1989).

Bell, Tom, *John Maclean: A Fighter for Freedom* (Glasgow: Communist Party, Scottish Committee, 1944).

Briggs, Asa, and Saville, John, *Essays in Labour History 1886–1923* (London: Springer, 1971).

Broom, John, *John Maclean* (Loanhead: MacDonald, 1973).

Cairns, Gerry, *The Red and the Green, A Portrait of John Maclean* (Glasgow: Connolly Books, 2017).

Callwell C. E. Sir, *Field Marshal Sir Henry Wilson, His Life and Diaries*, Volume Two (London: Cassell and Company, 1927).

Cameron, Jim, *Red Flag Over the Clyde* (Militant Labour, 1994).

Challinor, Raymond, *The Origins of British Bolshevism* (London: Croom Helm, 1977).

Clarke, John S., *The Man In Peterhead* (Glasgow: Women's Section of the Glasgow District Council of the British Socialist Party, 1918).

Connolly, James, and Ó Cathasaigh, Aindrias (eds), *The Lost Writings* (London: Pluto Press, 1997).

Craig, Maggie, *When the Clyde Ran Red* (Edinburgh: Mainstream Publishing: 2011).

Crawfurd, Helen, Unpublished Biography, edited by Fiona and Beryl Jack and available in the Glasgow Women's Library.

Crawford, Ian, and Moir, Peter, *Argyll Shipwrecks* (Wemyss Bay: Moir Crawford, 1994).

Darlington, Ralph, *Syndicalism and the Transition to Communism: An International Comparative Analysis* (Farnham: Ashgate Publishing, 2013).

Debs, Eugene Victor, Unpublished Scrapbook, Book One, Volume One, 31 July 1920, in the Tamiment Institute, New York.

Field, Gordon Lawrence, *The First World War* (Exeter: Wheaton of Exeter, 1966).

Fletcher, Anthony, *Life, Death, and Growing Up on the Western Front* (New Haven, CT: Yale University Press, 2013).

Gallacher, Willie, *Last Memoirs* (London: Laurence and Wishart, 1966).

Gallacher, Willie, *Revolt on the Clyde* (London: Laurence & Wishart, 1990).

Gibson, Corey, *Voice of the People* (Edinburgh: University of Edinburgh Press, 2015).

Gorinov, Mikhail, M., *The Preobrazhensky Papers: Archival Documents and Materials*. Volume I: 1886–1920 (Leiden: Brill, 2014).

Gray, Elle, *Red Clyde Goodbyed?* (Clydebank: Long Books, 2016).

Hardach, Gerd, *The First World War, 1914–1918* (Oakland: University of California Press, 1981).

Hattersley, Roy, *David Lloyd George: The Great Outsider* (London: Hachette, 2010).

Hay, John, M., *The Beardmore Vickers Octopus* (Glasgow: Socialist Information and Research Bureau, Glasgow).

Henderson, Hamish, and Finlay, Alec (eds), *The Armstrong Nose* (Edinburgh: Polygon, 1996).

HMSO, *Official History of the Ministry of Munitions*, Volume IV: *The Supply and Control of Labour 1915–1916* (London: HMSO, 2009).

Howell, David, *A Lost Left* (Manchester: Manchester University Press, 1986).

Hubler, Angela, E., *Little Red Readings: Historical Materialist Perspectives on Children's Literature* (Jackson: University Press of Mississippi, 2014).

James, C. L. R., *World Revolution* (Durham, NC: Duke University Press, 2017).

Kenefick, William, *Red Scotland!: The Rise and Fall of the Radical Left, c. 1872 to 1932* (Edinburgh: Edinburgh University Press, 2007).

Knox, William, *James Maxton* (Manchester: Manchester University Press, 1987).

Knox, William, ed., *Scottish Labour Leaders, 1918–39* (Edinburgh: Mainstream Publishing, 1984).

Kuhn, Gabriel, *All Power to the Councils!: A Documentary History of the German Revolution of 1918–1919* (Oakland, CA: PM Press, 2012).

Law, T. S. and Berwick, Thurso, *Homage to John Maclean* (Loanhead: John Maclean Society, 1973).

Lenin, V. I., *Collected Works*, Volume 24, April–June 1917 (Moscow: Progress Publishers, 1974).

Lenin, V. I., *Collected Works*, Volume 25, June–September 1917 (Moscow: Progress Publishers, 1974).

Lenin, V. I., *Collected Works*, Volume 27, February–July 1918 (Moscow: Progress Publishers, 1974).

Lenin, V. I., *Collected Works*, Volume 31, April–December 1920 (Moscow: Progress Publishers, 1974).

Luxemburg, Rosa, *The Rosa Luxemburg Reader* (New York: NYU Press, 2004).

MacDiarmid, Hugh, *The Company I've Kept* (Oakland: University of California Press, 1967).

MacDougall, Ian, *Voices from the Hunger Marches* (Edinburgh: Polygon, 1991).

McKay, J., Biography of William Gallacher (Unpublished), Glasgow Caledonian University Research Collections. William Gallacher Memorial Library, 1993.

Maclean, John, *In the Rapids of Revolution* (London: Allison & Busby, 1979).

Maclean, John, *Ireland's Tragedy, Scotland's Disgrace* (Glasgow: John Maclean Society, 1970).

Maclean, John, *The War After the War* (London: Socialist Reproduction, 1974).

Maclean, John, *The War After the War* (Bristol: Bristol Radical History Group, 2017).

McShane, Harry and Smith, Joan *No Mean Fighter* (London: Pluto Press, 1978).

Maley, Willy, and O'Malley-Younger, Allison (eds), *Celtic Connections: Irish Scottish Relations and the Politics of Culture* (Oxford: Peter Lang, 2012).

Malone, Cecil L'Estrange, *The Russian Republic* (New York: Harcourt, Brace & Howe, 1920).

Marx, Karl, *Capital*, Volume 1 (London: Laurence & Wishart, 1970).

Marx, Karl, and Engels, Frederick, *Collected Works*, Volume 47 (New York: International Publishers, 1995).

Melling, Joseph, *Rent Strikes: People's Struggle for Housing in West Scotland* (Edinburgh: Polygon, 1983).

Miller, Ian, *A History of Force Feeding, Hunger Strikes, Prisons and Medical Ethics, 1909–1974* (London: Palgrave MacMillan, 2016).

Milton, Nan, *John Maclean* (London: Pluto Press, 1979).

Montefiore, Dora, *From a Victorian to a Modern* (London: E. Archer, 1927).

Noonan, Gerry, *The IRA in Britain, 1919–1923* (Oxford, Oxford University Press, 2014).

Page, Ra, ed. *Protest* (Manchester: Comma Press, 2017).

Pankhurst, Sylvia, *The Home Front* (London: Hutchinson & Co., 1932).

Petroff, Peter, Unpublished Autobiography (available in the International Institute of Social History, Amsterdam).

Pitt, Bob, *John Maclean and the CPGB* (London: Pitt Publications, 1995).

Renshaw, Patrick, *Nine Days that Shook Britain: The 1926 General Strike* (New York: Anchor Press, 1976).

Ripley, B. J., and McHugh, J., *John Maclean* (Manchester: Manchester University Press, 1989).

Rodger, Richard (ed.), Scottish *Housing in the 20th Century* (Leicester: Leicester University Press, 1989).

Rothstein, Andrew, *The Soldiers' Strikes of 1919* (London: Springer, 1980).

Sheïnis, Zinoviï, *Maxim Litvinov* (Moscow: Progress Publishers, 1990).

Sherry, Dave, *John Maclean: Red Clydesider* (London: Bookmarks Publications, 2014).

Sherry, Dave, *Russia 1917: Workers' Revolution and the Festival of the Oppressed* (London: Bookmarks Publications, 2017).

Shipway, Mark, *Anti-Parliamentary Communism: The Movement for Workers' Councils in Britain 1917–1956* (London: Springer, 2016).

Stalin, Joseph, *Three Years of Proletarian Dictatorship; Report Delivered at a Celebration Meeting of the Baku Soviet*, 6 November 1920, http://neo democracy.blogspot.co.uk/2017/11/three-years-of-proletarian-dictatorship. html; accessed 18 May 2018.

Taudevin, A. J., *Mrs Barbour's Daughters* (London: Oberon Books, 2015).

Thomson, Basil, *The Scene Changes* (London: Collins, 1939).

Trotsky, Leon, *The First Five Years of the Communist International*, Volume 1 (London: New Park, 1973).

Weinbren, Daniel, *Generating Socialism: Recollections of Life in the Labour Party* (Stroud: Sutton, 1997).

Welshman, John, *Underclass: A History of the Excluded Since 1880* (London: Bloomsbury, 2006; 2013).

Wheeler-Bennet, John W., *Brest-Litovsk: The Forgotten Peace, March 1918* (London: W.W. Norton and Company, 1971).

Winslow, Barbara, *Sylvia Pankhurst, Sexual Politics and Political Activism* (London: Routledge, 2013).

Wrigley, Chris, *Arthur Henderson* (Cardiff: GPC Books, 1990).

Young, James, D., *John Maclean Clydeside Socialist* (Glasgow: Clydeside Press, 1992).

Articles

Foster, Gavin, 'Scotsmen Stand by Ireland', *History Ireland*, Vol. 16, No. 1 (January–February 2008).

Foster, John, 'Strike Action and Working-Class Politics on Clydeside 1914–1919'. *International Review of Social History*, Volume XXXV (1990), pp. 33–70.

Kendall, Walter, *Russian Emigration and British Marxist Socialism*, https://www.cambridge.org/core/services/aop-cambridge-core/content/view/S0020859000002364; accessed 9 October 2017

Milton, Nan, 'John Maclean and Ireland', *Socialist Scotland / Alba Soisealac*, Winter 1979.

Morgan, Kevin, 'In and Out of the Swamp: The Unpublished Autobiography of Peter Petroff', *Scottish Labour History*, Volume 48 (2013).

Thatcher, Ian D., 'Representations of Scotland in Nashe Slovo During World War One: A Brief Note', *Scottish Historical Review*, Volume 78, Number 206, Part 2 (October 1999).

Thompson, F. M. L., *The Cambridge Social History of Britain, 1750–1950*, Volume 1 (Cambridge University Press, 1992).

Young, James, D., *The May Day Celebrations in Scotland*, http://www.workers city.org/the_reckoning/james_d_young.html; accessed 13 January 2018.

Theses

Griffin, Paul (2015) 'The Spatial Politics of Red Clydeside: Historical Labour Geographies and Radical Connections', Glasgow University PhD thesis, http://theses.gla.ac.uk/6583/; accessed 17 May 2018.

Hogsbjerg, Christian John, 'CLR James in Imperial Britain, 1932–1938', PhD Thesis from the University of York, 2009.

Jenkinson, Jacqueline, 'Black Sailors on Red Clydeside: Rioting, Reactionary Trade Unionism and Conflicting Notions of 'Britishness' Following the First World War', Stirling University, http://storre.stir.ac.uk/bitstream/1893/1069/1/TCBHamendedversion.pdf; accessed 17 May 2018.

Recorded Music

Hulett, Alistair, *Red Clyde* (CD) (Australia: Red Rattler, 2002).

Index